THE NATIONAL CURRICULUM
... AND BEYOND

Big Edd

*A Big Edd Guide
to*

The National Curriculum

by

Barbara Young   **Andy Hamilton**

Illustrators
Matthew Staff and Jennifer Smith
Luke Young and Joanne Young

Acknowledgements
to the students and teachers who trialled this new approach,
who worked with enthusiasm
and made suggestions for improving
both content and presentation.

> Thanks to the Y7 students and teachers of:
>
> John Hanson School, Andover, Hants
>
> St. John's School, Episkopi, Cyprus, BFPO 53
>
> Tarporley High School, Tarporley, Cheshire

But, above all, thanks to Gill Burrows and Phil Navin
for all their support and encouragement.

© The 'Maths Is...' Jugglers
2, Millview Close, Bulkeley, Malpas, Cheshire, SY14 8DB

This edition was first published in Great Britain 1997
British Library Cataloguing–in–Publication Data

ISBN   1 – 874428 – 54 – 9

Printed and bound by PRINTCENTRE WALES, Mold, Flintshire

THE NATIONAL CURRICULUM ...
... AND BEYOND ...

The authors, **Barbara Young** and **Andy Hamilton**
are full-time teachers in comprehensive schools.

Our priorities have always been:
- to foster enjoyment of mathematics in students of all abilities;
- to develop mathematical self-confidence;
- to lay down sound mathematical foundations;
- to enable students of all abilities to be stretched mathematically – and enjoy the sensation;
- to promote mathematical understanding;
- to provide plenty of varied technique practice;
- to encourage students to decide for themselves how much practice they need at each technique;
- to give students a sense of achievement;
- to prepare students for NCTs at the end of KS3 and GCSE at the end of KS4;
- to prepare students well for A-Levels, GNVQs, mathematics at work and at home.
- to produce a system for teachers that is flexible, easy-to-use and, above all, delivers everything they have to do using the minimum of time and effort.

> **In Y7, all topics are independent.
> They can be done in any order.**

IMPORTANT

Each topic is in two parts:

The first part (all sections except the last) is for all students. Each student learns/reviews the basic ideas and techniques (DEVELOPMENT), then does as much PRACTICE as they need and, finally, attempts as many Star Challenges as they have time for.

The second part is the last section in each topic. Able students are expected to do the challenges that are provided in the last section (The High Level Challenge Section). It is <u>not</u> intended that these problems should be left until the first part of the topic is complete. Each of the High Level Challenges is labelled with the section that it is linked to, and may be done at any time after that section has been attempted.

Big Edd

CONTENTS

Topic Title	Main Sections	High Level Challenges
Sum Number Fun	pp05 – 30	pp31 – 38
Introducing Area	pp39 – 63	pp64 – 74
Journeys, Maps and Coordinates	pp75 – 93	pp94 – 98
Shape	pp99 – 113	pp114 – 120
Fractions and Decimals	pp121 – 152	pp153 – 160
Handling Data	pp161 – 176	pp177 – 184
Angle	pp185 – 211	pp212 – 224
Number Patterns	pp225 – 244	pp245 – 248
Nets, Cubes and Volumes	pp249 – 269	pp270 – 274
ANSWERS	pp275 – 304	

All topics are independent.
They can be done in any order.

Questions asked by our students

Why do you keep saying "Check your answers"?

You need to know whether you are doing the work correctly.
You should check your answers regularly and find out where you have gone wrong, if you cannot get the correct answer. If answers are checked some time after the work has been done (say when your teacher takes your book in), then you will have lost interest in any earlier problems that you have got wrong. You will only try to find out hwat you have done wrong, if it is the piece that you have just finished doing. If you rarely, or never, check your answers, then you could be getting things wrong and learning the wrong ways of doing things.

Headbanger

Why do we have to "Copy and complete"?
Why can't we just write down the answers?

To get some ideas to stick, the brain needs to repeat patterns.
It also needs to repeat the whole pattern, not just part of it.
So, when you "Copy and complete", you are repeating a technique that the brain needs to learn.

THE NATIONAL CURRICULUM ...
... AND BEYOND ...

Big Edd

Sum Number Fun

By the end of this topic, you should be able to:
Level 2
- recognise consecutive numbers
- recognise odd and even numbers

Level 3:
- + and – numbers up to 20
- remember tables up to 5x5 and 2, 5, 10 tables

Level 4
- remember tables up to 10x10
- find the sum and difference of two numbers
- + and – two digit numbers in my head
- solve problems
- order large consecutive numbers
- +, –, x & ÷ 2-digit numbers
- x & ÷ using table facts
- + three digit numbers
- – three digit numbers
- multiply a 2-digit number by a 1-digit number
- divide a 2-digit number by a 1-digit number
- read write and order numbers
- solve problems using addition of 2-digit numbers

A BIG EDD GUIDE TO THE NATIONAL CURRICULUM

Sum Number Fun
Section 1 : Using a calculator

In this section you will use a calculator to solve problems.

DEVELOPMENT

D1: The calculator with the broken 3 key

Task 1: Your calculator has a broken 3 key.
You need to work out $53 + 19$
Find two ways of working it out
without using the 3 key. Write down the key strokes.

Task 2: Your calculator still has a broken 3 key.
You need to work out $263 + 157$
Find two ways of working it out without using the 3 key.
Write down the key strokes.

Task 3: Your calculator still has a broken 3 key.
You need to work out $159 - 93$
Find one way of working it out without using the 3 key.
Write down the key strokes.

• *Check your answers.*

Star Challenge

Now the 3 key is OK. – but the 5 key is broken

Find one way of working out each sum without using the 5 key.
Write down the key strokes.

		All 3 correct = 1 star
Sum 1: $65 + 27$	Sum 2: $135 + 234$	Sum 3: $255 + 97$

		All 3 correct = 1 star
Sum 4: $45 - 14$	Sum 5: $501 + 276$	Sum 6: $356 - 47$

		All 3 correct = 1 star
Sum 7: $153 + 65$	Sum 8: 55×13	Sum 9: 85×126

• *Your teacher will need to check these.*

A BIG EDD GUIDE   *Sum Number Fun*

P1: Calculator crossnumber

Across
1. 13 + 8
3. 33 x 5
6. 248 + 176
7. 868 ÷ 4
8. 86 – 18
9. 287 + 164
13. 28 + 47
14. 301 – 47
16. 1630 ÷ 5
17. 84 x 9
19. 14 x 7
20. 708 ÷ 6
22. 112 + 123
23. 57 + 27

Down
2. 37 x 4
3. 16 x 9
4. 242 + 279
5. 875 ÷ 5
8. 13 x 5
10. 16 x 16 x 2
11. 594 – 238
12. 149 x 5
13. 182 x 4
15. 296 + 282
16. [12 + 13 + 14] x 10
18. 151 x 4
20. 156 ÷ 12
21. 555 ÷ 37

• Check your answers.

P2: Solving problems

For each problem:
  • write down a sum
  • work out the answer using a calculator
  • write down the answer

1. In four innings a batsman scores 41, 113, 201, 98. What is his total score ?
2. Dave had £218. He bought a Walkman for £79. How much did he have left ?
3. In one primary school, there are 147 boys and 158 girls. How many children are there in the school ?
4. Mary keeps 25 sheep, 11 goats and 28 pigs. How many animals does she keep ?
5. An old lady counts up the members of her family. She has 4 sons, 2 daughters, 19 grandchildren and 18 great-grandchildren. How many is this altogether ?

• Check your answers.

Star Challenge 2

6-8 marks = 1 star

For each problem: • write down a sum   (1 mark)
  • work out the answer using a calculator   • write down the answer (1 mark)

1. Pete collects 47 eggs from his chickens. 19 of them are brown. The rest are white. How many white eggs does he collect ?
2. There are 17 boys and 14 girls in 7JH. How many pupils are there in 7JH ?
3. 252 women and 142 men work in a factory. 174 of them belong to a union. How many do not belong to a union ?
4. A batsman scores 55, 31, 49, 104. How many must she score next time to reach a total of 300 ?

• Your teacher has the answers to these.

A BIG EDD GUIDE   page 7   Sum Number Fun

Section 2: Sum, difference, product

In this section you will:
- be reminded of the meaning of the words 'sum', 'difference', 'product';
- work out sums, differences and products of numbers.

DEVELOPMENT

D1: Arithmogons

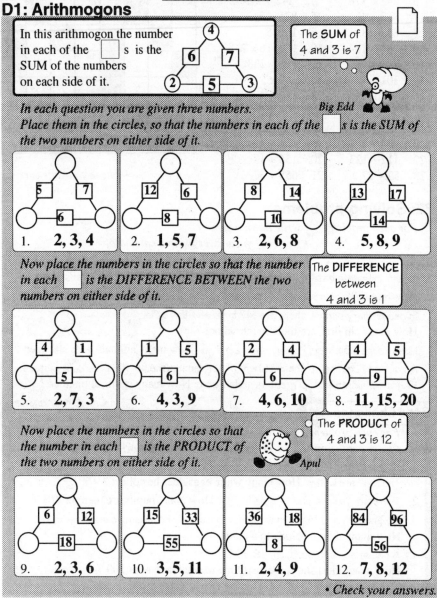

In this arithmogon the number in each of the ☐ s is the SUM of the numbers on each side of it.

The SUM of 4 and 3 is 7

Big Edd

In each question you are given three numbers.
Place them in the circles, so that the numbers in each of the ☐ s is the SUM of the two numbers on either side of it.

1. **2, 3, 4**
2. **1, 5, 7**
3. **2, 6, 8**
4. **5, 8, 9**

Now place the numbers in the circles so that the number in each ☐ is the DIFFERENCE BETWEEN the two numbers on either side of it.

The DIFFERENCE between 4 and 3 is 1

5. **2, 7, 3**
6. **4, 3, 9**
7. **4, 6, 10**
8. **11, 15, 20**

Now place the numbers in the circles so that the number in each ☐ is the PRODUCT of the two numbers on either side of it.

The PRODUCT of 4 and 3 is 12

Apul

9. **2, 3, 6**
10. **3, 5, 11**
11. **2, 4, 9**
12. **7, 8, 12**

• *Check your answers.*

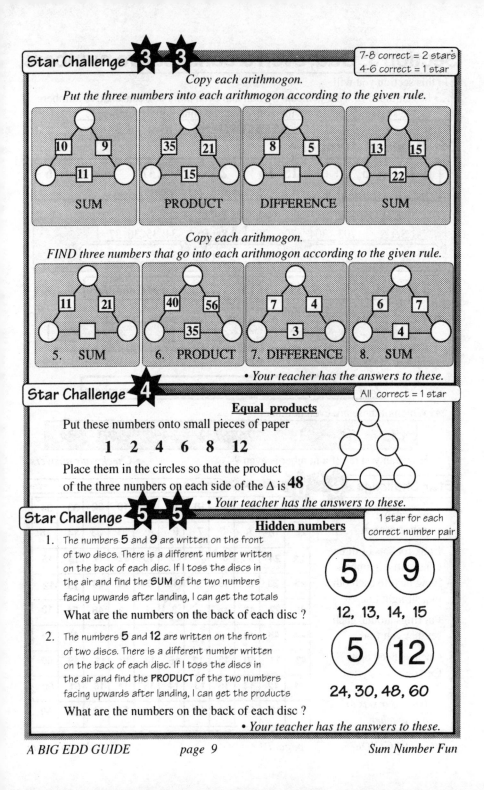

Section 3: Odd, even & consecutive numbers

In this section you will:
- be reminded of what is meant by odd and even numbers, consecutive numbers
- tackle some puzzles involving odd, even and consecutive numbers.

DEVELOPMENT

D1: Types of number

| 1 2 3 4 5 | 14 15 16 | 235 236 237 | 9 8 7 6 |

These are sets of **consecutive numbers.**

1. Which of these are sets of consecutive numbers?

   Set A: 703 704 706 707   Set B: 34 35 36 37
   Set C: 57 56 55 54   Set D: 10 11   Set E: 2 4 6 8

   1 3 5 7 9 11 13 15 .... are **odd numbers**

2. Which of these are odd numbers?

   49   44   57   768654   17   4321   26

3. How can you tell if a number is odd?

   2 4 6 8 10 12 14 .... are **even numbers**

4. Which of these are even numbers?

   18   54   15   2456732   3456   5491   34

5. How can you tell if a number is even?   • Check your answers.

Star Challenge 6 6   31-32 sets = 2 stars   25-30 sets = 1 star

Consecutive number search

Look for sets of three consecutive numbers lying next to each other in a straight line.

Put rings around each set that you find.

One has been done for you.

• Show your sets to your teacher.

7	2	3	4	8	9	10	32	33	34
22	6	8	5	7	9	8	31	33	14	16
23	24	5	6	7	9	10	32	17	16	15
25	23	8	48	7	48	31	33	33	13	12
45	22	47	48	49	8	11	13	48	34	13
44	46	48	49	48	10	11	12	47	49	14
43	11	50	15	12	15	13	12	13	49	50
34	12	14	16	13	14	15	14	16	51	52
31	13	14	15	14	13	15	51	52	53	50

A BIG EDD GUIDE   page 10   Sum Number Fun

Star Challenge 7

All correct = 2 stars

Task 1: **Avoiding consecutive numbers**

Put each of these numbers

2 3 4 5 6 7 8 9

onto a small piece of paper. Place each number onto a square in the diagram. Arrange the numbers so that no two consecutive numbers go in spaces that are directly connected by a line.

[If 4 is placed at H, then neither 5 nor 3 can go at E, F or G]

When you think you have a correct arrangement, ask you teacher to check it. If your teacher finds two consecutive numbers next to each other – try again.

• *Your teacher has the solutions to this.*

Star Challenge 8

All correct = 1 star

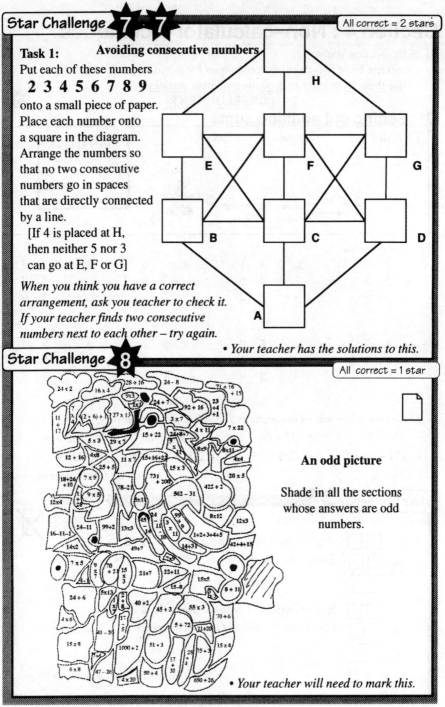

An odd picture

Shade in all the sections whose answers are odd numbers.

• *Your teacher will need to mark this.*

A BIG EDD GUIDE   page 11   *Sum Number Fun*

Section 4 : Non–calculator techniques

In this section you will :
- review basic non-calculator techniques for +, –, x;
- use these techniques to do some arithmetic puzzles

DEVELOPMENT

D1: Setting out addition sums

EXAMPLE 1   Q: Add 231, 37 and 5
A:
```
      2 3 1
    +   3 7
    +     5
      2 7 3
        1
```
Show your 'carried' numbers clearly.

WHEN ADDING, you must stack numbers with units under units, tens under tens ...

Big Edd

Copy and complete:

1.   3 6
   + 5 5
   _____

2.   2 3 1
      1 4 6
   +   2 2
   _____

3.   6 2
   + 2 0 9
   _____

4. 1 2 3
     1 3 7
   + 2 5 0
   _____

5.   4 5 2
   + 2 4 5
   _____

6. 5 6 0
      3 1
   + 2 2 4
   _____

7. 8 7 5
      2 5
   + 1 0 2
   _____

8.   2 4
     1 0 3
   +   7 5
   _____

Write each addition sum as in questions 1–8. Work out each answer.

9. 32 + 17
10. 35 + 66
11. 18 + 4 + 45
12. 135 + 36
13. 271 + 36 + 5
14. 209 + 75
15. 201 + 20 + 15
16. 722 + 271 + 72

- *Check your answers.*

Star Challenge 9

11-12 marks = 1 star

1. ☐☐
   + ☐☐
   _____
   Replace the boxes with the digits **1 2 3 5**
   Show how you can get six different answers. (6 marks)

2. ☐☐
   + ☐☐
   _____
   Repeat question 1 with the digits **1 2 3 4**
   Find as many different answers as possible. (6 marks)

- *Your teacher has the answers to these.*

A BIG EDD GUIDE   Sum Number Fun

D2: Multiplication using a table square

x	2	3	4	5	6	7	8	9	10
2	4	6	8	10	12	14	16	18	20
3	6	9	12	15	18	21	24	27	30
4	8	12	16	20	24	28	32	36	40
5	10	15	20	25	30	35	40	45	50
6	12	18	24	30	36	42	48	54	60
7	14	21	28	35	42	49	56	63	70
8	16	24	32	40	48	56	64	72	80
9	18	27	36	45	54	63	72	81	90
10	20	30	40	50	60	70	80	90	100

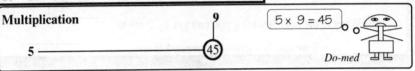

Copy and complete each of these multiplication sums:

1. 7 x 3 = ...
2. 8 x 5 = ...
3. 7 x 9 = ...
4. 7 x 4 = ...
5. 8 x 7 = ...
6. 9 x 8 = ...
7. 7 x 6 = ...
8. 8 x 8 = ...
9. 5 x 7 = ...
10. 6 x 9 = ...

• *Check your answers.*

D3: Setting out multiplication sums

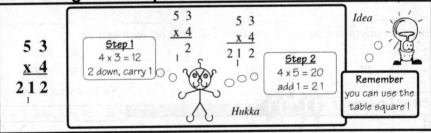

Copy and complete the following multiplication sums:

1. 1 5 x 3
2. 2 4 x 3
3. 4 7 x 2
4. 3 3 x 5
5. 6 4 x 6
6. 1 5 2 x 7

Write out each multiplication sum as in questions 1 – 6. Work out each answer.

7. 31 x 5
8. 63 x 7
9. 136 x 4
10. 572 x 3
11. 463 x 8
12. 308 x 3
13. 470 x 5
14. 679 x 8

• *Check your answers.*

A BIG EDD GUIDE — *Sum Number Fun*

Star Challenge 10 10

13-14 marks = 2 stars
10-12 marks = 1 star

1. Make multiplication sums like this using the digits **2, 3, 5, 6**
   There are six different totals.

   ☐☐☐
   ―――
   × 6

   (a) How many totals can you find? (6 marks) _____
   (b) What is the *largest* total you can get? (1 mark)

2. (a) Make six different multiplication sums like this using the digits **3, 4, 7** (6 marks)

   ☐☐
   × ☐
   ―――

   (b) What is the *smallest* total you can get? (1 mark)

   • *Your teacher will need to mark these.*

D4: Setting out subtraction sums

If you can't do these, ask your teacher.

```
   2 5 8          ⁵6̸ ¹5
  -  2 7         -  2 7
   ―――――          ―――――
   2 3 1           3 8
```

You can't take 7 from 5. So you borrow a 10 from the tens column!

Fission

Copy and complete:

1. 8 6   2. 8 1   3. 2 6 8   4. 1 4 1
   - 2 5   - 4 2   - 3 5   - 1 2 3
   ―――――   ―――――   ――――――   ――――――

Write each subtraction sum as in questions 1–4. Work out each answer.

5. 35 – 12   6. 46 – 28   7. 172 – 65   8. 247 – 53
9. 335 – 28   10. 257 – 124   11. 372 – 84   12. 476 – 128

• *Check your answers.*

Star Challenge 11 11

1 star for each correct Task

1. The digits **1 2 3** go into the boxes. You can get the answers **61, 52,** ▓▓▓ **48, 39.**
   What are the two answers under the ink blot?

   7 ☐
   - ☐ ☐
   ――――

   9 ☐ 4
   - 7 ☐ ☐
   ―――――

2. Replace the boxes by the digits **1 2 3**
   (a) What is the largest answer you can get?
   (b) What is the smallest answer you can get?

   • *Your teacher has the answers to these.*

A BIG EDD GUIDE   page 14   Sum Number Fun

Star Challenge 12-12 — Multiplying in pairs

43-45 marks = 2 stars
38-42 marks = 1 star

Rules:
- pair all the numbers using loops (across or down – not diagonal loops)
- write the product of each pair inside each loop
- add up all the products
- write the sum of the products underneath each box.
- REPEAT using as many different patterns of loops as possible
- find the largest sum of the products

2 x 2 box

```
2  4
5  7
```

Task 1: Fill in the products

Box A: 2 4 / 5 7 with 10 filled in
Box B: 2☐4 / 5☐7

sums of products ……   ………

largest sum of products = ☐   (6 marks)

3 x 3 box

```
4  7
5  6
8  9
```

Task 2 Draw the third loop pattern. Fill in the products

sums of products …… …… ……

largest sum of products = ☐   (13 marks)

Task 3: *Complete:*

(Five boxes, each containing:)
```
2   5
7   12
14  8
9   11
```

sums of products

……   ……   ……   ……   ……

largest sum of products = ☐   (26 marks)

• *Your teacher will need to mark these.*

A BIG EDD GUIDE   page 15   *Sum Number Fun*

Section 5 : Techniques for division

In this section you will review some non-calculator techniques for division.

D1: Sharing with counters

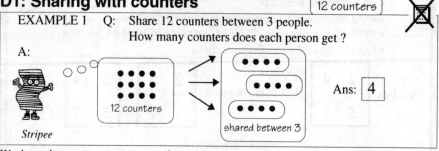

EXAMPLE 1   Q: Share 12 counters between 3 people.
                How many counters does each person get?
A: Ans: 4

Work out how many counters each person gets:
1. Share 6 counters between 2 people.
2. Share 6 counters between 3 people.
3. Share 8 counters between 2 people.
4. Share 8 counters between 4 people.
5. Share 10 counters between 5 people.
6. Share 12 counters between 4 people.

• *Check your answers.*

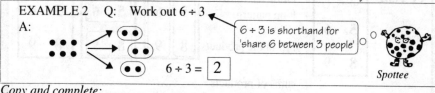

EXAMPLE 2   Q: Work out $6 \div 3$
A: $6 \div 3 = 2$

$6 \div 3$ is shorthand for 'share 6 between 3 people'

Copy and complete:

7. $15 \div 3 = ...$ 8. $12 \div 4 = ...$ 9. $20 \div 5 = ...$ 10. $8 \div 4 = ...$
11. $12 \div 2 = ...$ 12. $16 \div 4 = ...$ 13. $18 \div 6 = ...$ 14. $21 \div 3 = ...$
15. $15 \div 5 = ...$ 16. $20 \div 4 = ...$ 17. $18 \div 2 = ...$ 18. $14 \div 2 = ...$

• *Check your answers*

D2: Division using the table square

EXAMPLE 3   Work out $45 \div 5$

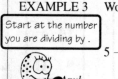

Start at the number you are dividing by.

$45 \div 5 = 9$

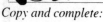

Copy and complete:

1. $16 \div 2 = ...$ 2. $12 \div 4 = ...$ 3. $15 \div 5 = ...$ 4. $18 \div 6 = ...$
5. $28 \div 4 = ...$ 6. $24 \div 3 = ...$ 7. $24 \div 6 = ...$ 8. $42 \div 7 = ...$
9. $64 \div 8 = ...$ 10. $72 \div 9 = ...$ 11. $54 \div 9 = ...$ 12. $25 \div 5 = ...$
13. $56 \div 7 = ...$ 14. $81 \div 9 = ...$ 15. $35 \div 5 = ...$ • *Check your answers*

A BIG EDD GUIDE   Sum Number Fun

D3: Setting out division sums

EXAMPLE 4   Work out $2\overline{)14}$ *(table square)*

A: 7 ← answer

$2\overline{)14}$

This means $14 \div 2$

Use the table square!

Taz

Copy and complete:

1. $3\overline{)15}$ 2. $5\overline{)30}$ 3. $6\overline{)48}$ 4. $7\overline{)28}$ 5. $6\overline{)36}$

6. $4\overline{)36}$ 7. $2\overline{)16}$ 8. $9\overline{)72}$ 9. $9\overline{)81}$ 10. $12\overline{)48}$

• *Check your answers.*

D4: More difficult division sums

EXAMPLE 5   Work out $148 \div 4$

If you need help with this technique, ASK YOUR TEACHER!

A: $3\;7$

$4\overline{)14^28}$

Step 1: 4 into 1 won't go

Step 2: 4 into 14 goes 3 times, with 2 left over. Carry 2 into next column

Step 3: 4 into 28 goes 7 times

Work out:

1. $5\overline{)75}$ 2. $4\overline{)224}$ 3. $5\overline{)275}$ 4. $3\overline{)222}$ 5. $7\overline{)623}$

6. $5\overline{)625}$ 7. $6\overline{)270}$ 8. $282 \div 2$ 9. $372 \div 4$ 10. $294 \div 6$

11. $5\overline{)515}$ 12. $3\overline{)273}$ 13. $357 \div 7$ 14. $168 \div 6$ 15. $126 \div 9$

• *Check your answers.*

Star Challenge 13 13

13 marks = 2 stars
10-12 marks = 1 star

1. $2\overline{)\square\square\,4}$ How many different answers can you get using the digits **6** and **8**? What are they?   (2 marks)

2. $3\overline{)\square\square\square}$ How many different answers can you get using the digits **6 6** and **9**? What are they?   (3 marks)

3. $3\overline{)\square\square\square}$ How many different answers can you get using the digits **6 7** and **8**? What are they?   (6 marks)

4. $5\overline{)\square\square\square}$ Use the digits **3 5 7** in this sum. How many answers can you get that have no remainder? What are the answers?   (2 marks)

• *Your teacher has the answers to these.*

A BIG EDD GUIDE   Sum Number Fun

Section 6: Use your head

In this section you will work out sums in your head.

PRACTICE

P1: Fill in the gaps

1.
3	+		=	12
+		+		+
	+		=	13
=		=		=
	+	10	=	

Put these numbers into the gaps to make the sums correct:
1 9 12 15 25

2.
18	−		=	3
−		÷		×
3	÷	3	=	
=		=		=
		÷		=

Put these numbers into the gaps to make the sums correct:
1 3 5 15 15

3.
	+	9	=	12
×		×		−
5	+		=	
=		=		=
		−	9	=

Find the numbers to put into the gaps to make the sums correct.

4.
8	+		=	14
×		−		+
2	+	3	=	
=		=		=
	+		=	

Find the missing numbers.

5.
	+		=	11
+		+		+
	+	9	=	17
=		=		=
	+	13	=	

Find the missing numbers.

6.
10		10	=	20
4		1	=	5
=				=
40		10	=	

Find the missing signs and numbers.

• *Check your answers.*

P2: Little problems

1. Abdul has 3 matchboxes. Each one has 6 marbles in it.
   How many marbles does he have?

2. Mary has 4 hutches. Each hutch has 2 rabbits in it.
   How many rabbits does she have?

3. Yusuf knows that he needs 3 eggs to make a cake.
   How many eggs does he need to make 2 cakes?

4. Ceri has a birthday. Each of her aunts gives her £5. She has 4 aunts.
   How much money does she get?

5. 6 cars are hired for a wedding. Each car can take 5 wedding guests.
   How many guests can go in the hired cars?

• *Check your answers.*

P3: Connect 4   *Four games for 1–3 people*

The rules for all four games are on the top of each of the next three pages.

CONNECT FOUR	You have to work out which numbers will give you the total you want, before you are allowed to use a calculator. So, these games will improve your mental arithmetic skills!						
86	42	58	109	98	61
125	70	109	36	65	138
66	38	81	50	53	114
28	40	118	97	108	153
166	133	84	51	122	94
105	177	110	95	56	120

CONNECT FOUR GAME 1 +

| 27 | 43 | 15 | 23 | 38 | 71 | 82 | 95 | 13 |

A BIG EDD GUIDE   page 19   *Sum Number Fun*

Rules: Each person
- chooses two numbers from the list on the left of the table
- says what they are before picking up the calculator
- adds them using a calculator (multiplies for games 3 & 4)
- puts a marker on the square with that total if it is available

The first person to get 4 markers in a straight line is the winner.

CONNECT FOUR GAME 2 +

You have to work out which numbers will give you the total you want, before you are allowed to use a calculator. So, these games will improve your mental arithmetic skills!

397	1528	1199	1380	603	1020
1111	1291	578	1797	1528	1174
1705	905	1022	643	1436	993
1259	840	928	1616	751	1109
816	1174	1617	668	997	1439
1085	1347	849	1355	1086	1266

166
231
412
585
762
943
437
674
854

A BIG EDD GUIDE   *Sum Number Fun*

Rules: Each person
- chooses two numbers from the list on the left of the table
- says what they are before picking up the calculator
- adds them using a calculator (multiplies for games 3 & 4)
- puts a marker on the square with that total if it is available

The first person to get 4 markers in a straight line is the winner.

You have to work out which numbers will give you the total you want, before you are allowed to use a calculator. So, these games will improve your mental arithmetic skills!

56	84	21	99	132	45
27	55	20	15	14	24
24	36	108	36	33	18
88	28	72	44	48	10
32	96	40	16	35	77
6	12	22	60	8	63

CONNECT FOUR GAME 3 x

2 3 4 5 7 8 9 11 12

A BIG EDD GUIDE — Sum Number Fun

Rules: Each person
- chooses two numbers from the list on the left of the table
- says what they are before picking up the calculator
- adds them using a calculator (multiplies for games 3 & 4)
- puts a marker on the square with that total if it is available

The first person to get 4 markers in a straight line is the winner.

CONNECT FOUR GAME 4 ×

You have to work out which numbers will give you the total you want, before you are allowed to use a calculator. So, these games will improve your mental arithmetic skills!

252	247	299	342	117	234
56	126	63	108	72	228
156	171	104	84	276	268
184	216	162	133	144	152
322	96	437	112	161	126
98	414	91	182	84	168

| 7 | 8 | 9 | 12 | 13 | 14 | 18 | 19 | 23 |

A BIG EDD GUIDE   page 22   *Sum Number Fun*

Star Challenge 14-14-14

Clock sums

1 star for each of Tasks 2, 3 and 4

Task 1: Work out the sum of the numbers on this clock face.

Task 2: Divide the clock face into TWO parts, so that the sum of the figures on each part is the same.

Task 3: Divide the clock face into THREE parts, so that the sum of the figures on each part is the same.

Task 4: Divide the clock face into SIX parts, so that the sum of the figures on each part is the same.

• *Your teacher will need to mark this.*

Star Challenge 15-15

Every which way you turn

11 correct = 2 stars
9-10 correct = 1 star

Find the missing digits that make all these sums correct:

```
 4  0  0    –    4  9    =  ☐☐☐
 ÷              +
☐☐              ☐☐
 1  6       x    6 ☐    =    ☐ 7  5
                                —
                              ☐☐
                =             
```

• *Your teacher will need to mark this.*

Star Challenge 16-16

Number jigsaw

All correct = 2 stars

Here are eight jigsaw pieces. Cut them out from the worksheet. Place them in the table so that the sums of the numbers in each row and column match the totals at the end of each row and column.

7	4		7	3		5	4		7	6
3	2		2	4		9	7		8	5

8	6		3	9		1	5		1	6
6	2		1	6		9	2		5	4

								39
								37
								43
								38
24	14	19	26	15	17	24	18	

• *Your teacher has the answers to this.*

Section 7: Some mental tricks

In this section you will meet some mental arithmetic tricks that may be new to you.

DEVELOPMENT

D1: Finger counting

Some additions are easy to do in your head. Others cause us some difficulty.

> To add 18 + 5, put 5 fingers up.
> Count on from 18, putting one finger down for each number.

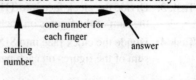

Use your fingers to work out the answers to these. Write down the answers.

1. **17 + 4** 2. **28 + 5** 3. **49 + 3** 4. **67 + 6** 5. **36 + 5**
6. **19 + 5** 7. **37 + 7** 8. **56 + 8** 9. **126 + 5** 10. **98 + 7**

> You can use a similar method to add on 20, 30, 40, ...
> Look at 46 + 50
> 50 is 5 tens. Put up five fingers – one for each ten.
> Count on in tens.

Use your fingers to work out the answers to these. Write down the answers.

11. **43 + 30** 12. **67 + 50** 13. **49 + 40** 14. **1123 + 200** 15. **257 + 400**

• *Check your answers.*

D2: Mental shortcuts

> Instead of adding 9, try adding 10, then taking 1 away.
> So, 37 + 9 becomes 37 + 10 – 1 = 47 – 1 = 46

Try doing these in your head. Write down the answers.

1. **46 + 9** 2. **87 + 9** 3. **38 + 9** 4. **9 + 24** 5. **9 + 66**

> Instead of adding 19, try adding 20, then taking 1 away.
> Instead of adding 29, try adding 30, then taking 1 away.

6. **58 + 19** 7. **67 + 29** 8. **14 + 59** 9. **35 + 49** 10. **69 + 23**

> Instead of adding 99, try adding 100, then taking 1 away.

11. **45 + 99** 12. **37 + 99** 13. **78 + 99**

14. What shortcut could you use for adding (a) 90 (b) 490 ?

15. **57 + 90** 16. **78 + 490** 17. **45 + 990** 18. **36 + 9** 19. **36 + 29**

20. **36 + 90** 21. **36 + 99** 22. **47 + 19** 23. **47 + 99**

• *Check your answers.*

A BIG EDD GUIDE   *Sum Number Fun*

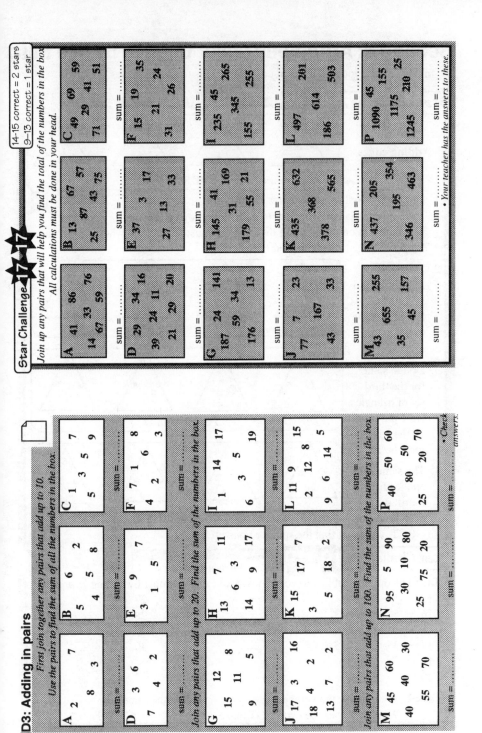

Section 8: Arithmetic never used to be like this

In this section you will use non-calculator skills to solve puzzles.

Star Challenge 18-18

EXTENSIONS

All correct = 2 stars
3 correct = 1 star

Adding edges

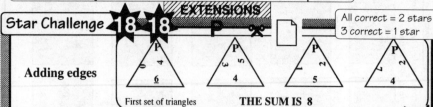

First set of triangles — THE SUM IS 8

1. Cut out the first set of triangles.
   Put the four triangles together to make a larger triangle.
   The numbers on the edges of the trianlges must add up to 8 where they meet.
   Stick the large triangle in your book.

2. Do the same for the second set of triangles. Here the sums on the edges must be 10.

Second set of triangles — THE SUM IS 10

3. Do the same for the third set of triangles. Here the sums on the edges must be 12.

   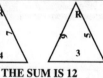

Third set of triangles — THE SUM IS 12

4. The same rule applies for the fourth set of triangles

  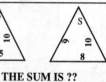

Fourth set of triangles — THE SUM IS ??

– BUT, you must find the sum for yourself !

Star Challenge 19-19

Threes and fives

21-22 marks = 2 stars
18-20 marks = 1 star

Task 1: Copy this table into your book. Make each number by adding 3s and 5s.

$15 = 5 + 5 + 5$ $21 =$ $27 =$
$16 = 5 + 5 + 3 + 3$ $22 =$ $28 =$
$17 =$ $23 =$ $29 =$
$18 = 3 + 3 + 3 + 3 + 3 + 3$ $24 =$ $30 =$
$19 =$ $25 =$
$20 =$ $26 =$

(13 marks)

Task 2: Try to make the numbers between 5 and 15 in the same way.
Which numbers can you NOT make ?   (9 marks)

A BIG EDD GUIDE — Sum Number Fun

Star Challenge 20

All correct = 2 stars
5 correct = 1 star

Place the numbers **1 2 3 4 5 6 7 8 9** into the circles so that:
- each number is only used once
- the sum of any three circles in a line, (connected by straight lines) is the number under the diagram.

A (contains 9) Sum = 14

B (contains 7) Sum = 14

C (contains 1) Sum = 15

D (contains 2) Sum = 15

E (contains 8) Sum = 15

F (contains 4) Sum = 16

• Your teacher will need to mark these.

Star Challenge 21

21-22 correct = 2 stars   17-20 correct = 1 star

Choose the numbers to fit in the boxes from **1 2 3 4 5**

No number is used twice in any question.

1. ☐ + ☐ − ☐ = 4
2. ☐ + ☐ − ☐ = 3
3. ☐ x ☐ − ☐ = 5
4. ☐ x ☐ + ☐ = 14
5. ☐ x ☐ − ☐ = 3
6. ☐ + ☐ − ☐ = 6

Choose the numbers to fit in the boxes from **3 5 6 7 9**

No number is used twice in any question.

7. ☐ + ☐ − ☐ = 10
8. ☐ + ☐ + ☐ = 15
9. ☐ − ☐ + ☐ = 12
10. ☐ + ☐ − ☐ = 5
11. ☐ x ☐ + ☐ = 21
12. ☐ − ☐ + ☐ = 5

Choose the numbers to fit in the boxes from **2 4 5 6 7**

No number is used twice in any question.

13. ☐ + ☐ − ☐ = 4
14. ☐ + ☐ − ☐ = 3
15. ☐ x ☐ − ☐ = 5
16. ☐ x ☐ + ☐ = 14
17. ☐ x ☐ − ☐ = 3
18. ☐ + ☐ − ☐ = 6

Choose the numbers to fit in the boxes from **2 3 4 5 8**

No number is used twice in any question.

19. ☐ x ☐ + ☐ − ☐ = 10
20. ☐ x ☐ − ☐ − ☐ = 2
21. ☐ x ☐ − ☐ − ☐ = 10
22. ☐ x ☐ + ☐ + ☐ = 25

• Your teacher will need to mark these.

Section 9: Maths is more than just numbers

In this section you will:
- practise using some mathematical words;
- order numbers using < and > signs.

DEVELOPMENT

D1: Getting the words right

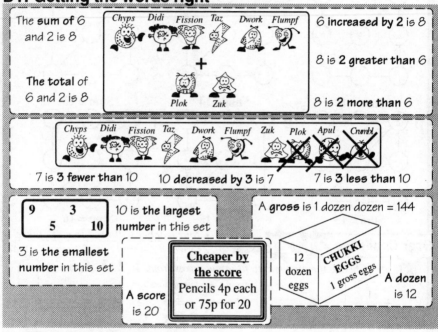

1. What is 3 more than 10 ?
2. What do you get if you increase 8 by 2 ?
3. Is 99 greater or less than 100 ?
4. What do you get if you increase your age by 2 years ?
5. What is 12 decreased by 2 ?
6. What is the total of 2, 3 and 5 ?
7. How many are there in 2 dozen ?
8. What is three more than a dozen ?
9. Eggs are sold in packs of half a dozen. I buy 3 packs. How many eggs do I get ?
10. How many are there in 2 score ?
11. What is 1 less than a score ?
12. What is the largest of these numbers : **304   403   34   43   433** ?
13. What is the smallest of the numbers in question 12 ?
14. How many are there in half a gross ?

Did you know ...
... that a baker's dozen is 13 ? In the Middle Ages, the Guild of Bakers fined bakers who sold short weight. As buns were generally of different sizes, a baker would put in an extra one, in case some of the buns in the dozen were too small.

• *Check your answers.*

Star Challenge 22

5-6 correct = 1 star

The numbers on a dartboard are
**1 2 3 4 5 6 7 8 9 10 11
12 13 14 15 16 17 18 19 20**

double 5 is 10
5 doubled is 10

treble 9 is 27
9 trebled is 27

1. What is the value of the largest double you can get on a dartboard?
2. What is the value of the smallest treble you can get on a dartboard?
3. When playing darts, Huw scored a double 10, a treble 5 and a 20 in one throw. What was his score for that throw?
4. The corner shop orders a gross of eggs each week. In Easter week, the egg order is doubled. How many eggs are ordered?
5. When asked her age, Ruth always decreases it by 10 years. How old will she say she is when she is actually 40?
6. The average lifespan of a human being is said to be 3 score and ten years. How old is that?

• *Your teacher has the answers to these.*

D2: Getting some order

$2 < 3$ means "**2** is less than **3**"
$7 > 6$ means "**7** is more than **6**"

State whether each of these is TRUE (T) or FALSE (F):

1. $5 > 4$ 2. $6 < 9$ 3. $4 < 7$ 4. $3 < 14$ 5. $4 = 5$

Replace each ☐ by <, > or = to make true sentences:

6. $2 \square 3$ 7. $3 \square 13$ 8. $34 \square 27$ 9. $12 \square 21$

10. one hundred and one $\square$ 101   11. one thousand and one $\square$ 101

• *Check your answers.*

Star Challenge 23

All correct = 1 star

We can put 2, 11, 3, 7 in order of size as
$$2 < 3 < 7 < 11$$
with the <u>smallest</u> number first.
Do the same with:
1. **46, 64, 35, 53, 56, 65**
2. **53, 35, 351, 531, 503**

We can put 2, 11, 3, 7 in order of size as
$$11 > 7 > 3 > 2$$
with the <u>largest</u> number first.
Do the same with:
3. **32, 23, 34, 43, 42**
4. **456, 546, 654, 465, 564**

A BIG EDD GUIDE   Sum Number Fun

Section 10: Palindromes

In this section you will work with palindromic numbers.

DEVELOPMENT

D1: What is a palindrome ?

small groups reporting back to class discussion

> A **palindrome** reads the same backwards as forwards
> **radar** and **deed** are **palindromic words**
> **12321** and **4774** are **palindromic numbers**

Discuss the answers to each of these questions.
Put the answers onto a large sheet of paper.
Only one set of answers needed for each group.

1. There is only one palindromic year this century.
   What year is it ?
2. 04.40 is a palindromic time on a digital clock.
   Find all the other palindromic times.
3. 18/4/81 is a palindromic date.
   Find all the palindromic dates between 1/1/90 and 31/12/92. *Your teacher has the answers to these.*

Star Challenge

15-16 marks = 2 stars
12-14 marks = 1 star

Square palindromes

Task 1: Using a calculator, if necessary, copy and complete:

$1 \times 1 =$
$11 \times 11 =$
$111 \times 111 =$
$1111 \times 1111 =$ (4 marks)

Look for a pattern.   Now, without a calculator, copy and complete:

$11111 \times 11111 =$
$111111 \times 111111 =$
$1111111 \times 1111111 =$
$11111111 \times 11111111 =$ (8 marks)

Task 2:   What is 7×9 ?
What is 77×99 ?
What is 777×999 ? Continue until you have spotted the pattern.
What is 7777777×9999999 ?   (1,1,1, 3 marks)

High Level Challenge Section
EXTENSIONS
YOUR TEACHER HAS THE ANSWERS TO THESE.

Ch 1: The calculator with two broken keys

SECTION 1

6 correct = 2 stars
4-5 correct = 1 star

How would you work out the answers to each of these:

1. **159 + 873**
2. **455 + 253**
3. **355 + 538**
4. **439 − 253**
5. **53 x 137**
6. **55 x 535**

Ch 2: The four fours challenge

SECTION 1

10 correct = 3 stars
8-9 correct = 2 stars
5-7 correct = 1 star

The only keys on your calculator that you are allowed to use are

Make up sums which give the numbers 1, 2, 3, 4, 5, 6, 7, 8, 9, 10 as answers.
However, for each sum, you must use the 4 key exactly four times.

For example   **0**

Ch 3: Find the numbers

SECTION 2

5 correct = 2 stars
4 correct = 1 star

1. The sum of two numbers is 8. Their product is 15.
   What are the two numbers ?

2. The sum of two numbers is 16. Their difference is 6.
   What are the two numbers ?

3. The sum of two numbers is 19. Their product is 48.
   What are the two numbers ?

4. Find two numbers whose sum is 9 and whose product is 20.25

5. Find two numbers whose difference is 4 and whose product is 16.25

Ch 4: Disc numbers

 SECTION 2 All correct = 2 stars

Two cardboard discs each have one number written on each side. The discs are tossed up into the air and the sums and products of the two numbers facing upwards are written down.

The possible SUMS of the these two numbers are **7 10 12 15**

The possible PRODUCTS of these two numbers are **12 21 32 56**

What numbers are written on each disc ?

A BIG EDD GUIDE   *Sum Number Fun*

Ch 5: Predicting odd and even numbers

9-10 correct = 2 stars

SECTION 3

1. If 2 is the first even number ...
   (a) ... what is the fifth even number ?
   (b) ... what is the fifteenth even number ?
   (c) ... what is the fiftieth even number ?
   (d) Explain how you worked out the answer to (c).

2. If 1 is the first odd number ...
   (a) ... what is the seventh odd number ?
   (b) ... what is the seventeenth odd number ?
   (c) ... what is the hundredth odd number ?
   (d) Explain how you worked out the answer to (c).

Ch 6: Odd and even number tables

All correct = 1 star

SECTION 3

2	3	O
4	5	O
E	E	

This table tells us that 2 + 3 is odd
4 + 5 is odd
2 + 4 is even
3 + 5 is even

1. Copy each of the following tables. Put O into the space if the sum is odd. Put E into the space if the sum is even.

5	3
6	4

6	1
4	2

2	4
8	6

1	3
5	7

2. Try some sets of numbers of your own.
   Try to make a table which gives you four Os.

3. What do you get if you add two even numbers ?

4. What do you get if you add two odd numbers ?

5. What do you get if you add an odd and an even number ?

Ch 7: Headscratcher – House numbers

2 correct answers = 1 star
3 correct answers = 2 stars

SECTION 3

1. The numbers of five houses next to each other add up to 135.
   What are the numbers of the houses ?

2. The numbers of six houses next to each other add up to 594.
   What are the numbers of the houses ?
   [There are two possible solutions to this.]

Ch 8: Odd and even addition & multiplication

All correct = 1 star
SECTION 3

O = an odd number   **E** = an even number
X = a number which is sometimes odd, sometimes even

1. Copy these sentences and replace the ☐ with **O, E** or **X**

    O + O = ☐   E + E = ☐
    O + O + O = ☐   E + E + E = ☐
    O + O + O + O = ☐   E + E + E + E = ☐

2. What would you get if you added 100 even numbers?
3. What would you get if you added 100 odd numbers?
4. Investigate the result of multiplying two odd numbers.
   Try at least four cases. When you multiply two odd numbers, do you:
   - always get an odd number **(O)**
   - always get an even number **(E)**
   - sometimes get an odd number, sometimes get an even number **(X)**?
5. Investigate multiplying two even numbers.
   Do you get **O, E** or **X**?
6. What happens when you multiply an odd number by an even number?
7. Complete this multiplication table with Os, Es and Xs.

×	O	E
O		
E		

Ch 9: How can you tell?

SECTION 4 *Correct explanation = 2 stars*

Putting **1 2 3 5** into the four boxes and adding gives six different totals.
But some sets of four digits only give five different totals.
The digits must all be different.
Experiment with some sets of four different digits.
How can you tell from the digits whether you will get five or six different totals?

Ch 10: What a difference a sign makes

Each correct Task = 1 star
SECTION 4

Task 1:   12 ☐ 34 ☐ 56 ☐ 67 ☐ 89 = ...
    Replace the boxes with two + signs and two − signs.
    How many different totals can you get? What are they?

Task 2: 12 ☐ 23 ☐ 34 ☐ 45 ☐ 56 ☐ 67 ☐ 78 ☐ 89 = ...
What is the highest score that you can get if you replace the boxes with four + signs and three − signs? What is the lowest score you can get?

A BIG EDD GUIDE   Sum Number Fun

Ch 11: Sum challenges [SECTION 4]   8-9 marks = 1 star

1. (a) Fill these boxes with the digits **4 5 6 7 8 9** so that the total is as large as possible. (1 mark)
   (b) Explain how you make the total as large as possible. (2 marks)
2. (a) What is the largest possible answer if you use the digits **1 2 3 5** in this sum? (1 mark)
   (b) What is the smallest possible answer? (1 mark)
   (c) Choose four digits of your own. Explain how you arrange the digits to get the largest possible answer. [Try some more sets of digits if it will help.] (2 marks)
   (d) Explain how you arrange the digits to get the smallest answer. (2 marks)

Ch 12: Reducing the difference [SECTION 4]   1 star for each correct answer.

The numbers **18   6   69   32   20   3   45   25**

can be split into two sets of numbers in many different ways.

One way is: **18   69   32**   and   **6   3   45   25   20**

The difference between the sums of these sets is 20.

1. Split the numbers into two sets so that the difference between the sums of the sets is as LARGE as possible. List the two sets.
2. Split the numbers into two sets so that the difference between the sums of the sets is as SMALL as possible. List the two sets.

Ch 13: How many did Zuleika get right? All correct = 1 star [SECTION 4]

In an examination there were 100 questions. Each question had to be attempted. Two marks are given for each correct answer. One mark is taken off for each wrong answer. If she gets 60 right, then Zuleika will be given 120 marks. But, if she gets 60 right, then she also gets 40 wrong, so she loses 40 marks. Her total would be 80.

        Zuleika scored 122. How many did she get right?

Ch 14: Figure this out   1 star for questions 1 & 2   1 star for question 3

1. Divide the number 459459 by 7. Divide the result by 11. Divide this result by 13. What do you get? [SECTION 5]
2. Find another number that is made in the same way and, when divided by 7, 11 and then 13 gives the same result.
3. Work out why this happens.

A BIG EDD GUIDE   Sum Number Fun

Ch 15: Headscratcher – Why ?

SECTION 8 — All correct = 1 star

☐ x 9 x 12345679

Replace the box with any single digit whole number and work out the answer to the sum.
Repeat with a different single digit whole number.
Explain why you get these answers.

Ch 16: Part sums

SECTION 8 — 20 marks = 2 stars / 17-19 marks = 1 star

1. This square has been divided into three parts. What is the sum of the numbers in each of the three parts ? (1 mark)

6	5	3
9	4	7
2	1	8

2. Divide the same square into three parts in a different way so that the sum of the numbers in each part is the same. (2 marks)

3.
6	9	5
7	3	10
2	8	4

   Divide this square into TWO PARTS so that the sum in each part is the same.
   Find three different ways of doing this. (6 marks)

4. Divide this rectangle into TWO PARTS so that the sum in each part is the same.
Do it in four different ways. (8 marks)

7	2	8	10
12	4	3	5
1	9	6	11

5.
7	2	8	10
12	4	3	5
1	9	6	11

   Divide this rectangle into THREE PARTS so that the sum in each part is the same.
   Do it in three different ways. (6 marks)

Ch 17: Getting your sums right

SECTION 8 — All correct = 1 star

Place the numbers

0 1 2 3 4 5 6 7 8 9 ③ ⑦

in the circles so that the totals

on the straight lines are

8 9 10 11 12 13

A BIG EDD GUIDE — *Sum Number Fun*

Ch 18: Headscratcher - What is the number?

Correct = 1 star

SECTION 9

This is a five digit number formed according to the following rules:
- the digit 7 is three places before the digit 5
- the digit 2 is three places before the digit 3
- the digit 3 comes after the digit 9 but before the digit 5.

What is the number?

Ch 19: You must end with a double

All correct = 1 star

SECTION 9

Ashram is playing darts.
She needs to score **15** to win.
She has two darts left to throw.
She must end with a double.
There are nine different ways she can score to win.

She uses the whole board – not just this board.

What are they?

Ch 20: Using two darts ...

26 or more marks = 3 stars
20-25 marks = 2 stars
14-19 marks = 1 star

SECTION 9

Using two darts ...
... you cannot score 1
... you can score 2 in only 1 way – as 1 & 1
... you can score 4 in five ways
– 2 & 2, double 1 & double 1, double 1 & 2, 3 & 1, treble 1 & 1

On a dartboard you can score 1, 2, 3, ... 20 and the doubles and trebles of these numbers. You can also score an outer bull, which is 25, and an inner bull which is 50.

Using two darts ...

1. ... what is the highest score you can get? (1 mark)
2. ... if each dart must make a different score, what is the highest possible total?
3. ... what are the scores between 114 and 120 that you cannot get? (1 mark)
4. ... find eight ways of scoring 6. (2 marks)
5. ... find nine ways of scoring 7. (2 marks)
6. Sunni reckons there are exactly 11 ways of scoring 8 with two darts. Show whether she is right or wrong. (2 marks)
7. Joel says there are 13 ways of scoring 9. Do you agree with him? (2 marks)
8. Find 23 ways of scoring 31 with two darts. (5 marks)
9. How many ways can you find of scoring 24 with two darts?
   Target: There are more than 34 possible ways – score 1 mark for every 4 ways you get.
10. Using two darts, what is the lowest score, other than 0 or 1, that you *cannot* get? (2 marks)

Ch 21: Digit reversals

[SECTION 9] *3 stars for correct answer to Task 4*

Task 1: Work out **21 x 48**   Work out **12 x 84**   What do you notice?

Task 2: Work out each of these products.

Write out each number sentence, replacing the ☐ by either < > or =

$26 \times 31 = ...$ and $62 \times 13 = ...$
Hence 26×31 ☐ 62×13

$46 \times 32 = ...$ and $64 \times 23 = ...$
Hence 46×32 ☐ 64×23

$39 \times 21 = ...$ and $93 \times 12 = ...$
Hence 39×21 ☐ 93×12

$68 \times 43 = ...$ and $86 \times 34 = ...$
Hence 68×43 ☐ 86×34

$54 \times 36 = ...$ and $45 \times 63 = ...$
Hence 54×36 ☐ 45×63

Task 3: Try some more multiplications of your own using digit reversal.
Find some more pairs of 2-digit numbers that give the same product when their digits are reversed.

Task 4: When digit reversal gives the same product, what is the relationship between the digits?

Ch 22: Palindromic multiples of seven

2 stars for all 3-digit palindromic multiples of 7
2 stars for all 4-digit palindromic multiples of 7

1. $7 \times 1 = 7$ $7 \times 2 = 14$ $7 \times 3 = 21$ ...

Copy out these multiples of 7 and continue them up to 7×10.   [SECTION 10]

$7 \times □□ = 3□4$
↑
What must this digit be?

[If you cannot tell, look at the multiples you have already written down.]
Now try multiplying 7 by numbers ending in this digit to find out what the whole sum is.

2. $7 \times □□ = 1□1$

Use the same technique to work out what this sum could be.
This is a palindromic multiple of 7, because the multiple reads the same backwards as forwards.

...continued on next page

3. Find the next four palindromic multiples of 7 and write them out in the form
   7 x ... = ...
   If you can see a pattern, describe it.
4. If you can see the pattern, use it to find all the 3-digit palindromic multiples of 7. If you cannot see the pattern, use the original method to find them.
5. Find two 4-digit palindromic multiples of 7 that start and end with a 1.
6. There are eighteen 4-digit palindromic multiples of 7. Find them.

SECTION 10

20 marks = 4 stars
17-19 marks = 3 stars
11-16 marks = 2 stars
9-10 marks = 1 star

Ch 23: Palindromic chains

1. Start with 19. You should get a palindrome after 2 steps.
2. How many steps does it take to get a palindrome starting with 12 ?
3. How many steps does it take to get a palindrome starting with 651 ?
4. Copy and fill in the table below, for all numbers from 11 to 49. (Look for shortcuts !)

Number	Number of steps	Palindrome found
11		
12		
.		
.		
.		
49		

Flowchart (one step):
- Write down the number
- Reverse the number
- Add the number and its reverse
- Write down the sum
- Did you get a palindrome? NO → loop back; YES → Write down how many steps it took

5. Look at the numbers that reach 121 in one stage. What are the sums of their digits ? (1 mark)
6. What is special about the digits of the numbers that reach 121 in two stages ? (1 mark)
7. What are the numbers below 50 that reach 363 in two stages ?
   Predict another two numbers less than 70 that will reach 363 in two stages and show that they do. Why did you choose those numbers ? (4 marks)
8. Which six 2–digit numbers will reach 484 in two stages ? (6 marks)
9. **Research challenge !**
   Find out what happens to 2–digit numbers with digit sums of 14, 15, 16 & 18. (8 marks)

THE NATIONAL CURRICULUM ...
... AND BEYOND ...

Big Edd

Introducing Area

By the end of this topic you should be able to:

Level 4
- find areas by counting squares
- find approximate areas of irregular shapes
- work out areas of rectangles

Level 5
- estimate areas

Level 6
- work out areas of compound shapes
- work out areas of parallelograms
- work out areas of triangles
- explain how to find areas of shapes (in words)
- explain how to find areas of shapes (in symbols)

Introducing Area
Section 1: Tiling and area

In this section you will :
- estimate how many tiles will exactly cover a shape;
- work out how many tiles will exactly cover a shape;
- meet the idea of area.

DEVELOPMENT

D1: Tiling

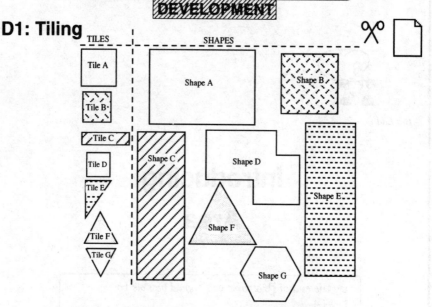

You are going to cover Shape A with Tile A, Shape B with Tile B ...
Tile A fits into Shape A a whole number of times.
Tile B fits into Shape B a whole number of times. ...

Task 1: *Copy this table into your book:*

Tile	A	B	C	D	E	F	G
Estimate							
Number							

Task 2: For each tile and shape pair, estimate (guess) how many tiles will fit into the shape. Put your estimates into the table.

Task 3: Cut out tile A. Work out how many times it fits onto Shape A.
[You can draw the tiles on the shape if you wish.]
Put the number of tiles onto the table.
Repeat for Tile B and Shape B, Tile C and Shape C ......
- *Check your answers.*

D2: Tiling with 1 cm squares   (1 cm square acetate overlay)

This is a 1 cm square. It is 1 cm long and 1 cm wide.

How many 1 cm squares will fit into each of the following shapes?

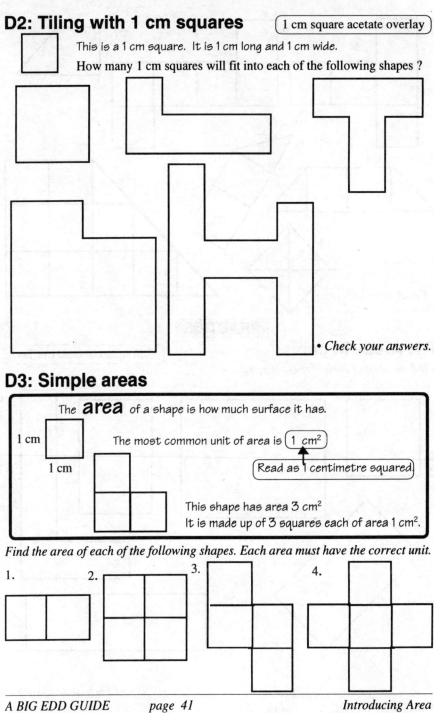

• Check your answers.

D3: Simple areas

The **area** of a shape is how much surface it has.

1 cm

1 cm

The most common unit of area is $1\ cm^2$

(Read as 1 centimetre squared)

This shape has area 3 cm^2
It is made up of 3 squares each of area 1 cm^2.

Find the area of each of the following shapes. Each area must have the correct unit.

1.   2.   3.   4.

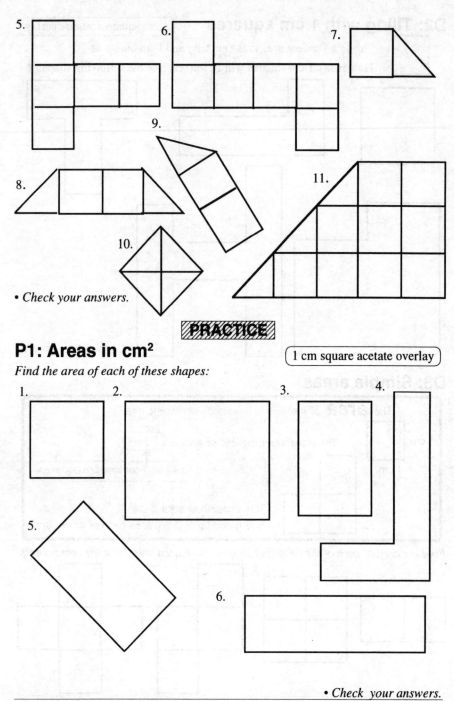

P1: Areas in cm²

1 cm square acetate overlay

Find the area of each of these shapes:

• *Check your answers.*

A BIG EDD GUIDE   page 42   Introducing Area

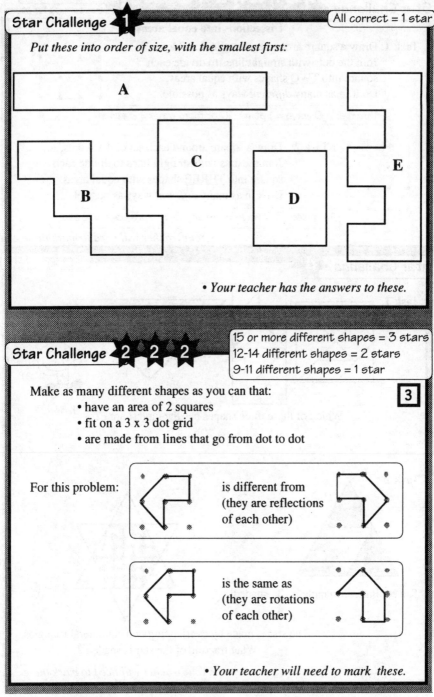

Star Challenge 1

All correct = 1 star

Put these into order of size, with the smallest first:

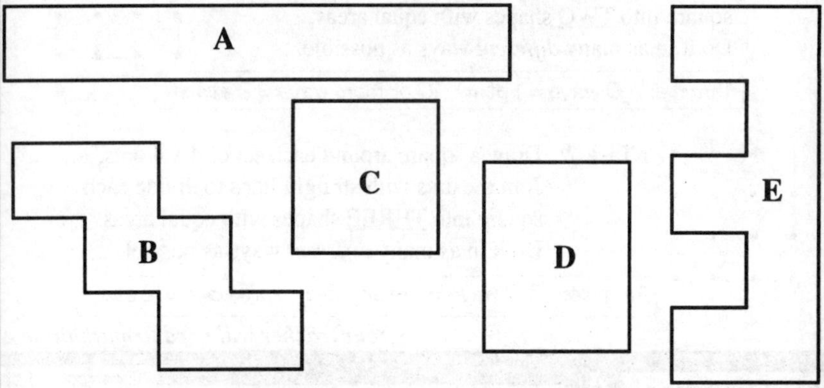

• *Your teacher has the answers to these.*

Star Challenge 2 2 2

15 or more different shapes = 3 stars
12-14 different shapes = 2 stars
9-11 different shapes = 1 star

3

Make as many different shapes as you can that:

- have an area of 2 squares
- fit on a 3 x 3 dot grid
- are made from lines that go from dot to dot

For this problem:

is different from (they are reflections of each other)

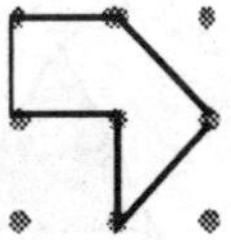

is the same as (they are rotations of each other)

• *Your teacher will need to mark these.*

Star Challenge 3 3 3 3   4 *See targets for stars*

Dissections into equal areas

Task 1: Draw a square around each set of 4 x 4 dots.
Join the dots with straight lines to divide each
square into <u>TWO</u> shapes with equal areas.
Do it in as many *different* ways as possible.

Targets: 7–9 ways = 1 star   10 or more ways = 2 stars

Task 2: Draw a square around each set of 4 x 4 dots.
Join the dots with straight lines to divide each
square into <u>THREE</u> shapes with equal areas.
Do it in as many *different* ways as possible.

Targets: 5–7 ways = 1 star   8 or more ways = 2 stars

• *Your teacher will need to mark these.*

Star Challenge 4

All correct = 1 star

Task 1

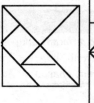 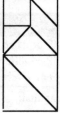 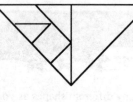

Which of these three shapes has the largest area ?   *Yerwat*

Task 2

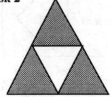

The equilateral triangle is $\underline{3}$ shaded.
                              4

The star is made by overlapping two equilateral triangles.
What fraction of the star is shaded ?

• *Your teacher will need to mark these.*

A BIG EDD GUIDE — *Introducing Area*

Section 2: Approximate areas

In this section you will :
- work out areas using a 1 cm square overlay grid and squared paper;
- work out approximate areas of irregular shapes.

DEVELOPMENT

D1: Squares and part squares

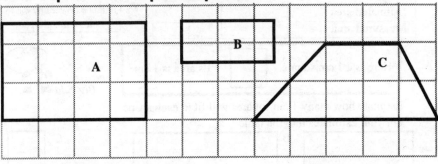

What is the area of each of these shapes ? • *Check your answers.*

D2: Awkward areas

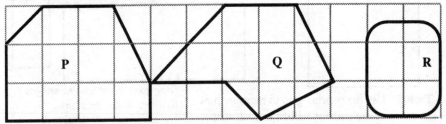

Work out the approximate area of each of these shapes.
• *Check your answers.*

Star Challenge 5 5   1 star for each correct Task

Approximate areas

Task 1: Collect a leaf from a tree or plant.
Place the leaf on centimetre squared paper.
Draw round the leaf.
Work out the approximate area of the leaf.
[Don't forget the bits of squares!]

Task 2: Place your hand on a sheet of centimetre squared paper.
Draw round your hand.
Work out the area covered by your hand.
• *Your teacher will need to mark these.*

Section 3: Estimating areas

In this section you will estimate areas using cm squares.

DEVELOPMENT

D1: Estimating areas

Task 1: *Copy this table:*

1 cm square acetate overlay

Shape	A	B	C	D	E
Estimated area					
Measured area					

Look at the 1 cm square. Imagine how many will fit into each shape.

Here is a 1 cm square. Its area is 1 cm²

Big Edd

Estimate how many 1 cm squares will fit in each shape.
Put your estimates into the table.

A   B   C
D   E

Task 2: Use the overlay grid to measure how many 1 cm squares will fit in each shape. Put the measured number of squares into the bottom row of the table.

How good at estimating are you?
- 4-5 right   excellent
- 3 right   satisfactory
- 2 or less   find out what you doing wrong

• *Check answers.*

Star Challenge 6

1 star for 3-4 reasonable estimates and 3-4 correct areas

1.
2.
3.
4.

Task 1: Put an estimate for each area into a table, like in D1

Task 2: Use an overlay grid to measure each area. Put areas into the table.

• *Show your teacher.*

A BIG EDD GUIDE   *Introducing Area*

Section 4: Areas of rectangles

In this section you will :
- find and use a rule for the area of a rectangle;
- work with different units of area.

DEVELOPMENT

D1: Investigating rectangles

Task 1: *Copy this table. Do not complete it yet.[It is for the results of Tasks 2 & 3]*

	Rectangle area 12 squares			Rectangle area 24 squares		
length						
width						

Task 2: Draw three *different* rectangles whose area is 12 squares.
Write the length and width on each rectangle.

Task 3: Draw three *different* rectangles whose area is 24 squares.
Write the length and width on each rectangle.

Task 4: Complete the table you drew in Task 1.

Task 5: There is a rule for working out the area of a rectangle.

Rule 1	Rule 2
area of rectangle = length + width	area of rectangle = length x width

Which of these is the correct rule ?

• *Check your answers.*

D2: Areas by rule

Task 1: *Write the rule for working out the area of a rectangle into your book.
Colour or highlight the rule so that it stands out.*

Task 2: *Use the rule to work out the area of each of these rectangles.
Write your answer in the form   Area of A = ... squares*

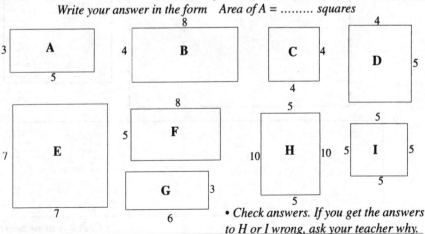

• *Check answers. If you get the answers to H or I wrong, ask your teacher why.*

D3: Measure and work out the area

For each rectangle:
- *measure the length and breadth*
- *work out the area*
- *write your answer in the form* $Area = \ldots\ldots cm^2$

1.

2.

3.

4.

5.

6.

7.

8.

• *Check your answers.*

A BIG EDD GUIDE — *Introducing Area*

Star Challenge 7

7-8 correct = 1 star

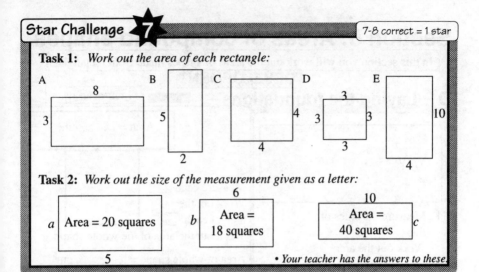

Task 1: Work out the area of each rectangle:

Task 2: Work out the size of the measurement given as a letter:

• Your teacher has the answers to these.

D4: Units of area

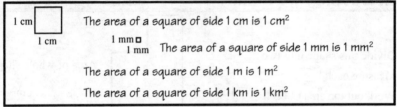

The area of a square of side 1 cm is 1 cm^2
The area of a square of side 1 mm is 1 mm^2
The area of a square of side 1 m is 1 m^2
The area of a square of side 1 km is 1 km^2

Work out the area of each of these rectangles.
They are not drawn to scale.
Each answer must have the correct unit, (mm^2, cm^2, m^2, or km^2)

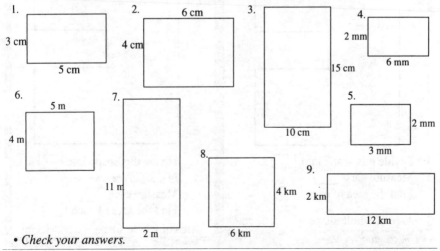

• Check your answers.

A BIG EDD GUIDE   *Introducing Area*

Section 5: Areas of compound shapes

In this section you will work out the areas of shapes made from rectangles.

DEVELOPMENT

D1: Laying the foundations (1 cm overlay)

Area = ………cm²

1. Measure the sides of this ☐
Work out the area.

Area = ………cm²

2. Measure each ☐
Work out the area of each ☐

Area = ……cm²

Work out the area of the whole shape.

Area of whole shape = ………… cm²

• *Check your answers.*

D2: Developing skills (1 cm overlay)

1.
Divide this shape into two ☐s.
Measure each ☐
Work out the area of each ☐
AND the area of the whole shape.

Area of whole shape = ………… cm²

2.
Divide this shape into ☐ s.
Measure each ☐
Find the area of each ☐

Area of whole shape = ……… cm²

3.
Divide this shape into ☐ s
in a different way.
Measure each ☐
Find the area of each ☐

Area of whole shape = ……… cm²

• *Check your answers.*

A BIG EDD GUIDE   *Introducing Area*

D3: Areas without measuring

Each given measurement is in cm.
Divide each shapes into rectangles.
Put the area of each rectangle inside it.
Work out the area of each whole shape.

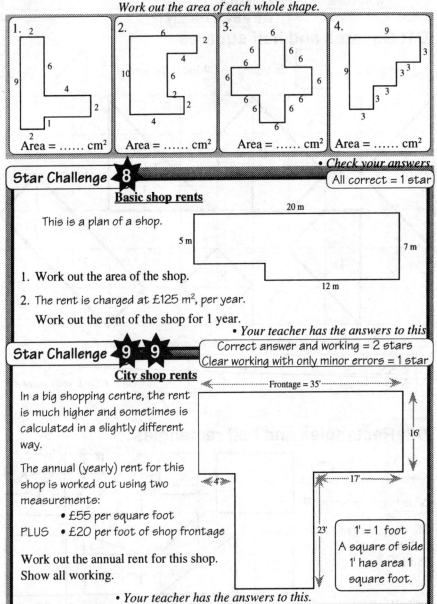

1. Area = …… cm²
2. Area = …… cm²
3. Area = …… cm²
4. Area = …… cm²

• Check your answers

Star Challenge 8 All correct = 1 star

Basic shop rents

This is a plan of a shop.

Dimensions: 20 m (top), 5 m (left), 7 m (right), 12 m (bottom).

1. Work out the area of the shop.
2. The rent is charged at £125 m², per year.
   Work out the rent of the shop for 1 year.

• Your teacher has the answers to this

Star Challenge 9 9
Correct answer and working = 2 stars
Clear working with only minor errors = 1 star

City shop rents

In a big shopping centre, the rent is much higher and sometimes is calculated in a slightly different way.

The annual (yearly) rent for this shop is worked out using two measurements:
  • £55 per square foot
PLUS • £20 per foot of shop frontage

Work out the annual rent for this shop. Show all working.

Dimensions: Frontage = 35', 16', 17', 4', 23'.

1' = 1 foot
A square of side 1' has area 1 square foot.

• Your teacher has the answers to this.

Section 6: Areas of right-angled triangles

In this section you will:
- find the connection between areas of rectangles and areas of right-angled Δs;
- work out areas of right-angled Δs.

DEVELOPMENT

D1: Squares and half squares

1. The area of ☐ is 1 cm². What is the area of ?

2. *Copy the table into your books. Fill in the area of each shape:*

Shape	A	B	C	D	E	F
Area						

• *Check your answers.*

D2: Rectangles and half rectangles

Each Δ is half the area of one of the rectangles.

ΔF is half of rectangle D.

Match up each rectangle and the triangle which is half its area.

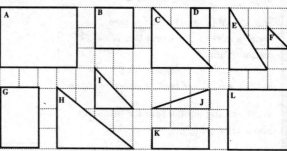

• *Check your answers*

D3: Areas of right-angled triangles

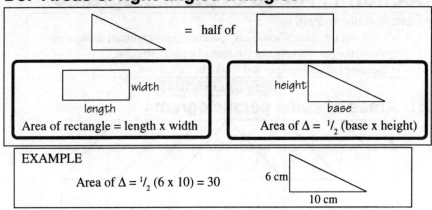

EXAMPLE

Area of $\Delta = \frac{1}{2} (6 \times 10) = 30$

Work out the area of each triangle:

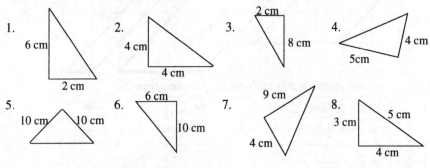

• *Check your answers.*

Star Challenge 10

7-8 correct = 1 star

Work out the area of each shape:

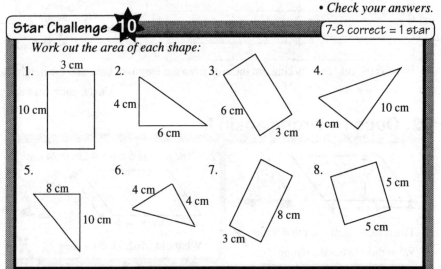

A BIG EDD GUIDE — Introducing Area

• *Your teacher has the answers to these.*

Section 7: Areas of parallelograms

In this section you will :
- work out the area of some easy parallelograms without using a rule;
- use a rule for working out the area of a parallelogram;
- measure parallelograms and work out their areas.

DEVELOPMENT

D1: Areas of some parallelograms

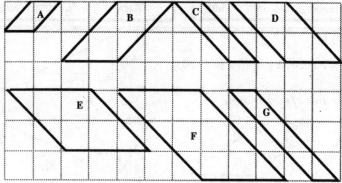

1. Copy and complete this table for the parallelograms:

	length of base	height	area
A	1	1	1
B			
C			
D			
E			
F			
G			

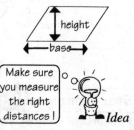

Make sure you measure the right distances ! *Idea*

2. What is the rule for working out the area from the length of base and the height ?

• *Check your answers.*

D2: Oops ! – wrong again !

1.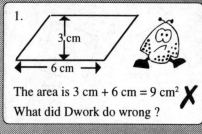

The area is 3 cm + 6 cm = 9 cm² ✗

What did Dwork do wrong ?

2. The area is 6 cm x 4 cm = 24 cm²

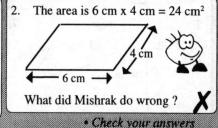

What did Mishrak do wrong ? ✗

• *Check your answers*

A BIG EDD GUIDE   *Introducing Area*

PRACTICE

P1: Areas of parallelograms

RULE
Area of parallelogram = base x height

Work out the area of each of these parallelograms:

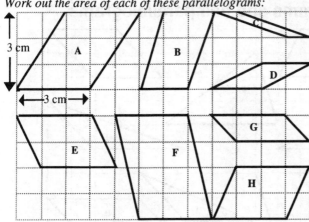

Copy the rule into your book. Highlight the rule.

Kooldood

• *Check your answers.*

Star Challenge 11
(7-8 correct = 1 star)

Work out the area of each of the parallelograms described below.
Each answer must have the correct unit of area.

1. base = 4 cm   height = 1 cm
2. base = 5 mm   height = 3 mm
3. base = 10 m   height = 3 m
4. base = 20 cm   height = 6 cm
5. base = 11 m   height = 5 m
6. base = 6 mm   height = 6 mm

Copy and complete the data for the following parallelograms.

7. base = 9 cm   height = …… cm   area = 45 cm^2
8. base = …… mm   height = 15 mm   area = 90 mm^2

• *Your teacher has the answers to these.*

Star Challenge 12
(Correct explanation = 1 star)

Draw a 6 cm by 4 cm rectangle on a piece of card. Cut it out.
Cut a triangle from one side (as shown).
Move the triangle and put it on the other end of the rectangle.

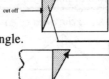

EXPLAIN how this shows that the area of a parallelogram is length of base x height.

Section 8: Areas of triangles

In this section you will:
- find the connection between the areas of parallelograms and triangles;
- learn how to measure the three heights of a triangle;
- work out the area of any triangle.

DEVELOPMENT

D1: Parallelograms and half parallelograms

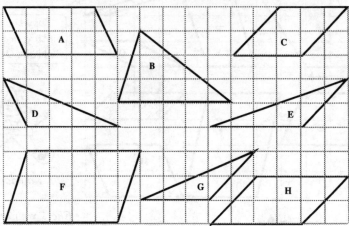

Each triangle is half the area of one of the parallelograms.

△ D is half the area of parallelogram A.

Match up each parallelogram and the triangle which is half its area.

• *Check your answers.*

D2: Rule for the area of a triangle

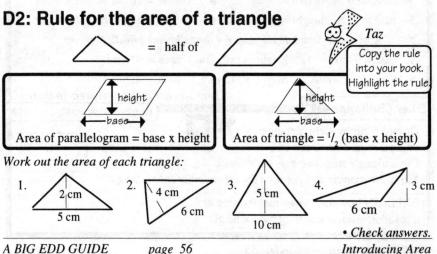

Taz: Copy the rule into your book. Highlight the rule.

Area of parallelogram = base × height

Area of triangle = ½ (base × height)

Work out the area of each triangle:

1. base 5 cm, height 2 cm
2. 4 cm, 6 cm
3. base 10 cm, height 5 cm
4. base 6 cm, height 3 cm

• *Check answers.*

A BIG EDD GUIDE   *Introducing Area*

PRACTICE

P1: Areas of triangles

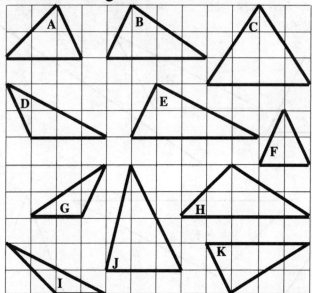

Task 1: *Copy and complete this table:*

Δ	Length of base	height	area
A			
B			
C			
D			
E			
F			
G			
H			
I			
J			
K			

Task 2:

Work out the area of each of these triangles:

1. base = 3 cm   height = 4 cm
2. base = 6 mm   height = 3 mm
3. base = 5 m   height = 4 m
4. base = 7 m   height = 3 m

• *Check your answers.*

Star Challenge 13

All correct = 1 star

Work out the area of each triangle:

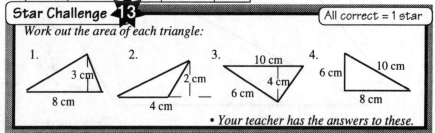

• *Your teacher has the answers to these.*

A BIG EDD GUIDE   Introducing Area

P2: No measurements given

For each of these triangles:
- *measure the base and height;*
- *calculate the area*

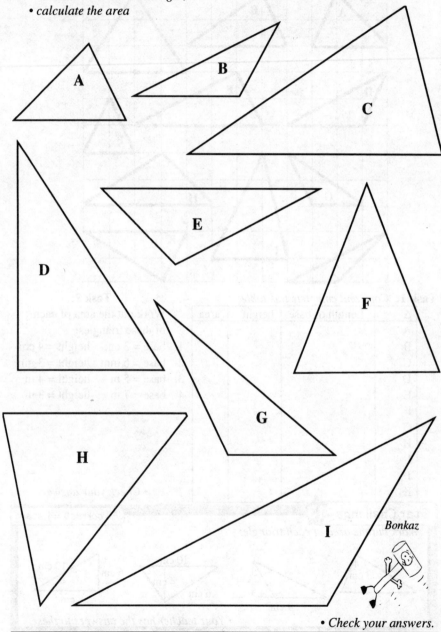

Bonkaz

• *Check your answers.*

Section 9: Perimeters

In this section you will:
- find the distance around shapes;
- find perimeters of a variety of shapes;
- tackle problems involving area and perimeter.

DEVELOPMENT

D1: Distance round the edge

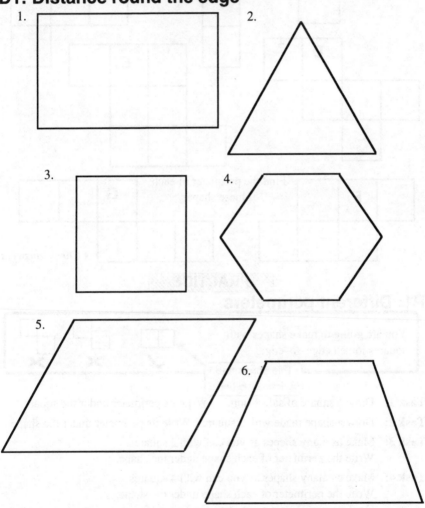

Measure the distance round the edge of each shape.

• *Check your answers.*

D2: Finding perimeters

> The **perimeter** of any shape is the distance round the edge of the shape.

Find the perimeter of each of these shapes.

• Check answers.

PRACTICE

P1: Different perimeters

> You are going to make shapes with squares joined edge-to-edge.
>
> This shape has perimeter 6 units

Task 1: Draw a square of side 1 unit. Write its perimeter under the square.

Task 2: Draw a shape made with 2 squares. Write its perimeter under the shape.

Task 3: Make as many shapes as you can with 3 squares.
Write the perimeter of each shape under the shape.

Task 4: Make as many shapes as you can with 4 squares.
Write the perimeter of each shape under the shape.
How many different perimeters can you get?

• Check answers.

A BIG EDD GUIDE   *Introducing Area*

Make ten different shapes with 5 squares.

> **Star Challenge 14** — All correct = 1 star
>
> Make ten different shapes with 5 squares.
> Under each shape, write its perimeter.
> • *Your teacher has the answers to these.*

P2: Rectangle perimeters

Work out the perimeter of each of these rectangles:

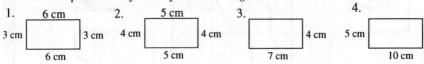

1. 6 cm × 3 cm
2. 5 cm × 4 cm
3. 7 cm × 4 cm
4. 10 cm × 5 cm

5. Rectangle with length 20 m and breadth 10 m.

6. Rectangle with length 12 mm and breadth 8 mm. • *Check your answers.*

> **Star Challenge 15 15 15** 4G
> 16 shapes = 3 stars
> 14-15 shapes = 2 stars
> 11-13 shapes = 1 star
>
> **Shapes with the same perimeter**
>
>
>
> This is a shape that can be made on a 4 x 4 geoboard, whose perimeter is 12 units. Draw it in your book like this.
>
> There are 16 different shapes that can be made on a 4 x 4 geoboard with a perimeter of 12 units. How many can you find ?
>
> • *Your teacher has the answers to these.*

> **Star Challenge 16 16**
> 20 marks = 2 stars
> 15-19 marks = 1 star
>
> **Task 1:** Imagine that you have a piece of wire 20 cm long.
> Sketch five different rectangles that you could make with this wire.
> Inside each rectangle, write its area.
>
> **Task 2:** Sketch five different rectangles each with an area of 36 cm².
> Under each rectangle, write its perimeter.
>
> 2 marks for each correct rectangle and area/perimeter
> • *Your teacher has the answers to these.*

Section 10: Altogether now

In this section you will use the skills developed in earlier sections.

EXTENSIONS

Star Challenge 17-17

30-33 marks = 2 stars
25-29 marks = 1 star

Rectangular pairs

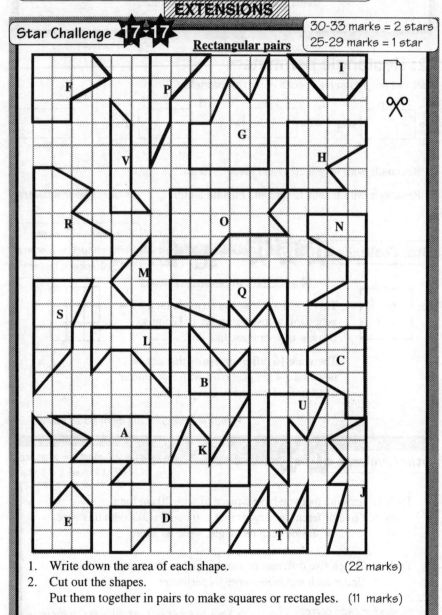

1. Write down the area of each shape. (22 marks)
2. Cut out the shapes.
   Put them together in pairs to make squares or rectangles. (11 marks)

• *Your teacher will need to mark these.*

A BIG EDD GUIDE   page 62   *Introducing Area*

Star Challenge 18

Equal areas

5 correct shapes = 2 stars
4 correct shapes = 1 star

Draw
- a rectangle
- a square
- a parallelogram
- a right-angled triangle
- a triangle which is not right-angled

each with an area of 16 squares

- *Your teacher will need to mark this.*

Star Challenge 19

Mixed bag

8 correct = 2 stars
6-7 correct = 1 star

Task 1: Work out the area of each shape:

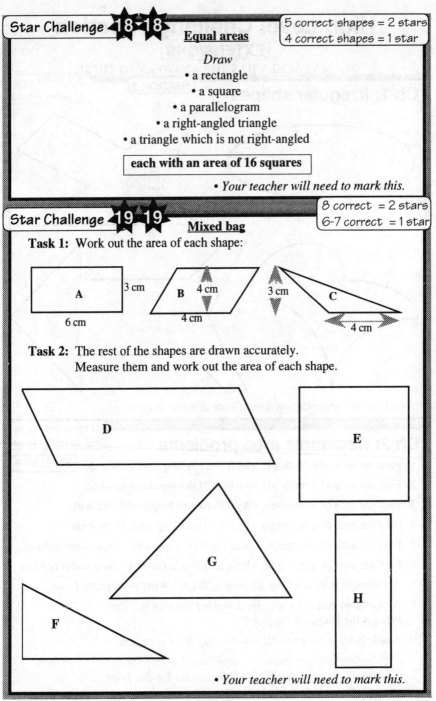

A: 6 cm × 3 cm
B: 4 cm × 4 cm
C: 4 cm, 3 cm

Task 2: The rest of the shapes are drawn accurately. Measure them and work out the area of each shape.

- *Your teacher will need to mark this.*

A BIG EDD GUIDE — *Introducing Area*

High Level Challenge Section
EXTENSIONS

YOUR TEACHER HAS THE ANSWERS TO THESE

Ch 1: Irregular shapes *SECTION 3*

3-4 reasonable answers = 1 star

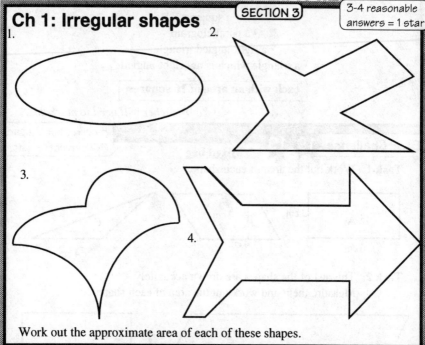

1.
2.
3.
4.

Work out the approximate area of each of these shapes.

Ch 2: Rectangle area problems

10 correct = 2 stars
7-9 correct = 1 star

1. Find the area of a rectangle which is 5 cm long and 4 cm wide. *SECTION 4*
2. Find the area of a rectangle which is 20 m long and 4 m wide.
3. Find the area of a rectangle which is 10 mm long and 6 mm wide.
4. Find the area of a rectangle which is 10 cm long and 10 cm wide.
5. Find the area of a rectangle whose length is 4 mm and whose width is 3 mm.
6. Find the area of a rectangle whose length is 2 km and whose width is 3 km.
7. A rectangle is 10 cm long. Its area is 50 cm². What is its width ?
8. A vegetable plot is a rectangle 3 m wide. Its area is 60 m².
   What is the length of the plot ?
9. A lawn is 20 m long and 10 m wide.   (a) What is its area ?
   On the fertiliser packet it says "Use 4 grams for each 1 m² of lawn."
   (b) How much fertiliser will be needed for this lawn ?

A BIG EDD GUIDE   *Introducing Area*

Ch 3: Equal area problems (SECTION 4)

5 correct = 2 stars
3-4 correct = 1 star

1. Rectangle A has area 24 cm². Complete rectangle B so that it has the same area as A.

2. A rectangle has length 15 cm and width 2 cm. Another rectangle has the same area. Its length is 10 cm. What is its width ?

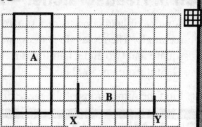

3. A rectangle has length 18 cm. A square of equal area has sides that are 6 cm long. What is the width of the rectangle.

4. A rectangle is 16 cm by 4 cm. A square has the same area as the rectangle. What is the length of the side of the square ?

5. A gardener has enough grass-seed to seed a lawn 12m by 3 m. If, instead, she uses all of it to seed a 4 m wide rectangular lawn, how long is the lawn ?

Ch 4: Ever decreasing squares

Q3,4,5 correct = 1 star
SECTION 4

1. Draw a square of side 16 cm. What is the area of this square ?

2. (a) Mark the midpoint of each side. Join the midpoints to make a second square.
   (b) Join up the midpoints of the second square to make a third square.
   (c) Repeat the process until you have eight squares, nested inside each other.

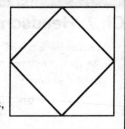

3. *Copy and complete this table:*

Square	Area in cm²
largest	
second	
third	
fourth	
fifth	
sixth	
seventh	
smallest	

4. If we drew another square around the outside of the largest square, what would its area be ?

5. The smallest square is too small to keep on drawing squares inside. But, imagine that you drew two more squares. What would be the area of the smaller of these two squares ?

A BIG EDD GUIDE   page 65   *Introducing Area*

SECTION 4 — All correct = 2 stars

Ch 5: Headscratcher – find the dimensions

A piece of land consists of a square on the side of a rectangle. The rectangle is the same width of the square and two and a half times as long. The total area is 5600 m².

The dimensions of a shape are the lengths of its sides.

Find the dimensions of the piece of land.

SECTION 4 — All correct = 1 star

Ch 6: Mixing the units

1. [rectangle: 10 mm by 2 cm]   2. [rectangle: 12 mm by 3 cm]

What is the area of this rectangle

(a) in cm²   (b) in mm²

What is the area of this rectangle

(a) in cm²   (b) in mm²

3. A rectangle is 1 m long and 50 cm wide. What is its area in (a) cm² (b) m²?

4. What is the area of a rectangle that is 1 cm 4 mm long and 1 cm 1 mm side?

---

2 solutions = 2 stars
1 solution = 1 star

Ch 7: Headscratcher – Equivalent areas (SECTION 4)

A rectangle is 3 cm by 8 cm. The total area of this rectangle and a square is equal to the area of another rectangle, which is 10 cm long and as wide as the square.

What is the length of the side of the square?
There are two possible solutions.
Can you find both?

---

1 star for each Task

Ch 8: Design a maths problem (SECTION 5)

Task 1: Design an area problem like those at the beginning of section 5. Make it suitable to be solved by an 11-year-old, without a calculator.

Use only rectangles but make the shape difficult.

Show clearly enough measurements for the problem to be solved.

Task 2: Draw a detailed solution to your problem on a separate page.

Ch 9: Find the lengths

SECTION 5 | All correct = 1 star

All the lengths given here are in cm.

Work out the measurements marked a, b, c, d, e, f.

Copy each diagram. Replace each letter with the correct measurement.

Work out the area of each shape.

• *Check your answers.*

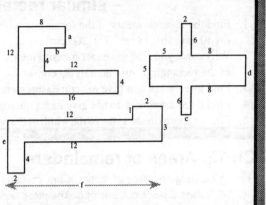

1 star for each Task. All work must be explained in detail, following the instructions given.

Ch 10: Who is right ?

SECTION 5

Letmewin and Sureshot were arguing about the correct way to do a certain kind of problem. They asked the teacher to say which one of them was correct. The problem was to find the area of the path surrounding a rectangular pond. They chose as an example a pond which is 4 m by 5 m and a path which is 1 m wide. Letmewin and Sureshot agreed that the diagram would look like this and that the outer rectangle would be 6 m by 7 m.

Letmewin: Find the area of the outer rectangle. Then find the area of the inner rectangle (the pond). Take away the area of the pond from the area of the outer rectangle. This give the area of the path.

Sureshot: You just add up the numbers 4 + 5 + 6 + 7

Task 1: Which of them is correct ? Investigate both methods for different sized ponds with paths 1 m wide. Consider at least five ponds. Show all your working out.

Task 2: Investigate what happens if you take paths 2 m, 3m, ... wide. Explain using diagrams. Find a rule that works for all widths of paths.

A BIG EDD GUIDE   page 67   *Introducing Area*

Ch 11: Headscratcher
– similar rectangles

SECTION 5 — All 5 correct = 2 stars / 4 correct = 1 star

1. Find the measurements of the rectangles with areas
   (a) 50 cm² (b) 18 cm² (c) 200 cm²
2. Why can't you find the exact measurements of the rectangle whose area is 20 cm² ?
3. Find three areas that give exact measurements.
4. Find three areas that do not give exact measurements.
5. Find an approximate value of the width of the rectangle whose area is 20 cm².

All rectangles in this problem are formed using the rule that the length must be twice the width.

Ch 12: Areas of remainders

SECTION 5 — 15 marks = 2 stars / 10-14 marks = 1 star

1. A rectangular piece of metal, 10cm long and 8 cm wide, has a piece cut out of it. The piece removed is also a rectangle, 5 cm long and 3 cm wide.
   Find: (a) the area of the original piece of metal.
   (b) the area of the piece that is cut out.
   (c) the area of metal left. (3 marks)

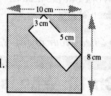

2. 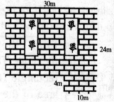 A rectangular lawn, 20 m by 10 m, has 4 square flower beds in it. Each flower bed has sides 4 m long.
   (a) What is the area of the grass ?

   Autumn fertiliser is to be applied at a rate of 50 grams to each square metre of grass.

   (b) Should the gardener buy the 8 kg bag or the 6 kg bag ? (4 marks)

3. This is a plan of a new patio. It will have two holes in it for flower beds, each 8 m long and 2 m wide. What area of concrete will be needed ?
   (4 marks)

   30m, 24m, 4m, 10m

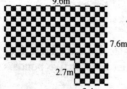

9.6m, 7.6m, 2.7m, 2.4m

4. This floor is to be covered with carpet tiles.
   Work out : (a) the area of the floor
   (b) the number of square carpet tiles, 1m by 1m, that will be needed
   [Be careful – the answer is *not* 53 or 54 !]
   (4 marks)

Ch 13: Carpeting the bungalow

SECTION 5 — 6 correct = 2 stars / 5 correct = 1 star

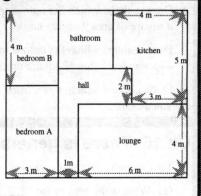

1. Find the cost of carpeting the lounge if the carpet costs £10 per m².
2. The carpet for bedroom A is half the price of the lounge carpet per m². Work out the cost of carpeting bedroom A.
3. The cost of the carpet in bedroom B is £72. How much is this carpet for 1 m²?
4. The carpet tiles in the kitchen cost £5 per m². What does it cost to tile the kitchen floor?
5. Work out the cost of carpeting the hall with carpet costing £8 per m².
6. The owners had £600 to carpet the whole bungalow. They do the bathroom last. What is the dearest carpet (per m²) that they can afford to buy?

Ch 14: Land problems

SECTION 6 — 1 star for each Problem / All working must be clearly shown

Problem 1: A builder wants to buy this plot of land to build houses on. He is told that it has an area of 18.75 acres. He is not sure that the figure is correct.

Check it for him.

Show all your working clearly so that the builder could see how you worked it out.

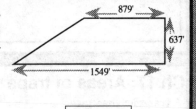

$1' = 1$ foot

1 acre = 43,560 square feet

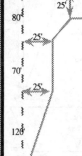

Problem 2: The County Council intends to buy some private land to make a road junction safer. The dotted line represents the original boundary. The solid line represents the new boundary. The land to be bought lies between the two boundaries.

The council will pay £3,000 an acre.

How much will this piece of land cost, to the nearest pound?

A BIG EDD GUIDE   *Introducing Area*

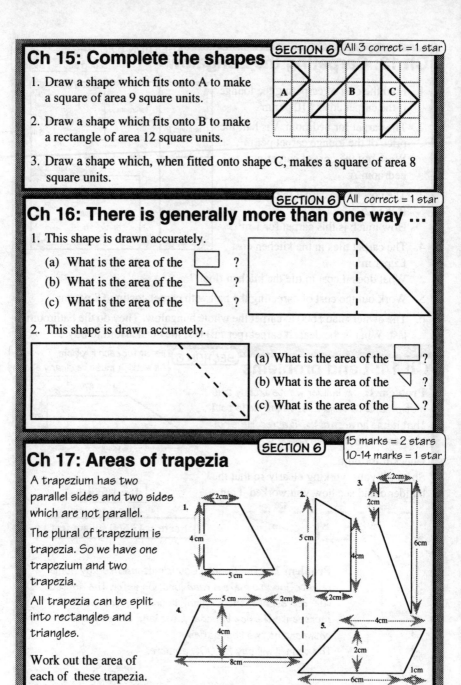

Ch 18: Find the missing measurements

SECTION 7 — 5-6 correct = 1 star

Find one missing measurement for each of these shapes.
Each measurement must have the correct unit of length.

1. Rectangle with area 12 cm² and length 4 cm.
2. Parallelogram with area 16 cm² and base 4 cm.
3. Rectangle with area 15 m² and width 3 m.
4. Rectangle with area 15 cm² and length 2 cm.
5. Parallelogram with area 18 m² and height 3 m.
6. Parallelogram with area 16 cm² and length 5 cm.

Ch 19: Investigating the areas of kites

SECTION 8 — 1 star for 4 correct areas. 1 star for Task 3 investigation and correct rule

Task 1: Work out the area of this kite.

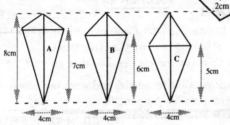

The dotted lines in this kite are called its **diagonals**.

Task 2: Make a table showing the area, the length of the long diagonal and the length of the short diagonal for each of these three kites.

Task 3: Investigate the areas of several more kites with diagonals of different lengths.
Find a rule connecting the area with the lengths of the diagonals.

Ch 20: Given an area of 4 squares

SECTION 8

Task 1: Make as many different shapes as you can with an area of 4 squares.
You can only use lines that go across or up the page. The lines must go from dot to dot.
Here are two to start with.

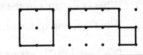

Targets: 10-13 shapes = 1 star
14 or more shapes = 2 stars

Task 2: Make as many different shapes as you can with an area of 4 squares.
You can use *any* lines that go from dot to dot.
Here are two to start with.

You cannot use any shapes that you made in Task 1.

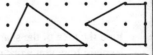

Targets: 15-19 shapes = 1 star
20 or more shapes = 2 stars

Ch 21: How long is the training run ?

SECTION 9 — 4 marks = 2 stars / 3 marks = 1 star

Tarporley United Football Team always start each period of training with 10 laps round the perimeter of the football pitch. The exact size of the pitch is not known. However, FA rules state that the length of the pitch must be at least 100 yards and not more than 130 yards. It must be at least 50 yards but nor more than 100 yards wide.

There are 1760 yards in 1 mile.

1. What is the shortest possible length of their training run ?
   Give your answer (a) in miles and yards (1 mark)
   and (b) as a decimal to the nearest 0.1 of a mile. (1 mark)

2. What is the longest possible length of their training run ?
   Give your answer (a) in miles and yards (1 mark)
   and (b) as a decimal to the nearest 0.1 of a mile. (1 mark)

Ch 22: The pig pen

SECTION 10 — Good investigation = 1 star / Correct rule and answer = 1 star

A rectangular pig pen is to be made with a wall as one side of the pen. There are 30m of fencing to make the other three sides. The farmer wants to make the pig pen as large as possible. Investigate some possible rectangles and work out how to get the largest possible pig pen. Show all working.

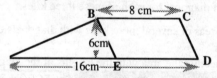

Ch 23: Compound areas

SECTION 10 — 9 marks = 2 stars / 6-8 marks = 1 star

BCDE is a parallelogram

1. What is the area of the shape ABCDE ? (2 marks)
2. What fraction of the total area is the area of $\triangle$ ABE ? (1 mark)

3. PQRV and PSTU are parallelograms.
   In $\triangle$RSV, the shortest distance of the point S from the line VR is 6 cm.

   Find the area of the shape PQRTU. (2 marks)
   Explain how you work it out. (4 marks)

A BIG EDD GUIDE — *Introducing Area*

Ch 24: Irregular polygons

SECTION 10 — 5 correct = 2 stars / 4 correct = 1 star

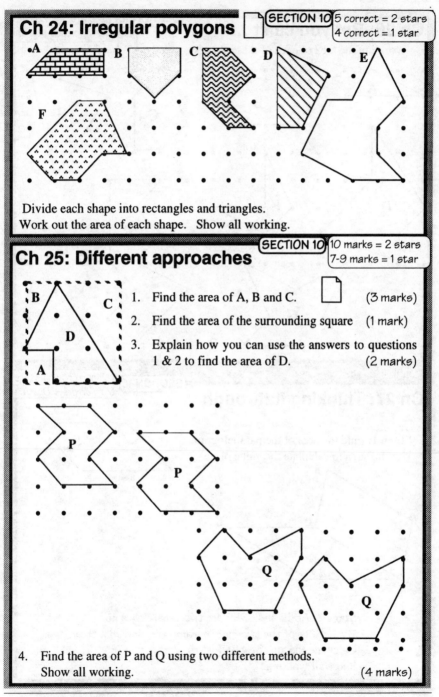

Divide each shape into rectangles and triangles.
Work out the area of each shape. Show all working.

Ch 25: Different approaches

SECTION 10 — 10 marks = 2 stars / 7-9 marks = 1 star

1. Find the area of A, B and C. (3 marks)
2. Find the area of the surrounding square (1 mark)
3. Explain how you can use the answers to questions 1 & 2 to find the area of D. (2 marks)

4. Find the area of P and Q using two different methods. Show all working. (4 marks)

A BIG EDD GUIDE   page 73   *Introducing Area*

Ch 26: Bet you can't …

SECTION 10 — 8 correct = 2 stars / 6-7 correct = 1 star

… work out the area of each of these shapes correctly.

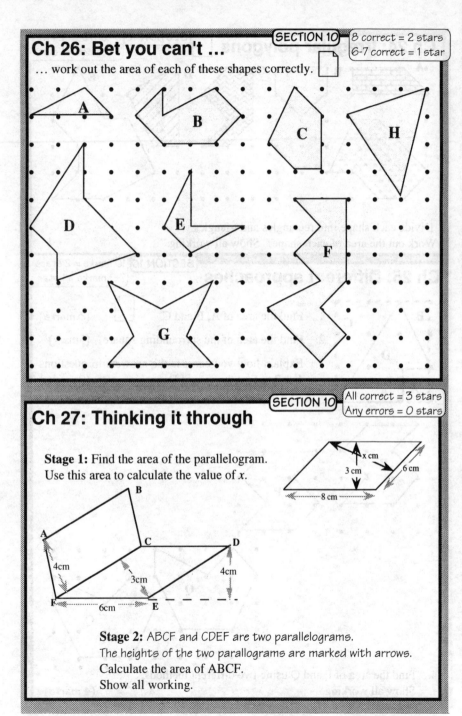

Ch 27: Thinking it through

SECTION 10 — All correct = 3 stars / Any errors = 0 stars

Stage 1: Find the area of the parallelogram.
Use this area to calculate the value of x.

Stage 2: ABCF and CDEF are two parallelograms.
The heights of the two parallograms are marked with arrows.
Calculate the area of ABCF.
Show all working.

A BIG EDD GUIDE   *Introducing Area*

THE NATIONAL CURRICULUM ...
... AND BEYOND ...

Big Edd

Journeys, Maps and Coordinates

> By the end of this topic you should be able to:
> - give directions
> - recognise relative positions of places
>
> Level 3
> - use compass directions
>
> Level 4
> - use coordinates in the first quadrant
> - find x– and y–coordinates
> - give coordinates of points in the first quadrant
> - recognise that points have the same x– or y– coordinates
> - plot points given coordinates in the first quadrant
>
> Level 6
> - draw and label simple lines with their equations
> - use coordinates in all four quadrants
> - plot points in all four quadrants

Journeys, Maps and Coordinates EXTRA
Section 1 : Giving directions

> In this section you will :
> • give directions in a variety of situations;
> • follow directions that you have been given.

DEVELOPMENT

D1: Can you tell me the way to ...   - *Class activity*

1. You have a new pupil in your class. She wants to go to the school office.
   Tell her how to get there from the door of your classroom.
2. Give her directions to get to the staffroom from the main school entrance.
3. ...
   The teacher (or someone in the class) chooses a starting point and a finishing point in the school. A student has to explain how to get from the start to the finishing point.
   This continues until everyone has had a chance to give directions.

D2: Youngsville, Tennessee   - *Small groups*

You are walking down Felix Avenue in Youngsville, Tennessee.
You turn right into Lorton Road.

1. What is the name of the road on your right ?
2. What is the name of the second road on your left ?
3. You turn left into St. Paul's Road and left again into "The Sandings".
   What kind of road is the Sandings ?

• *CHECK YOUR ANSWERS TO Q1–3*

4. Each person in the group should now :
   • choose a place on the map to start
   • choose a place on the map to finish
   • do NOT tell anyone else where the finish is
   • write down how to get from start to finish
5. Try to follow each others' instructions.
   Did you end up where you were meant to?
   If not, correct the instructions.

A BIG EDD GUIDE   *Journeys, Maps and Coordinates*

P1: Save Indiana Jones
Individual work

Indiana Jones is trapped in a dark cavern. The floor is covered with trapdoors to crocodile infested rivers below. He cannot see anything. He is in radio contact with you. You have the secret map and know where he is standing. You have marked his position with an X.

He is standing with his back to the cavern wall. One of his footsteps will take him from the centre of one square to the centre of the next.

The instructions to get him out start like this:
    2   TR 1   TL 2   ...

[TR means turn right   TL means turn left]

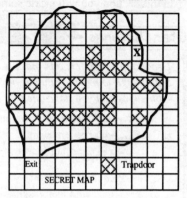

Complete the instructions that will get him safely out.

• Check your answers. If you went wrong, start again. If you need help, talk to your teacher.

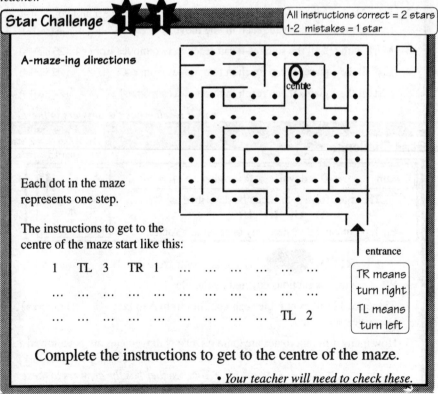

A BIG EDD GUIDE   Journeys, Maps and Coordinates

Section 2 : Route puzzles

In this section you will tackle some puzzles involving directions.

EXTENSIONS

Star Challenge 2 2

80–100 marks = 2 stars
50–79 marks = 1 star

Draw a grid like this and make it big enough to move a counter on – or a knight if you have one.

In chess a knight's move is an L-shape:
EITHER: 2 squares left/right
   and 1 up/down

OR: 2 squares up/down
   and 1 left/right.

1. A knight starts at the square e4. Mark with a 1 on your diagram all the squares it can reach in one move. (12 marks)

2. Two of these squares are already shown. Their labels are g3 and f6. List all the squares it can reach in one move. (14 marks)

3. Mark with a 2 all the squares it can reach in two moves from e4 (25 marks)

4. List all the squares it can reach in two moves from e4. (25 marks)

5. List all the squares it can reach in three moves from e4. (24 marks)

• *Your teacher has the answers to these.*

Star Challenge 3 3

14-15 marks = 2 stars
10-13 marks = 1 star

| U = up | D = down | R = right | L = left |

The route from A to B can be described as
R1 U1 R1 U1
Each point can be visited only once on any route.

1. **U1 R1 D1** ▬▬▬ is another route from A to B. (2 marks)
   What are the instructions covered by the blot ?

2. There are 12 different routes can you find from A to B. (12 marks)
   Describe each route.

3. How many different routes are there if DOWN movements are not allowed ?
   (1 mark)

• *Your teacher has the answers to these.*

A BIG EDD GUIDE   *Journeys, Maps and Coordinates*

Section 3 : Relative position

In this section you will :
- meet some words used to explain positions;
- use compass directions;
- find a place when you know where it is from another place;
- give the position of a place from another place.

DEVELOPMENT

D1: Who sits where ? — *Class activity*

Teacher's Desk	FRONT OF CLASS		
Mary Ranjit	Adi Gary	Fahzad Tracy	
Yoko Dave	Sara Afzal	Ben Mio	
Karl Sam	John Jenny	Yukio Sunay	

Sara sits • in front of John • behind Adi • left of Afzal • right of Dave

Who sits...
1. ...behind Mio?
2. ...to the left of Sam?
3. ...two seats in front of Yukio?
4. ...behind Jenny?
5. ...in front of Ranjit?
6. ...in front of and to the left of Sam?
7. Afzal was hit on the head from behind. Who could have hit him?
8. One day, Adi moved two seats back and two seats to the right. Whose seat did he take?

D2: North, South, East or West? - *Individual work*

1. Plymouth is further south than Southampton. Which town is further south, Liverpool or Cardiff?
2. Which town is further west, Glasgow or Aberdeen?
3. Which town is further east, Brighton or Carlisle ?
4. Which town is further north, Leeds or Manchester?
5. To travel from Oxford to Brighton you must go south-east (SE). In which direction do you travel to get <u>from</u> Leeds <u>to</u> Manchester ?
6. In which direction do you travel to get <u>from</u> Newcastle <u>to</u> Carlisle?
7. In which direction do you travel to get <u>from</u> Aberdeen <u>to</u> Glasgow?
8. In which direction do you travel to get <u>from</u> Nottingham <u>to</u> Liverpool?

• *Check your answers.*

P1: Around the counties

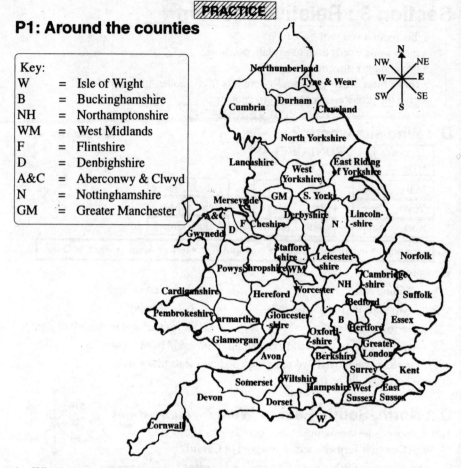

1. What county is directly West of Cheshire?
2. What county is directly East of Cheshire?
3. Six counties lie next to Cheshire. Name them.
4. What county is directly South of Durham?
5. Which two counties are directly North of Durham?
6. Name all the counties which lie next to Durham.
7. Name the county which is North–East (NE) of Greater London.
8. Name the county which is South–East (SE) of Greater London.
9. I am in a county NE of Leicester. Where am I?
10. I am in a county NW of Staffordshire. Where am I?
11. I am in a county SW of Wiltshire. Where am I?
12. I am in a county NW of Derbyshire. Where am I?
13. I am in a county E of Avon. Where am I?

• *Check your answers.*

A BIG EDD GUIDE　　　　*page 80*　　　　*Journeys, Maps and Coordinates*

D3: The Lake District

Each square is 5km wide and 5km high

From Sellafield, Workington is 20 km North

Fill in the gaps:
1. From Branthwaite, Maryport is ......km North
2. From Maryport, Branthwaite is ......km South
3. From Penrith, Workington is ......km West
4. From Workington, Penrith is ......km East
5. From Kendal, Carlisle is ......km ....
6. From Carlisle, Kendal is ......km .... • *Check your answers before going on.*

From Kendal, Penrith is 5 km East and 25 km North

7. From Workington, Maryport is   5 km East   and ......km North
8. From Sellafield, Whitehaven is   ......km West   and ......km ....
9. From Keswick, Maryport is   ......km ....   and ......km ....
10. From Whitehaven, Maryport is   ......km ....   and ......km ....
11. From Sellafield, Keswick is   ......km ....   and ......km ....
12. From Keswick, Silloth is   ......km ....   and ......km ....

• *Check your answers before going on.*

13. From Workington, Keswick is   ......km ....   and ......km ....
14. From Carlisle, Keswick is   ......km ....   and ......km ....
15. From Keswick, Kendal is   ......km ....   and ......km ....
16. From Kendal, Ambleside is   ......km ....   and ......km ....
17. From Keswick, Ambleside is   ......km ....   and ......km ....

• *Check your answers.*

Star Challenge 4

4-5 correct = 1 star

1. From Whitehaven, Sellafield is ......km ...... and ......km ......
2. From Keswick, ... is 25 km West and 5 km South.
3. .... is 15 km East and 20 km South from Keswick.
4. From Q, P is 30 km W and 30 km N. P is .... Q is ....
5. From T, R is 35 km W and 35 km S. R is .... T is ....

• *Your teacher has the answers to these.*

EXTENSION

E1: Compass shapes

The compass 'shape code' for this boat is
SW, W, NW, E, E, E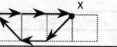

1. Copy and complete the compass 'shape code' for this shape:

SE   SE   E   ...

• *Check your answers.*

Star Challenge 5 5

14 marks = 2 stars
11-13 marks = 1 star

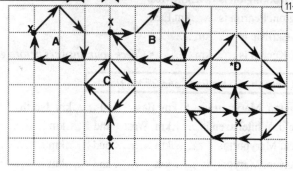

2. Write down the compass 'shape code' for each of these four shapes. (8 marks)

3. Draw the shape that is given by the 'shape code'   (2 marks)
   S S S E E N W N N W

4. Draw the shape that is given by the 'shape code'   (2 marks)
   S SE NE N SW NW

5. Draw the shape given by   (2 marks)
   NE NE NW NW SW SW SE SE N NE NW SW SE

• *Your teacher will need to mark this.*

Star Challenge 6

7-8 marks = 1 star

Pretend that the direction North is straight up your classroom to the front.

1. Who is the nearest person to you in the North direction ?   (1 mark)
2. Who is the nearest person to you in the South direction ?   (1 mark)
3. Who are the nearest persons to you in the E, W, NE, NW   (5 marks)
   and SE directions ?
4. Find out which way is North for your school.
   Which is the nearest building which is North of your classroom ? (1 mark)

• *Your teacher will need to mark this.*

Section 4: Coordinates in the first quadrant

In this section you will :
- meet coordinates as a way of fixing position;
- learn some of the words used with coordinates;
- use coordinates in the first quadrant.

DEVELOPMENT

D1: Painting by numbers *Small groups reporting back to a class discussion*

A firm of 12 painters are going to paint some of the window frames of a local hotel.

A ladder is placed against each set of windows. The ladders are joined together with ropes attached to ladder Ø. This is fixed to the edge of the building to hold the others in place. Here is a plan showing the positions of the windows and ladders.

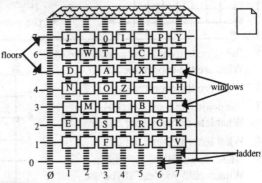

1. The window, letter code W is at position (2,6). Which ladder is W on ? ....
2. Which floor is W on ? ....
3. What is the letter of the window at (6,2) ? ....
4. What is the letter of the window at (7,1) ? ....
5. What is the letter of the window at (1,7) ? ....
6. What is the position of the window A ? (..., ...)
7. What is the position of the window B ? (...,...)
8. The foreman is a WEST HAM supporter.
   He tells the painters to paint the windows with the letter codes of his team.
   Give the instructions which would do this in the right order.

W	E	S	T	H	A	M
(...,...)	(...,...)	(...,...)	(...,...)	(...,...)	(...,...)	(...,...)

9. The gang of painters have a name for themselves.
   They paint the windows in the order of this name. Work out what the name is.

...	...	...	...	...	...	...	...	...	...	...
(5,6)	(7,4)	(4,7)	(5,2)	(6,7)	(7,7)	(1,5)	(3,4)	(4,4)	(1,2)	(1,4)

10. Sorry Sid is told to clean window (5,3).
    He is later found dead between the bottom of ladder Ø and ladder 1. His bucket is found on ladder Ø on the fifth floor. What happened to him?

D2: Coordinates

Individual work

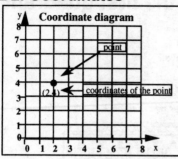

In a set of coordinates:
- the first number tells you how far ACROSS to go
- the second number tells you how far UP to go
- the order is important [Sorry Sid got the order wrong !]
- the point (0,0) is called the ORIGIN

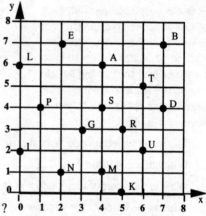

1. The coordinates of the point M are (4,1). What are the coordinates of R?
2. What are the coordinates of D ?
3. The point P is found at (1,4). What letter is found at (2,1) ?
4. What letter is found at (2,7) ?
5. "TEA" is (6,5), (2,7), (4,6). What would you 'eat' if you 'ate' the points (1,4), (2,7),(4,6), (4,4) ?
6. What would you 'eat' if you 'ate' the points (6,5), (6,2), (2,1), (4,6) ?
7. What would you 'eat' if you 'ate' the points (4,4), (6,5), (2,7), (4,6), (5,0) ?
8. Write the following "meal" as coordinates: BREAD AND DRIPPING.
9. What are the coordinates of the origin ?

• Check your answers.

PRACTICE

P1: Treasure Map

Individual work

Long John Silver buried his pirate gold on Skull Island. THIS IS HIS MAP.

What are the coordinates of ...
1. ... the Old Wreck ?
2. ... the centre of the Seething Swamp ?
3. ... Horrible Henry's Hut ?

What would be found at ...
4. ...(3,7) ?   5. ... (6,2) ?   6. ... $(4\frac{1}{2}, 6\frac{1}{2})$?

7. Long John marked the spot where he buried the Treasure with an X. What are the coordinates of the Treasure's position ?
8. What would be found halfway from Hangman's Hill to Deadman's Dyke?

• Check answers.

D3: Axes and Coordinates

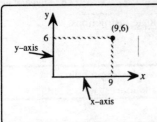

Always label your axes as x and y

X IS ALWAYS A-CROSS

For the point (9,6)
- (9,6) are the **coordinates**
- 9 is the **x-coordinate**
- 6 is the **y-coordinate**

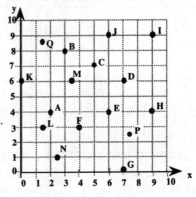

1. What is the *x*-coordinate of the point A ?
2. Give the *x*-coordinates of the points B,C,D,E.
3. What is the *y*-coordinate of the point F ?
4. Give the *y*-coordinates of the points G,H,I,J.
5. What are the coordinates of the point K ?
6. Give the coordinates of the points L,M,N,P,Q.
7. I choose a point with *x*-coordinate 7. Which two points could I have chosen ?
8. I choose a point with *x*-coordinate $1\frac{1}{2}$. Which points could I have chosen ?
9. I choose a point with *y*-coordinate 6. Which points could I have chosen ?
10. I choose a point with *y*-coordinate 4. Which points could I have chosen ?

• *Check your answers.*

Star Challenge 7 7

19-20 marks = 2 stars
14-17 marks = 1 star

MAKE YOUR OWN TREASURE MAP !

It must have:
- interesting places with drawings   (6 marks)
- buried treasure   (1 mark)
- a compass rose, real or invented   (1 mark)
- a name   (1 mark)
- coordinate axes   (2 marks)

The coordinates must be on the lines not in the gaps !

You should also have five questions about the map and their answers.
Each question or answer must have something to do with coordinates.

(5 marks)

For quality of map, plenty of colour, lots of detail   (4 marks)
Suggestion – can you make the map look old ?

• *Your teacher will need to mark this.*

A BIG EDD GUIDE   page 85   *Journeys, Maps and Coordinates*

Section 5: Plotting points

All individual work

In this section you will draw pictures from coordinate instructions.

DEVELOPMENT

D1: Plotting pictures

Marking the position of a point is called **plotting a point**
To **plot a point**, find its position on the grid and mark it with a small •

For each group of points in a picture set:
- *plot the points in the given order*
- *join them with straight lines as you go along*

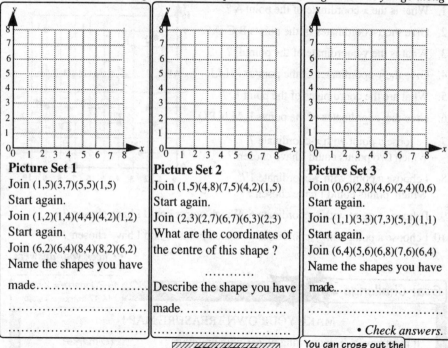

Picture Set 1
Join (1,5)(3,7)(5,5)(1,5)
Start again.
Join (1,2)(1,4)(4,4)(4,2)(1,2)
Start again.
Join (6,2)(6,4)(8,4)(8,2)(6,2)
Name the shapes you have
made............................
....
....

Picture Set 2
Join (1,5)(4,8)(7,5)(4,2)(1,5)
Start again.
Join (2,3)(2,7)(6,7)(6,3)(2,3)
What are the coordinates of
the centre of this shape?

....
Describe the shape you have
made. ....
....

Picture Set 3
Join (0,6)(2,8)(4,6)(2,4)(0,6)
Start again.
Join (1,1)(3,3)(7,3)(5,1)(1,1)
Start again.
Join (6,4)(5,6)(6,8)(7,6)(6,4)
Name the shapes you have
made............................
....

• *Check answers.*

PRACTICE

P1: More pictures

You can cross out the coordinates as you polot them – on the worksheet only!

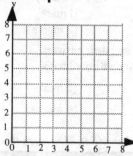

Picture Set 4
Join (4,0)(1,5)(7,5)(4,0)
Start again. Join (1,2)(4,7)(7,2)(1,2)
What are the coordinates
of the centre of this shape?

. . . .
Describe the shape you have made

....

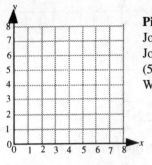

Picture Set 5
Join (5,7) to (4,6).
Join (3,7)(4,6)(4,4)(6,8)(8,4)
(5,0)(4,2)(3,0)(0,4)(2,8)(4,4).
What have you drawn ? ....

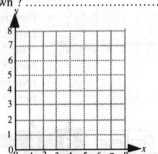

Picture Set 6
Join (1,7)(0,6)(1,5)(5,5)(5,6)
($5\frac{1}{2}$,5) (7,4)(7,3)(5,$3\frac{1}{2}$)(4,1)
(3,3)(2,3)(1,1) (0,3)(1,5)

What have you made ? ....
What should the coordinates of the eye be? ....

• *Check your answers.*

P2: Yet more pictures

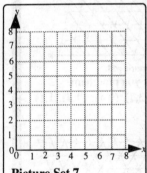

Picture Set 7
Join (1,2)(7,2)(7,6)(1,6)(1,2)
(3,6)(5,2)(7,6)
Start again.
Join (1,6)(3,2)(5,6)(7,2)

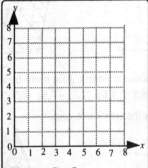

Picture Set 8
Join (8,1)(6,4)(7,4)(5,6)(6,6)
(4,8)(2,6)(3,6)(1,4)(2,4)
(0,1)(8,1)
Start again.
Join (5,1)(5,0)(3,0)(3,1)

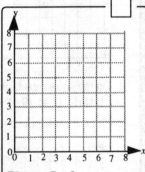

Picture Set 9
Join (8,5)(8,1)(0,1)(0,5)(8,5)
(6,7)(2,7)(0,5)
Start again.
Join (1,2)(2,2)(2,4)(1,4)(1,2)
Start again.
Join (6,2)(7,2)(7,4)(6,4)(6,2)
Start again.
Join (5,1)(5,4)(3,4)(3,1)

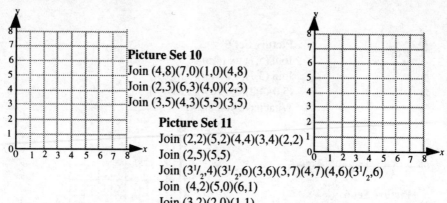

Picture Set 10
Join (4,8)(7,0)(1,0)(4,8)
Join (2,3)(6,3)(4,0)(2,3)
Join (3,5)(4,3)(5,5)(3,5)

Picture Set 11
Join (2,2)(5,2)(4,4)(3,4)(2,2)
Join (2,5)(5,5)
Join (3½,4)(3½,6)(3,6)(3,7)(4,7)(4,6)(3½,6)
Join (4,2)(5,0)(6,1)
Join (3,2)(2,0)(1,1)

• *Check your answers.*

Star Challenge

diagrams on square grids correct = 1 star
diagrams on isometric grids correct = 1 star

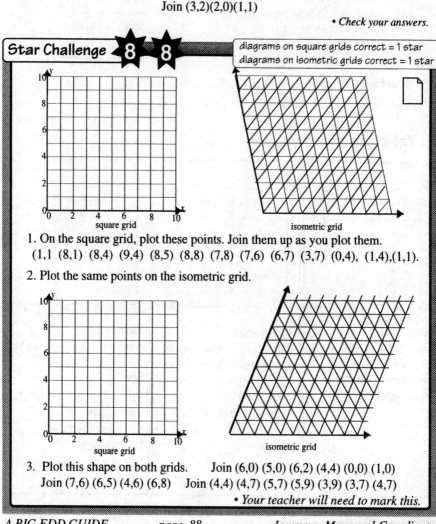

1. On the square grid, plot these points. Join them up as you plot them.
(1,1) (8,1) (8,4) (9,4) (8,5) (8,8) (7,8) (7,6) (6,7) (3,7) (0,4), (1,4),(1,1).

2. Plot the same points on the isometric grid.

3. Plot this shape on both grids.   Join (6,0) (5,0) (6,2) (4,4) (0,0) (1,0)
Join (7,6) (6,5) (4,6) (6,8)   Join (4,4) (4,7) (5,7) (5,9) (3,9) (3,7) (4,7)

• *Your teacher will need to mark this.*

A BIG EDD GUIDE   page 88   *Journeys, Maps and Coordinates*

Section 6: Negative numbers & coordinates

In this section you will:
- meet and use negative numbers;
- use negative numbers with coordinates;
- draw pictures using coordinate instructions using negative numbers.

DEVELOPMENT

D1: It's going to be cold tonight
Small groups leading back to class discussion
Only one set of answers needed for each group.

1. What does **–4** on the weather map mean ?
2. At which city will the temperature be 3 degrees below freezing point tonight ?
3. Which city will be the coldest tonight ?
4. Which city will be the least cold tonight ?
5. Place the cities in order of "coldness" with the coldest first.
6. This is a thermometer scale.

   What are the numbers that go at a, b, c and d ?

D2: Extending the coordinate grid

Small groups leading back to class discussion.
ONLY ONE SET OF ANSWERS NEEDED FOR EACH GROUP.

Copy and complete:

A is (1,2)   I is (…, …)
B is (3, …)   J is (…, …)
C is (…, …)   K is (…, …)
D is (…, –2)   L is (…, …)
E is (…, …)   M is (…, …)
F is (…, …)   N is (…, …)
G is (–3, …)   P is (…, …)
H is (…, …)   Q is (…, …)

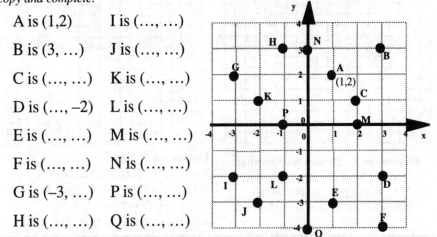

A BIG EDD GUIDE   *Journeys, Maps and Coordinates*

D3: Four-quadrant picture sets

All individual work

For each group of points in a picture set:
- *plot the points in the given order;*
- *join them together with straight lines, as you go along.*

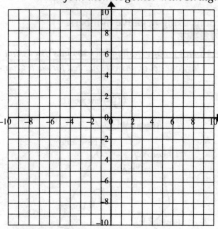

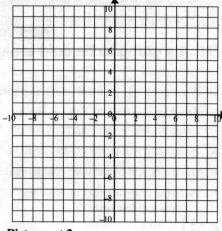

Picture set 1
Plot and join: (0,0)(6,3)(9,9)(0,0)
Plot and join: (0,0)(–6,3)(–9,9)(0,0)
Plot and join: (0,0)(–6,–3)(–9,–9)(0,0)
Plot and join: (0,0)(6,–3)(9,–9)(0,0)

Picture set 2
Plot and join: (4,0)(8,4)(3,4)(0,10)(–3,4)
(–8,4) (–4,0)(–8,–4)(–3,–4)(0,–10)(3,–4)
(8,–4)(4,0)

You may cross out each set of coordinates as you plot it.

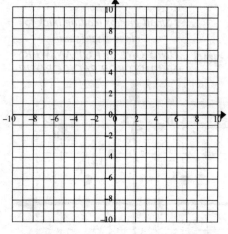

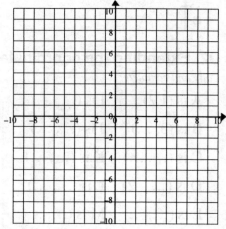

Picture set 3 – British Rail symbol
Join (–1,–1)(2,–4)(4, –4)(1,–1)(6,–1)(6,0)
(1,0)(3,2)(6,2)(6,3)(3,3)(0,6)(–2,6) (1,3)
(–4,3)(–4,2)(1,2)(–1,0)(–4,0)(–4,–1)(–1,–1)

- *Check your answers.*

Picture set 4 – Duck
Join (0,0)(1,1)(1,6)(2,7)(3,7)(4,6)(6,5)
(4,4)(2,4)(2,1)(3,0)(3,–2)(2,–3)(–5,–3)
(–7,–1) (–7,3)(–4,0)(0,0)

Join (0,–1)(–1,–2)(–5,–2)(–3,–1)(0,–1)

P1: Now you draw the grids

For each group of points in a picture set:
- *DRAW A GRID with values of x and y from –10 to 10*
- *plot the points in the given order;*
- *join them together with straight lines, as you go along.*

Picture set 1 – 8 petalled flower
Plot and join: (0,0)(5,3)(8,8)(3,5)(0,0)
Plot and join: (0,0)(2,6)(0,8)(–2,6)(0,0)
Plot and join: (0,0)(–3,5)(–8,8)(–5,3)(0,0)
Plot and join: (0,0)(–6,2)(–8,0)(–6,–2)(0,0)
Plot and join: (0,0)(–5,–3)(–8,–8)(–3,–5)(0,0)
Plot and join: (0,0)(–2,–6)(0,–8)(2,–6)(0,0)
Plot and join: (0,0)(3,–5)(8,–8)(5,–3)(0,0)
Plot and join: (0,0)(6,–2)(8,0)(6,2)(0,0)
Mark in any lines of symmetry.

Picture set 2 – Sail boat
Join (1,5)(5,1)(1,1)(1,7)(–4,1)(1,1)(1,–1)
(–4,–1)(–3,–3)(5,–3)(8,0)(3,0)(3,–1)(1,–1)

> The numbers must be ON THE LINES – not in the gaps!

- *Check your answers.*

Star Challenge 9

Face outline correct = 1 star
Face features correct = 1 star

Challenge picture set – The Face of the Monster King

Draw a grid with values of x and y from –8 to 8.

Plot and join: (–1,–5) (0,–3) (2,–3) (3,–5) (2,–4) (0,–4) (–1,–5)

Plot and join: (0,1) (2,1) (1,–2) (0,1)

Plot and join: (2,3) (5,2) (5,5) (4,5) (4,8) (3,5) (2,5) (1,8) (0,5) (–1,5) (–2,8) (–2,5)
(–3,5) (–3,2) (0,3) (–3,0) (–3,–2) (–2,–6) (0,–6) (4,–6) (5,–2) (5,0) (2,3)

- *Your teacher will need to mark this.*

Star Challenge 10

5 correct = 2 stars
4 correct = 1 star

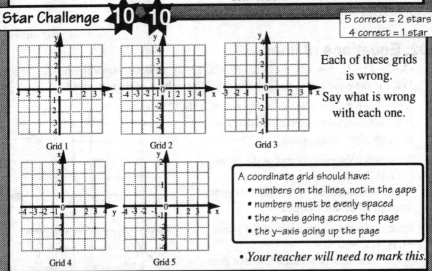

Each of these grids is wrong. Say what is wrong with each one.

A coordinate grid should have:
- numbers on the lines, not in the gaps
- numbers must be evenly spaced
- the x-axis going across the page
- the y-axis going up the page

- *Your teacher will need to mark this.*

Section 7: Lines

In this section you will:
- look at what is special about some sets of points;
- find equations for some lines;
- draw lines given their equations.

DEVELOPMENT

D1: Related coordinates

> **The equation of a line** is what is special about the coordinates of the points on the line.

1.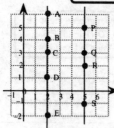

    (a) Write down the coordinates of the points A, B, C, D & E.

    (b) What is special about this set of coordinates?

    (c) The equation of the line through these points is $x = 2$

    What is the equation of the line through the points P, Q, R & S?

2. (a) Write down the coordinates of the marked points on line A.

    (b) What is special about the coordinates of line A?

    (c) What is the equation of line A?

    (d) What is the equation of line B?

    (e) What is the equation of line C?

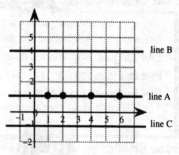

• *Check your answers.*

D2: Equations of lines

1. $(4,-2)$, $(1,-2)$, $(-4,-2)$, $(-3,-2)$, $(0,-2)$, $(2,-2)$ all have y-coordinate -2.
   What is the equation of the line that goes through all of these points?

2. Write down the coordinates of the points A, B, C, D and E.
   What is the equation of the line that goes through all of these points?

3. Write down the coordinates of the points F, G, H, I and J.
   What is the equation of the line that goes through all of these points?

4. Write down the coordinates of the points M, N, P, Q and R.
   What is the equation of the line that goes through all of these points?

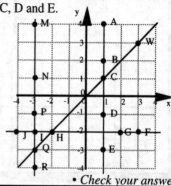

• *Check your answers.*

P1: Intersections of lines

> The point of intersection of two lines is the point where they cross.
>
> The lines $x = 2$ and $y = 3$ cross at the point (2,3)

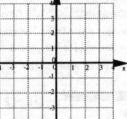

1. Where do the lines $x = 4$ and $y = -2$ cross ?
2. Where do the lines $x = -2$ and $y = 3$ cross ?
3. Where do the lines $x = -2$ and $y = -2$ cross ?
4. Where would $x = -4$ and $y = 2$ cross ?
5. Where would $x = -6$ and $y = 1$ cross ?
6. Where would the lines $x = 3$ and $y = -4$ cross ?
7. Where would the lines $y = -1$ and $x = 7$ cross ?
8. Where would the lines $y = -4$ and $x = -2$ cross ?
9. Where would the lines $x = 3$ and $x = 7$ cross? Explain your answer.
10. Where would the lines $y = 7$ and $y = -4$ cross? Explain your answer.

• *Check your answers.*

P2: Drawing lines

Task 1: Copy this grid. Draw and label these lines:
- $x = 3$
- $y = 4$
- $x = -1$
- $y = -4$

Task 2: Make a second copy of the grid. Draw and label these lines:
- $y = 2$
- $x = 0$
- $x = -2$
- $y = 0$

• *Check your answers.*

Star Challenge

7 correct = 2 stars
5-6 correct = 1 star

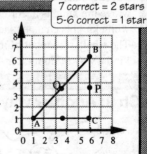

1. Write down the coordinates of A, B and C.
2. P is the midpoint of BC. What are the coordinates of P ?
3. Write down the coordinates of the midpoint of AC.
4. Write down the coordinates of the midpoint of AB.
5. Which of these is the equation of AC ?
   $y = 1 \quad x = 1 \quad y = 6 \quad x = 6$
6. Which of these is the equation of BC ?
   $y = 1 \quad x = 1 \quad y = 6 \quad x = 6$
7. Write down the coordinates of A, B and Q. Which of these is the equation of AB ? $\quad y = x \quad y = -x$

• *Your teacher will need to mark this.*

A BIG EDD GUIDE   *Journeys, Maps and Coordinates*

High Level Challenge Section
EXTENSIONS
YOUR TEACHER HAS THE ANSWERS TO THESE.

Ch 1: The West Country   [SECTION 1] All correct = 1 star

1. Demelza left Penzance on the A30. She turned left at the first major junction and right at the next. She stopped for the night at the next town. Where did she stop?
2. Ione travelled to Falmouth. The roads she took were the A38, the A30 and finally the A39. Name two towns that she could have started from.
3. Susan wants to know the shortest route from Torquay to Bude. Give her the directions she will need for her journey.
4. Unfortunately the A38 is blocked by a fallen tree just outside Exeter. Give an alternative route for Susan to take.

Ch 2: Dancing knights   [SECTION 2] Done in 16 moves and sensibly recorded = 2 stars

Draw a 3 x 3 grid, making it large enough to move knights on.
Put two black and two white knights in opposite corners as shown.
Move the knights according to the rules of chess so that black and
white knights change places. Devise a way of recording your moves.
The smallest number of moves to change places is 16.
Find a way of doing it in 16 moves. Record your moves.

B		B
W		W

Ch 3: Another way of looking at things   [SECTION 3] 8-9 correct = 1 star

A BIG EDD GUIDE   *Journeys, Maps and Coordinates*

On Natcur Island, what compass directions do you travel in to go …
1. …from the harbour to the hills
2. …from Deecity to the hills
3. …from Beetown to the forest
4. …from Seeford to the lake
5. …from Aville to the forest
6. …from the lake to Seeford

On Natcur island, where would I be if I was …
7. … south of Beetown and east of the hills
8. … west of Beetown and north-east of the hills
9. … north–west of the lake and north of the forest.

Ch 4: Herbs, Spices and Directions

SECTION 3
25 marks = 2 stars
20-24 marks = 1 star

A wisewoman had a herb and spice garden.
The herbs and spices were grown in a grid like this:

R	C	CA	D	S
CH	T	P	B	TA
A	G	RU	O	BL
SO	CU	SP	FE	H
FG	L	CW	BE	FV

N ↑

R = Rosemary	C = Comfrey	FV = Feverfew
CA = Camomile	D = Dill	BE = Bergamot
S = Sage	CH = Chives	CW = Caraway
T = Thyme	P = Parsley	L = Lemon balm
B = Basil	TA = Tarragon	FG = Fenugreek
A = Allspice	G = Garlic	H = Hyssop
RU = Rue	O = Oregano	FE = Fennel
BL = Bayleaf	SO = Sorrel	SP = Spearmint
CU = Cumin		

The wisewoman asked her husband to give her customers the herbs they required. She gave her husband directions based on this layout of the garden. She knew that he could recognise the herbs Thyme and Garlic. If he went N1 from T he could collect some Comfrey; NE2 from G and he could get some Dill.

1. She told him always to start at Thyme before collecting any herb.

   His instructions for one regular customer were:
   (a) E1 S1   (b) S1 E2 S1   (c) N1 W1 S3 E2
   (d) E3 S1 W2 N2   (e) W1 N1 E3 S4 E1

   Which herbs and spices should he have collected? (5 marks)

2. He made a mistake and started each time from the G square.
   What herbs and spices did he actually collect? (5 marks)

3. Which herb or spice is:
   (a) NW1 of G   (b) SW3 of B   (c) NE2 of G   (d) SE4 of R   (4 marks)

4. Then he started from Thyme and went E1 S3.
   What route would he take from this square to get back to Thyme? (2 marks)

5. He started from G and went N2 E3 SW1 S3 W2.
   (a) What herb or spice did this bring him to?
   (b) Write down a simpler route that he could have followed.
   (c) Give his return route to G for both routes. (4 marks)

6. Which of the following collection routes bring him to the same herbs or spices if he starts from Thyme on each occasion? (5 marks)

   Route A: E2 N1 W1   Route B: SE1 NE2 S3   Route C: S1 SW1 N2 NE1 E1
   Route D: SE2 N1 NW1 N1   Route E: NE1 W2 S2 SE2 E2 N1

Ch 5: Isometric coordinates

SECTION 4 36 marks = 2 stars
30-35 marks = 1 star

Coordinates are not always given on perpendicular axes.
On isometric paper (triangle spotty paper or triangle lined paper), axes are drawn at an angle to one another.
Position is still given using a pair of coordinates:
- the first number is the distance parallel to the axis *across* the page;
- the second number is the distance parallel to the axis *up* the page.

1. A has coordinates (4,2). (1 mark)
   What are the coordinates of B ?
2. What are the coordinates of C ? (1 mark)
3. What are the coordinates of
   D, E, F, G, H and I ? (6 marks)
4. What letter is at (1,7) ? (1 mark)
5. What letter is at (5,1) ? (1 mark)
6. What letter is at (3,3) ? (1 mark)
7. What are the coordinates of M, N, P and Q ? (4 marks)
8. What are the coordinates of the points midway between :
   (a) A & D (b) A & R (c) C & R (d) E & G (e) H & G ? (5 marks)
9. What type of triangle is $\triangle$ BAD ? (1 mark)
10. Joe found 7 triangles congruent (identical) to $\triangle$ BAD.
    How many can you find ? List them. (7 marks)
11. Sue found 7 triangles congruent (identical) to $\triangle$ HIJ.
    How many can you find ? List them. (7 marks)
12. If $\triangle$ HIJ was drawn with the same coordinates on an ordinary grid,
    what kind of triangle would it be ? (1 mark)

Ch 6: Picture challenges

SECTION 6 1 star for each correct picture (maximum 3 stars)

Challenge set 1: Coffee pot	Challenge set 2: Space ship	Challenge set 3: Windmill
Draw a grid with values of x and y from –8 to 8. Plot and join: (2,4) (–1,4) (–2,2) (–3,3) (–4,3)(–5,1) (–5,–1) (–4,–3) (–2,–3)(–2,–2) (–3,–2) (–4,–1) (–4,1) (–3,2) (–2,1) (–2,–4) (3,–4) (3,–3) (6,4) (5,4) (3,1) (3,2) (2,4) (2,5) (1,5) (0,6) (1,6) (0,5) (–1,5) (–1,4)	*Draw a grid with values of x and y from –8 to 8.* Plot and join: (1$^1/_2$,–4) ($^1/_2$,–4) (0,–3) (0,–2) (2,–2) (2,–3) (1$^1/_2$,–4) (1$^1/_2$,–5) ($^1/_2$,–5) ($^1/_2$,–4) Plot and join: (–1,3) (–1,4) (0,4) (0,1) (–1,1) (–1,3) (–3,–1) (0,–2) ($^1/_2$,2) (1,1) (1$^1/_2$, 2) (2,–2) (5,–1) (3,3) (3,1) (2,1) (2,4) (3,4) (3,3) Plot and join: (–$^1/_2$,4) (0,5) (1,8) ($^1/_2$,2) (1,1) (1$^1/_2$,2) (1,8) (2,5) (2$^1/_2$,4)	*Draw a grid with values of x and y from –8 to 8.* Plot and join: (1$^1/_2$,–1) (–1,–1) (–1,0) (1,2) (3,0) (3,–1) (1$^1/_2$,–1) (1$^1/_2$,1)($^1/_2$,1) ($^1/_2$,–1) Plot and join: (–1,2) (0,3) (–1,4) (–1,2) (–3,0) (–2,–1) (1,2) (–3,6) (–2,7) (5,0) (4,–1) (1,2) (1,4) (4,7) (5,6) (2,3) (3,2) (3,4) Plot and join: (1$^1/_2$,5$^1/_2$) (1$^1/_2$,4) ($^1/_2$, 4) ($^1/_2$,5$^1/_2$) (–$^1/_2$,5$^1/_2$) (1,7) (2$^1/_2$, 5$^1/_2$), (1$^1/_2$, 5$^1/_2$) (1$^1/_2$, 6) ($^1/_2$,6) ($^1/_2$,5$^1/_2$)

Ch 7: Distortion challenge

SECTION 6 — 1 star for each correct picture (maximum 2 stars)

1. *Draw a set of coordinate axes from –8 to 8 along each axis on squared paper.*
   Plot and join: (1,3) (2,2) (0,–6) (1,–7) (2,–6) (0,2) (1,3)
   Plot and join: (5,2) (5,1) (–3,–5) (–3,–6) (–2,–6) (4,2) (5,2)
   Plot and join: (–3,2) (–2,2) (4,–6) (5,–6) (5,–5) (–3,1) (–3,2)
   Plot and join: (–4,–2) (–3,–1) (5,–3) (6,–2) (5,–1) (–3,–3) (–4,–2)

2. *Draw a set of coordinate axes on isometric paper (triangle spotty or triangle lined).* Plot the same coordinates on this grid.

Ch 8: Midpoints of lines

SECTION 7 — 20 marks = 2 stars / 14-19 marks = 1 star

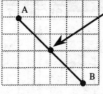

Draw a grid with the x-axis and the y-axis numbered from 0 to 8.

1. Plot the following points – *but do not join them up yet!*
   A(4,2) B(8,2) C(6,1) D(6,7) E(2,4)
   F(8,4) G(3,0) H(3,8) I(0,6) J(7,6)
2. Join up and label the line segments: AB, CD, EF, GH and IJ.
3. Mark the midpoints of these line segments on your diagrams.
   Label them P, Q, R, S and T.
4. Write down the coordinates of each of these midpoints.   (5 marks)

Draw a grid with the x-axis and the y-axis numbered from –8 to 8.

5. Plot the points and draw in the lines which join:
   (a) (3,0) to (3,3)   (b) (5,2) to (7,–4)   (c) (0,–5) to (–5,5)
   (d) (1,2) to (1,–7)   (e) (–3,6) to (7,2)   (f) (–2,4) to (4,-6)
6. Mark the midpoints of these line segments on your diagrams.
   Label them P, Q, R, S, T and U.
   Write down the coordinates of each of these midpoints.   (6 marks)

7. Look for a method that will give you the coordinates of the midpoints of a line segments without drawing?
   Find the midpoint M of the line joining L(2,5) and N(4,1) without drawing.
   Then check by drawing it !   (2 marks)

8. Without drawing, now find the midpoint of the line segments joining :
   A(4,8) to B(6,12)   and C(3,4) to D(7,6)   and   E(2,5) to F(3,10)
                                                                   (4 marks)

9. Explain your method.   3 marks)

A BIG EDD GUIDE   page 97   *Journeys, Maps and Coordinates*

Ch 9: Intersection challenge

SECTION 7 — 1 star for each Task

Task 1: Find where each of these pairs of lines cross:
1. $x = -4$ & $y = -2$
2. $x = -4$ & $y = -3.5$
3. $x = -5.5$ & $y = 3$
4. $x = 3$ & $y = -2.5$
5. $x = -3.2$ & $y = 2.6$
6. $y = 3.4$ & $x = 1.8$
7. $x = -4$ & $x = 2$
8. $y = -3.5$ & $y = 5.1$

Task 2: Find a way of working out where two lines (with equations of the form $x = k$ or $y = p$) cross, WITHOUT drawing the lines. Explain your method.

Ch 10: More midpoints

SECTION 7 — 14 marks = 2 stars / 10-13 marks = 1 star

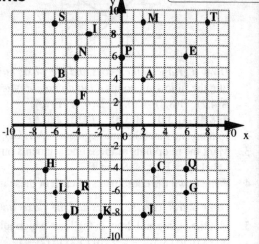

1. Find the coordinates of the midpoints of the line segments joining:
   (a) N to R
   (b) R to Q
   (c) G to E
   (d) L to E
   (e) N to Q
   (f) S to J

   (6 marks)

2. A line segment has endpoints (a,b) and (c,d).
   What are the coordinates of the midpoint of this line segment.

   (4 marks)

3. Use the answer to Q2 to find the midpoints of the following lines:
   (a) (3, 5) to (−1, 17)
   (b) (2.2, 4.6) to (−4, −2.6)
   (c) (5.4, −8.8) to (−10, −4.2)
   (d) (1.2, −2.7) to (−3, 4.9)

   (4 marks)

A BIG EDD GUIDE   *Journeys, Maps and Coordinates*

THE NATIONAL CURRICULUM ...
... AND BEYOND ...

Big Edd

Shape

By the end of this topic you should be able to:

Level 3
- classify triangles

Level 4
- recognise congruent triangles
- make a tesselation
- construct circles to fit given information

Level 5
- construct equilateral triangles

Level 6
- name geometric shapes
- draw named quadrilaterals
- match polygons with their properties

A BIG EDD GUIDE TO THE NATIONAL CURRICULUM

Shape
Section 1: Triangles

In this section you will:
- learn what is meant by congruent shapes;
- learn what is meant when you are asked to find 'different' shapes;
- make and classify triangles.

DEVELOPMENT

D1: Congruent triangles 3G [3]

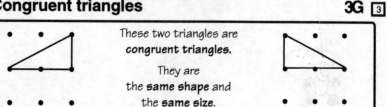

These two triangles are **congruent triangles**.

They are the **same shape** and the **same size**.

1. Make 4 more triangles that are congruent to these two triangles. Draw them on the spotty paper.

   Congruent means 'exactly the same'

2. Make 3 triangles that are congruent to this triangle. Draw them on the spotty paper.  *Optymistic*

- *You must ask your teacher if your triangles are congruent, BEFORE DOING D2.*

D2: Classifying triangles 3G [3]

You can recognise triangles that are the same (congruent).
Now you are going to make triangles that are **all different**.

Task 1: There are 8 possible different triangles that can be made on a 3 x 3 geoboard. Make all 8.

When you have made them, ask your teacher to check that they are all different, before doing Task 2.

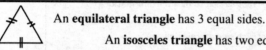
An **equilateral triangle** has 3 equal sides.
An **isosceles triangle** has two equal sides.
Scalene triangles have sides of different lengths.
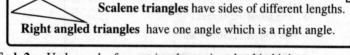
Right angled triangles have one angle which is a right angle.

Task 2: Under each of your triangles, write what kind it is.

- *Your teacher will need to check these.*

P1: Matchstick triangles

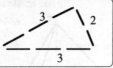

There is only one triangle that can be made with 8 matches.
It is an isosceles triangle.
It is a 3 3 2 triangle.

1. Make an equilateral triangle with 9 matches. Draw it.
2. Make a scalene triangle with 9 matches. Draw it.
3. Explain why you *cannot* make a 2 3 1 triangle?
4. This is an isosceles triangle made using 10 matches.
   Make a different triangle using 10 matches. Draw it.
   Under the triangle, write what kind it is.
5. This is one kind of triangle that can be made using 11 matches.

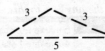

   Make three different triangles, each using 11 matches.
   Draw them.
   Under each triangle, write what kind it is.

• *Check your answers.*

Star Challenge

11 marks = 2 stars
9-10 marks = 1 star

6. Make three different triangles, each using 12 matches.
   Draw them.
   Under each triangle, write what kind it is.

   (1 mark for each correct triangle. 2 marks for each correct classification.)

7. Imagine that you have a number of matches.
   You count the matches.
   How can you tell, just by the number, whether you can make an
   equilateral triangle?   (2 marks)

• *Your teacher will need to mark these.*

P2: Show me how…

Show me how…

1. … to divide a square into 2 identical right-angled isosceles triangles using 1 straight line.
2. … to divide a square into 4 identical right-angled isosceles triangles using 2 straight lines.
3. … to divide a square into 8 identical right-angled isosceles triangles.
4. … to divide a square into 16 identical right-angled isosceles triangles.
5. *Copy and complete this table :*

number of Δs	2	4	8	16
number of lines	1			

6. How many lines would you use to divide a square into 64 right angled triangles ?

• *Check your answers.*

A BIG EDD GUIDE   page 101   Shape

Star Challenge 2·2

Can you beat Kazuo ?

23 triangles = 2 stars
15-22 triangles = 1 star

Kazuo made a list of all the triangles he could find in this diagram.

His list started   ABE
ABF
ABH
ACE......

He found 15 triangles.
His sister, Mio, said that she could find 23 triangles.

How many can you find ?

[If you label your triangles in alphabetical order (that is ABE rather than EBA) it will make them easier to check.]

• *Your teacher has the answers to this.*

Star Challenge 3·3

5 marks = 2 stars
4 marks = 1 star

Equilateral triangle puzzles

Task 1: There are 5 equilateral triangles in this triangle.

How many equilateral triangles are there in each of these two triangles ?   (2 marks)

Task 2: Arrange nine matches (as shown) to form three equilateral triangles.

Now move three matches <u>only</u> to make <u>five</u> equilateral triangles.   (2 marks)

Task 3: Arrange 6 matches to make 4 equilateral triangles.   (1 mark)

• *Your teacher has the answers to these.*

Star Challenge 4·4·4

27 (or more) triangles = 3 stars
24-26 triangles = 2 stars
20-23 triangles = 1 star

Triangle challenge !

A class of 15 year-olds were asked to find as many different triangles as possible that could be made on a 4 by 4 geoboard.
They found 27 different triangles.
How many can you find ?

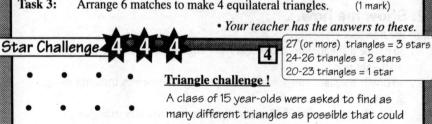

• *Your teacher has the answers to these.*

A BIG EDD GUIDE — Shape

Section 2: Rectangles and squares

In this section you will investigate some properties of rectangles and squares.

DEVELOPMENT

D1: Truths, untruths and halftruths

Small groups leading back to whole class discussion.

For each of these, state whether it is
always true, never true, sometimes true ?

A1: A rectangle has 4 straight sides	A2: Shapes that have 4 straight sides are rectangles
B1: A rectangle has 2 pairs of equal sides	B2: Shapes that have 2 pairs of equal sides are rectangles
C1: The opposite sides of a rectangle are parallel	C2: Shapes with opposite sides parallel are rectangles
D1: A rectangle has 4 right angles	D2: Shapes with 4 right angles are rectangles
E1: A square is a rectangle	E2: A rectangle is a square

Headbanger

D2: Finding the exact centre of a rectangle

Class discussion.

In a craft lesson, Sara needs to drill a hole <u>exactly</u> in the centre of a rectangular piece of metal.

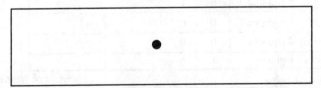

Find several different methods of getting the exact centre of the rectangle.

Get your teacher to draw each method on the board for you.

Discuss which is the best method.

A BIG EDD GUIDE   page 103   *Shape*

D3: How many different rectangles can you find?

Individual work

Rules: Rectangles must cover whole squares

Rectangles can go across or up/down - but not diagonally

Task 1: Make 6 copies of this 3 by 3 grid.
There are six different shaped rectangles that you can draw on this grid.
Find all 6.
Shade one on each grid.
Kooldood

Remember: a square is a rectangle

- *Check your answers.*

Star Challenge 5 5

10 triangles = 2 stars
8-9 triangles = 1 star

Task 2: There are 10 different rectangles that can be drawn on a 4 by 4 grid.
How many can you find? Draw them!

• *Your teacher has the answers to these.*

PRACTICE

P1: Systematic counting

1. *Copy and complete this table for each of the squares:*

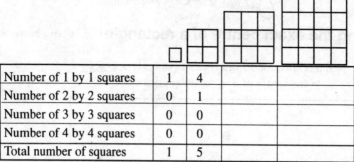

Number of 1 by 1 squares	1	4		
Number of 2 by 2 squares	0	1		
Number of 3 by 3 squares	0	0		
Number of 4 by 4 squares	0	0		
Total number of squares	1	5		

• *Check your answers*

Star Challenge 6

All correct = 1 star

2. Without drawing it, predict the total number of squares in a 5 by 5 square.

3. Without drawing it, predict the total number of squares in a 10 by 10 square.

• *Your teacher has the answers to these.*

A BIG EDD GUIDE   *Shape*

Star Challenge 7

17 marks = 2 stars
11-16 marks = 1 star

Square problems

Task 1:
How many squares can you find in this diagram?
You must not draw in any more lines. (3 marks)

Task 2:

A 2 by 3 rectangle can be covered in squares in two different ways:

6 squares   3 squares

1. What is the smallest number of squares needed to cover a 2 by 4 rectangle?
   Show how you do it. (2 marks: 1 for the number and 1 for the diagram)

2. What is the smallest number of squares needed to cover a 2 by 5 rectangle?
   Show how you do it. (2 marks: 1 for the number and 1 for the diagram)

3. What is the smallest number of squares needed to cover an 8 by 6 rectangle?
   Show how you do it. (2 marks: 1 for the number and 1 for the diagram)

4. What is the smallest number of squares needed to cover a 10 by 6 rectangle?
   Show how you do it. (2 marks: 1 for the number and 1 for the diagram)

5. Show how you can cover an 8 by 5 rectangle with 5 squares. (3 marks)

6. Show how you can cover a 13 by 8 rectangle with just 6 squares. (3 marks)

• *Your teacher will need to mark these.*

Star Challenge 8

12-13 marks = 2 stars
6-10 marks = 1 star

Square dissections

This square has been dissected into four congruent shapes each bounded by one straight line and two quarter circles.

This square has been dissected into four congruent smaller squares.

Dissect a square into 4 congruent pieces which are ...

1. ... rectangles (1 mark)
2. ... isosceles triangles (2 marks)
3. ... T shapes (3 marks)
4. ... L shapes (3 marks)
5. ... shapes bounded by two straight lines and two semicircles (4 marks)

• *Your teacher will need to mark these.*

Section 3: Quadrilaterals

In this section you will make and classify quadrilaterals.

DEVELOPMENT *All individual work*

> A **polygon** is a flat shape with straight sides
> A **triangle** is a polygon with 3 sides
> A **quadrilateral** is a polygon with 4 sides

Star Challenge 9

30-32 marks = 2 stars
22-29 marks = 1 star

A **quadrilateral** has 4 straight sides

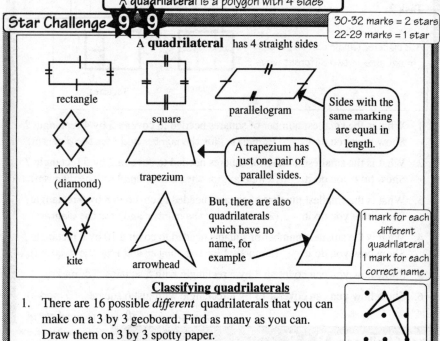

Sides with the same marking are equal in length.

A trapezium has just one pair of parallel sides.

But, there are also quadrilaterals which have no name, for example

1 mark for each different quadrilateral
1 mark for each correct name.

Classifying quadrilaterals

1. There are 16 possible *different* quadrilaterals that you can make on a 3 by 3 geoboard. Find as many as you can. Draw them on 3 by 3 spotty paper.

- *You may ask your teacher to check that they are all different.*

This is a 'crossed quadrilateral'. It is not allowed.

2. Name as many of your quadrilaterals as possible. If they have no name, write "no name".

- *Your teacher will need to mark these.*

Star Challenge 10

14-16 correct names = 1 star

Diagonals

On the worksheet are diagonals of quadrilaterals.

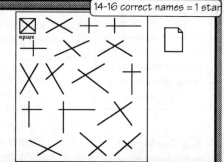

Draw the quadrilaterals.
The first one has been done for you.

Name the quadrilaterals.
There are two that have no name.

- *Your teacher will need to mark these.*

Star Challenge 11, 11, 11, 11 4G 4

38 marks	= 4 stars
34-37 marks	= 3 stars
30-33 marks	= 2 stars
28-29 marks	= 1 star

Quadrilateral challenge

Make the following shapes.
They must each fit on a 4 by 4 geoboard.
Draw them on 4 by 4 spotty paper.
Shade them in.

1. 4 different rectangles which are not squares. (4 marks)
2. 5 different squares (5 marks)
3. 4 different kites (4 marks)
4. 5 different arrowheads (there are at least 12) (5 marks)
5. 10 different parallelograms which are not rectangles or squares (10 marks)
6. one rhombus which is not a square (3 marks)
7. as many different trapezia as you can

TARGETS	8 trapezia	good	(4 marks)
	10 trapezia	very good	(5 marks)
	12 trapezia	excellent	(6 marks)
	14 or more	brilliant	(7 marks)

one trapezium
two trapezia

Gizmo

• *Your teacher has the answers to these.*

Star Challenge 12

All correct = 1 star

Take 4 triangles and make ...

1. Draw a square of side 8 cm on a piece of paper.
   Cut it out.
   Cut along the diagonals to make 4 right-angled triangles.
   Arrange the 4 pieces to make **a triangle**.
   Stick them in your book.

2. Draw and cut another square in the same way.
   Make **a rectangle** with the four triangles.
   Stick the rectangle in your book.

3. Draw and cut another square.
   Make **a parallelogram** from the triangles.
   Stick it in your book.

4. Draw and cut another square.
   Make **a trapezium** from the triangles.
   Stick it in your book.

• *Your teacher has the answers to these.*

A BIG EDD GUIDE   Shape

Section 4: More polygons

In this section you will:
- learn to recognise different sorts of polygons;
- construct equilateral triangles and regular hexagons.

DEVELOPMENT

D1: Can you find ... ?

> A **polygon** is a flat shape with straight sides
> A **triangle** is a polygon with 3 sides
> A **quadrilateral** is a polygon with 4 sides
> A **pentagon** is a polygon with 5 sides
> A **hexagon** is a polygon with 6 sides
> An **octagon** is a polygon with 8 sides
> A **decagon** is a polygon with 10 sides
> A **regular polygon** has equal sides and equal angles

Big Edd

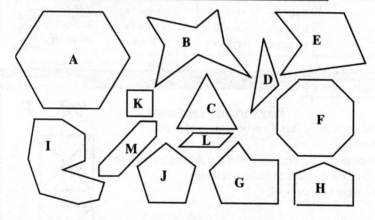

Can you find... *(Write down their letters)*
1. ...3 pentagons
2. ...3 hexagons
3. ....2 octagons
4. ...1 decagon
5. ...2 quadrilaterals
6. ...a regular octagon
7. ...a regular hexagon
8. ...a regular pentagon
9. ...a regular triangle
10. ...a regular quadrilateral ?
- *Check your answers.*

D2: Make a regular hexagon

1. Join some of the dots to make an equilateral triangle whose sides are 2 cm long.
   Make six of these equilateral triangles.
   Cut them out.

2. Make a regular hexagon with your six triangles.
   Stick it in your book.

- *Check your shape with the answers.*

D3: Compass constructions

1. Draw a line 4 cm long across the middle of your paper.
   Using a pair of compasses, construct an equilateral triangle whose sides are 4 cm long.
   Leave the compass marks on the diagram. If you need help, talk to your teacher.

2. In the same way, construct 6 equilateral triangles with sides 4 cm long, so that they make a regular hexagon.
   Leave the compass marks on the diagram. • *Show the hexagon to your teacher.*

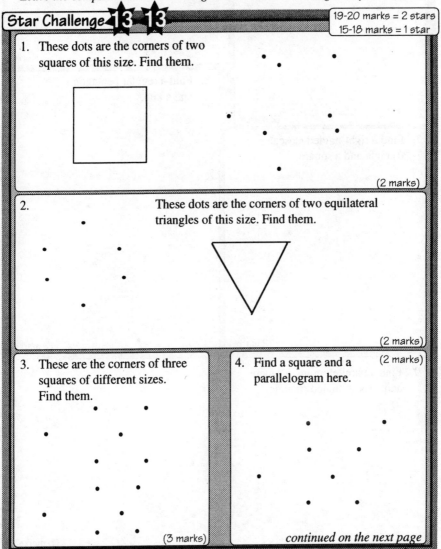

A BIG EDD GUIDE   *Shape*

5. Find a parallelogram and a right-angled triangle.

(2 marks)

6. Find a regular hexagon and a square

(2 marks)

7. Find a right-angled isosceles triangle and a square.

(2 marks)

8. Find a regular pentagon and a kite.

(2 marks)

9. Find a parallelogram, a square and a right-angled triangle.

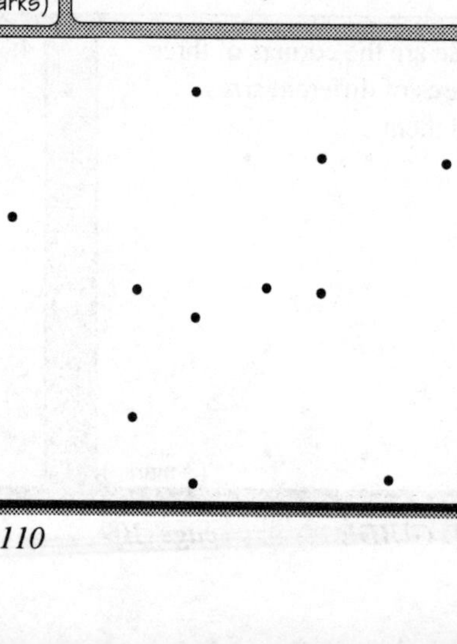

(3 marks)

Section 5: Circles

In this section you will:
- use words associated with circles;
- develop expertise with a pair of compasses.

DEVELOPMENT

D1: Introducing circles

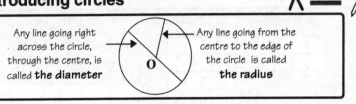

Any line going right across the circle, through the centre, is called **the diameter**

Any line going from the centre to the edge of the circle is called **the radius**

1. Put the point of the compass and its pencil 3 cm apart. Draw a circle with radius 3 cm.
2. Draw another circle with radius 5 cm.
3. What is the diameter of the circle you have just drawn?
4. A circle has diameter 8 cm. What is its radius?
5. Draw a circle with radius 4 cm.
6. Draw a circle with diameter 4 cm.

• *Check your answers.*

D2: Concentric circles

1. Draw a circle with radius 6 cm. Label its centre O.
   Draw another circle, with the same centre O, with radius 4 cm.
   Shade the ring formed between the two circles.
2. Two circles with the same centre are called **concentric circles**.
   Draw two concentric circles, one of radius 4 cm and the other of radius 3 cm.
3. Draw two concentric circles, one of *radius* 5 cm and the other of *diameter* 6cm.

• *Check your answers.*

> **Star Challenge 14**
>
> 5-6 correct = 1 star
>
> **Touching and overlapping circles**
>
> 1. Draw two circles, each with radius 3 cm, whose centres are 6 cm apart.
> 2. Draw two circles, each with radius 3 cm, whose centres are 5 cm apart.
> 3. Draw two circles, each with radius 3 cm, whose centres are 7 cm apart.
> 4. Draw two circles, each with radius 4 cm, that just touch each other.
> 5. Draw two circles, one with radius 3 cm, and one with radius 4 cm, that just touch each other. How far apart are their centres.
> 6. If two circles with radii 15cm and 20 cm are to be drawn so that they just touch each other, at what distance apart must you put the centres?
>
> • *Your teacher will need to mark this.*

Section 6: Tessellations

In this section you will:
- learn what is meant by a tessellation;
- experiment to find which shapes tessellate.

DEVELOPMENT

D1: Why not ?
Class discussion

> A **tessellation** is a regular repeating pattern with no gaps
>
> Here are two tessellations of squares
>
> Here are two tessellations of rectangles
>
> This is a tessellation of squares and rectangles
>
> *Big Edd*

1. Why is this not a tessellation ?

2. Why do circles not tessellate ?

PRACTICE

P1: Tessellating squares and rectangles
Individual work — crayons or coloured pens/pencils

1. Make a tessellation using at least 8 of these.
   Colour the tessellation to show the pattern clearly.

2. Make a different tessellation using at least 8 of these.
   Try and make it a more interesting pattern. Colour it.

3. Make a tessellation using at least 8 of ▭ and ☐ together.
   Colour the tessellation to show the pattern clearly.

4. Make a tessellation using at least 8 of ▯ and ▭ together.

5. A tessellation starts like this:
   Copy it and continue it to cover about $1/4$ of your page.
   Use colour to show the pattern.

   • *Show your tessellations to your teacher.*

A BIG EDD GUIDE   *Shape*

Star Challenge 15

2-3 correct Tasks = 1 star

Tessellating triangles and hexagons

Task 1: Draw a triangle on a piece of card.
Cut it out.
Draw round the triangle on a piece of paper.
Make a tessellation with at least 6 copies of your triangle.
Do you think all triangles tessellate ?

Task 2: Make a tessellation using at least 8 equilateral triangles.
Use triangular spotty or triangular lined paper.
Colour the tessellation to show the pattern clearly.
Stick the tessellation into your book.

Task 3: Make a tessellation using at least 8 hexagons.
Use triangular spotty or triangular lined paper.
Colour the tessellation to show the pattern clearly.
Stick the tessellation into your book.

• *Show your tessellations to your teacher.*

Star Challenge 16 16 16

8-10 marks = 2 stars
5-8 marks = 1 star
plus 1 star for a good display

Now try these ...

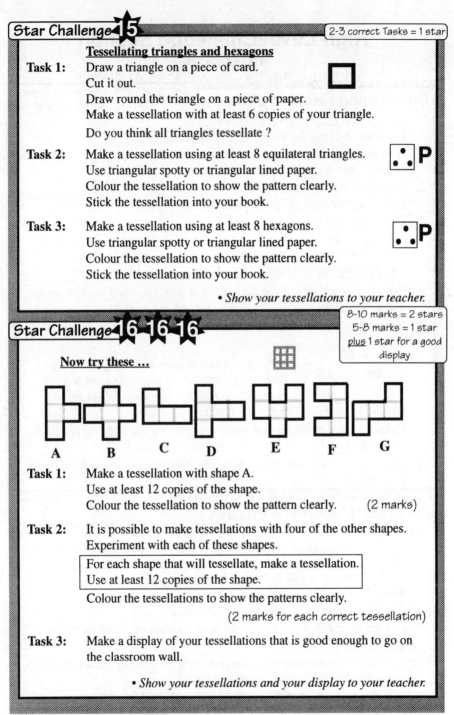

A   B   C   D   E   F   G

Task 1: Make a tessellation with shape A.
Use at least 12 copies of the shape.
Colour the tessellation to show the pattern clearly.   (2 marks)

Task 2: It is possible to make tessellations with four of the other shapes.
Experiment with each of these shapes.

> For each shape that will tessellate, make a tessellation.
> Use at least 12 copies of the shape.

Colour the tessellations to show the patterns clearly.

(2 marks for each correct tessellation)

Task 3: Make a display of your tessellations that is good enough to go on the classroom wall.

• *Show your tessellations and your display to your teacher.*

High Level Challenge Section
EXTENSIONS
YOUR TEACHER HAS THE ANSWERS TO THESE.

Ch 1: Going round in circles `SECTION 1`
7-8 correct = 2 stars
6 correct = 1 star

1. Draw 5 dots roughly in the form of a circle.
   Label two dots that are next to each other A and B.
   How many triangles can you make that have A, B
   and one other dot as its corners?
2. Repeat the experiment with 9 dots.
   How many triangles can you make this time?
3. *Complete this table:*

Number of dots	6	7	9	10	12
Number of triangles using A, B and one other dot					

4. Explain in words how, given the number of dots, you could say how many triangles there are.
5. If there are n dots (n is an unknown number), how many triangles would there be?
6. Now let us make the rules more difficult.
   How many triangles can you make using any three dots, provided at least two of them are next to each other?
7. Using the same condition, how many triangles can you make using a circle of 10 dots?
8. If you have a circle with n dots, how many triangles can you make with the same condition?

Ch 2: MacMahon Tile Puzzles `SECTION 1`
1 star for a solution to Puzzle No.1,
plus
2 stars for a solution to Puzzle No. 2

Puzzle number 1

Take a square. Divide it into 4 right angled isosceles triangles by drawing the diagonals of the square. This is a MacMahon tile.
Make 24 tiles.   You will need 3 colours.
For each tile   • colour in all the isosceles triangles
                • use 1, 2 or 3 colours

Each tile must be different. There are 24 different ways of colouring the tiles.

Puzzle number 2

Take the set of MacMahon tiles. Arrange them to make a 4 by 6 rectangle so that: • edges that touch have the same colour
   • the outside edge of the rectangle is the same colour all round

A BIG EDD GUIDE   *page 114*   *Shape*

Ch 3: Investigating 3–dot triangles

4 correct = 2 stars
3 correct = 1 star

SECTION 1

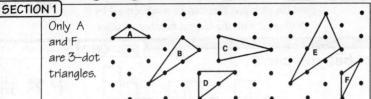

Only A and F are 3–dot triangles.

1. Copy shape G onto spotty paper and divide it up into 3-dot triangles. Count the number of triangles. Make two more copies of G and divide each one up into 3-dot triangles. Count the number of triangles.

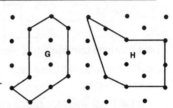

2. Repeat the instructions given for G, for shape H.

3. What do you notice about the number of 3-dot triangles in G and H? Do you think this will be true for any shape? Test your answer by making a shape of your own. Split it up into 3-dot triangles in three different ways. Say whether you were right.

4. Draw the equilateral triangle X onto your spotty paper. Make several copies of it. In how many different ways can you split the equilateral triangle into 3-dot triangles?

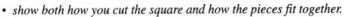

SECTION 2

Ch 4: Mega-challenging problem

1 star for solutions to Q1 & 2
plus
1 star for solutions to each of Q3-5

In each of the following cases
- *you start with a square and a rectangle;*
- *you may cut the square into 2 pieces only but you must not cut the rectangle at all;*
- *combine the 2 pieces of the square with the rectangle to make the given, larger, rectangle;*
- *show both how you cut the square and how the pieces fit together.*

1. Make a 2 by 5 rectangle from a 3 by 3 square and a 1 by 1 rectangle.

2. Make a 3 by 6 rectangle from a 4 by 4 square and a 2 by 1 rectangle.

3. Make a 4 by 7 rectangle from a 5 by 5 square and a 3 by 1 rectangle.

4. Make a 5 by 8 rectangle from a 6 by 6 square and a 4 by 1 rectangle.

5. Make a 9 by 12 rectangle from a 10 by 10 square and an 8 by 1 rectangle.

Ch 5: The ultimate polygon challenge

SECTION 3 All correct = 2 stars

Find the polygon that can be made on a 4 by 4 geoboard with the largest number of sides.

4G [4]

Ch 6: I bet you can't ...

SECTION 3 All correct = 1 star

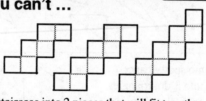

P ✹ ▦

1. ... cut the first staircase into 2 pieces that will fit together to make a rectangle.
2. ... cut the second staircase into 2 pieces that will fit together to make a parallelogram.
3. ... cut the third staircase into 3 pieces that will fit together to make a square.

Ch 7: Dissections of an equilateral triangle

All correct = 1 star

SECTION 4

This equilateral triangle has been dissected into three congruent isosceles triangles.

This equilateral triangle has been dissected into three congruent shapes, each bounded by two curves and a straight line.

Construct two equilateral triangles with sides 4 cm long.

Task 1: Dissect one triangle into 3 congruent kites.

Task 2: Dissect one triangle into 3 congruent trapezia.

trapezia is the plural of trapezium

Ch 8: Crossed hexagons

SECTION 4

16 hexagons = 3 stars
14-15 hexagons = 2 stars
12-13 hexagons = 1 star

In your book, mark the six corner dots of a regular hexagon as here.

You could make a regular hexagon if you joined them up round the outside.

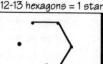

BUT.. if you joined them up in a different order you could get a crossed hexagon.

For example:

Make as many *different* crossed hexagons as you can.
You can visit each dot once only.
You start and end at the same point.
Reflections are allowed but ...
...only if they are not rotations.

A BIG EDD GUIDE   page 116   *Shape*

Ch 9: Tetrahexes

sheet of hexagons **P** ✂

SECTION 4

Task 1: 10 correct = 1 star
Task 2: 2 correct = 1 star
4 correct = 2 stars

If you join 4 hexagons together, edge to edge, you can make different shapes.

These shapes are called **tetrahexes**.

Two of them are 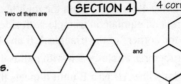 and

Task 1: There are 10 possible different tetrahexes.

In this problem the rules are slightly different :
• if one tetrahex can be *turned round* to fit on another tetrahex, it is the same.
• if one tetrahex can be *turned over* to fit on another tetrahex, it is different.

Find all 10 tetrahexes.
Colour each one in a different way.

Task 2: The ten tetrahexes can be fitted together to make these four shapes.
Make the shapes with your tetrahexes and stick them in your books.

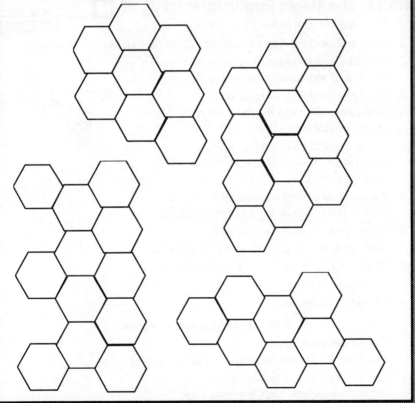

A BIG EDD GUIDE   page 117   *Shape*

Ch 10: Compass capers

SECTION 5 — All correct = 1 star

1. Draw a line 4 cm long across the middle of the page.
   Construct an equilateral triangle with sides 4 cm long.
   Label the corners of the triangle A, B and C.

2. Construct three circles, each with radius 4 cm, whose centres are A, B and C.

3. Extend the line AB past B until it meets the other side of the circle.
   Label the end of this line D.

4. Extend the line AC past C until it meets the other side of the circle.
   Label the end of this line E.

5. In exactly the same way
   - extend BC to the point F
   - extend BA to the point G
   - extend CA to the point H
   - extend CB to the point I

6. Join up the points DEFGHID in order with straight lines.
   What is the name of this shape?

7. How many equilateral triangles are there?

Ch 11: The Magic Egg tangram P ∧ ✂ ☐

1 star for correct egg
1 star for bird
SECTION 5

1. Draw a circle with radius 6 cm, centre O.

2. Draw and label the diameters AC and BD at right angles to each other.

3. Join A to B and continue the line on past B.
   Join C to B and continue the line on past B.

4. Put the point of your compass on C.
   With radius CA, draw the arc of the circle AE.
   Do not go past E.

5. Put the point of your compass on A.
   With radius AC, draw the arc of the circle CF.
   Do not go past F.

6. Put the point of your compass on B.
   With radius BE, draw the arc of the circle EF.

7. Put the point of your compass on D.
   With the same radius as BE, mark the point G.

8. Draw a circle, centre G, going through D.

9. Draw GH and GI.

10. Extend OB to the point J.

Your magic egg is now complete.

11. Cut out the magic egg.
    Cut along the lines in the diagram to make 9 pieces

12. Use all of the pieces to make a bird
    of your own design. Stick it in your book.

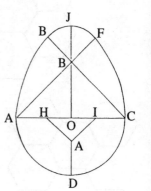

A BIG EDD GUIDE   page 118   *Shape*

Ch 12: A famous combinatorial problem

Task 1 correct = 1 star
Task 2 correct = 1 star
Task 3 correct = 2 stars

Combinatorics is a branch of mathematics.
One kind of problem that is often tackled is that of finding all possible arrangements of a given type.
This particular problem is one that is generally attributed to the British mathematician Percy A. MacMahon.

Draw 24 square tiles with sides 4 cm long.
For each square tile
- mark the midpoints of each side
- join the midpoints of each side with one of these three lines

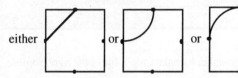

The curves are quarter circles with centres at either the corner or the centre of the square.

There are 24 possible different patterns.
Rotations are not allowed.
Reflections are allowed but only if they are not rotations too.
For example :

 is the same as but is different from

Task 1: Find all the 24 different tiles.
Use 3 colours to colour same-shaped corner sections.

Task 2: Cut out the 24 patterned tiles.
Make a rectangle from the tiles matching same-coloured edges.
There are many possible solutions.

Task 3: In the rectangles you made, the corners of the tiles should show one of these three patterns:

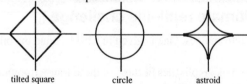

tilted square   circle   astroid

Now, make a rectangle where the colours on the edges of the tiles match *and* there are equal numbers of each of these patterns at the corners.

A BIG EDD GUIDE   page 119   *Shape*

Ch 13: Repli–tiles

All correct = 1 star

Four dominoes like this [ ] will fit together to make [ ]

[ ] and [ ] are both twice as long as they are wide.

[ ] and [ ] are **similar shapes**.

[ ] **is a repli–tile** of [ ]

1. [ ] is a right tromino.
   Put four of these together to make a repli–tile of the right tromino.
   Draw it.
   Shade the four trominoes so that you can see where they are.

2. [ ] A tetromino is made from 4 squares.
   This is the square tetromino. Make a repli–tile of it.
   Shade in the smaller tetrominoes,
   so that you can see where they are.

Polyominoes are shapes made from fitting squares
together, edge-to-edge.

A **domino** is made from 2 squares.
A **tromino** is made from 3 squares.
A **tetromino** is made from 4 squares.
A **pentomino** is made from 5 squares.
A **hexomino** is made from 6 squares.

Yerwat

Do you know that a domino is sometimes ...

... a light cloak often worn with a half-mask at a masquerade (a masked ball)

... the half-mask warn at a masquerade

One star for each correct repli-tile

Ch 14: The ultimate repli–tile challenge !

1. There are five tetrominoes. One is given in Ch 13. Find the other four.

2. It is possible to make repli–tiles of three of these four tetrominoes.
   Try to find all three repli–tiles.

   *Warning : Do not assume that you will always need four copies of each tile.
   One of these repli–tiles, at least, needs 16 copies.*

A BIG EDD GUIDE   page 120   *Shape*

THE NATIONAL CURRICULUM ...
... AND BEYOND ...

Big Edd

Fractions
and Decimals

By the end of this topic you should be able to:

Level 3
- use decimals to work with money

Level 4
- shade fractions of shapes
- recognise fractions of shapes

Level 5
- find fractions of amounts

Level 6
- find fractions equivalent to a half, a quarter and a third
- know the decimals equivalent to half, quarter and three quarters
- work with decimals
- change fractions to decimals
- change decimals to fractions

Fractions and Decimals EXTRA
Section 1 : Fractions of shapes

In this section you will work with fractions of shapes.

DEVELOPMENT

D1: Equal divisions - *Class discussion*

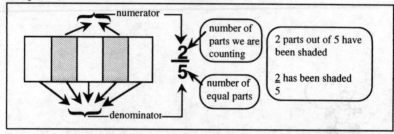

1. A B C D E

   Four of these shapes have half the area shaded.
   Which one does not ?
   Why is it *not* half shaded ?

2. P Q R S T U

   Which of these have $\frac{1}{3}$ shaded ?

3. U V W X Y Z

   What fraction of each of these has been shaded ?

4. Spottee was asked to shade $\frac{1}{4}$ of a △

   This is what Spottee shaded.

   Teacher marked it wrong. Why ?

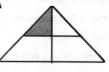

Spottee

Star Challenge 1.1

How many different ways can you shade half of each rectangle? *Individual work*

$\frac{1}{2}$ $\frac{1}{2}$ $\frac{1}{2}$ $\frac{1}{2}$

30 different correct diagrams = 2 stars

20 different correct diagrams = 1 star

$\frac{1}{2}$ $\frac{1}{2}$ $\frac{1}{2}$ $\frac{1}{2}$

$\frac{1}{2}$ $\frac{1}{2}$ $\frac{1}{2}$ $\frac{1}{2}$

$\frac{1}{2}$ $\frac{1}{2}$ $\frac{1}{2}$ $\frac{1}{2}$

$\frac{1}{2}$ $\frac{1}{2}$ $\frac{1}{2}$ $\frac{1}{2}$

How many different ways can you shade a quarter of each rectangle?

$\frac{1}{4}$ $\frac{1}{4}$ $\frac{1}{4}$ $\frac{1}{4}$

$\frac{1}{4}$ $\frac{1}{4}$ $\frac{1}{4}$ $\frac{1}{4}$

$\frac{1}{4}$ $\frac{1}{4}$ $\frac{1}{4}$ $\frac{1}{4}$

• Your teacher will mark this.

A BIG EDD GUIDE   *Fractions and Decimals*

D3: How many squares do I shade?

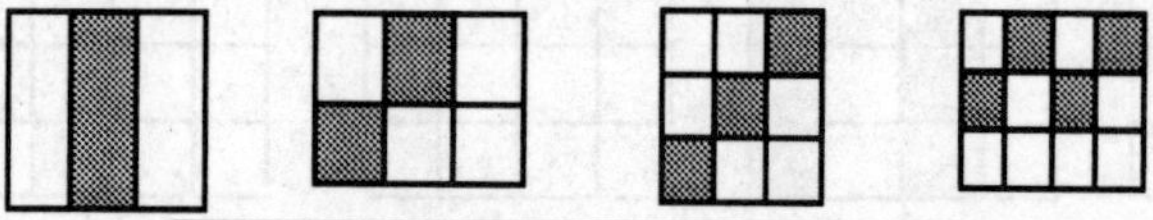

1 in every 3 squares has been shaded.
$\frac{1}{3}$ has been shaded

1. (a) Shade 1 out of every 4 squares.
   (b) What fraction has been shaded? …………

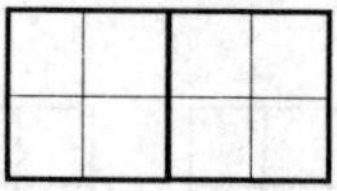

2. 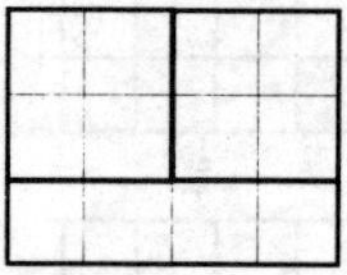 (a) Shade 3 out of every 4 squares.
   (b) What fraction have you shaded? ………

   Big Edd

3. 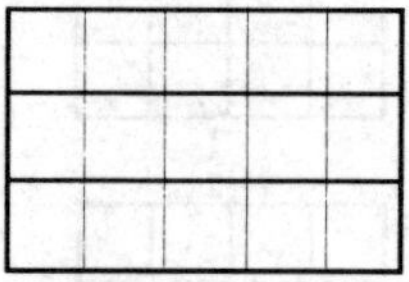 (a) Shade $\frac{1}{5}$ of the rectangle. [1 out of every 5 squares]
   (b) How many squares did you shade? …………

4. (a) Shade $\frac{3}{5}$ of this rectangle. [3 out of every 5 squares]
   (b) How many squares did you shade? ……………

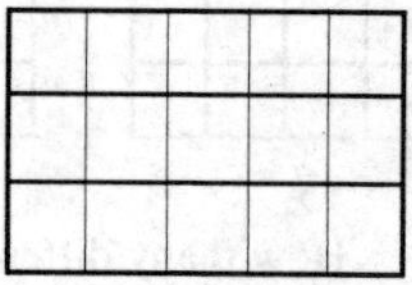

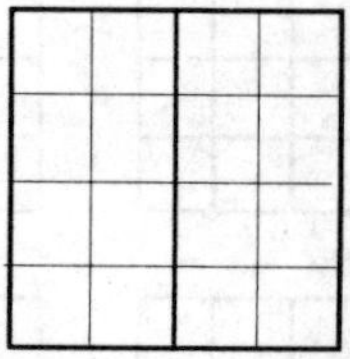

5. (a) Shade $\frac{3}{8}$ of this square. [3 out of every 8 squares]
   (b) How many squares did you shade? …………

6. Shade $\frac{3}{4}$

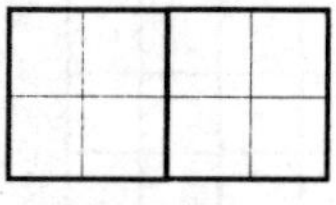

7. Shade $\frac{2}{3}$

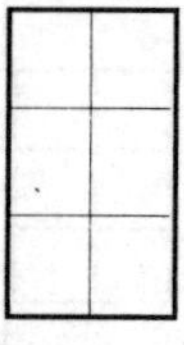

8. Shade $\frac{5}{6}$

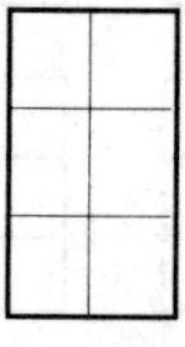

• *Check your answers.*

A BIG EDD GUIDE   *Fractions and Decimals*

P1: Shading fractions

1.

   Find two more different ways of shading $\frac{1}{2}$

2.

   Shade $\frac{1}{2}$ of each of these shapes.

3.

   Shade $\frac{1}{3}$ of each of these shapes.

4.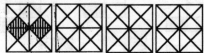

   Find 3 more *different* ways of shading $\frac{1}{4}$

   • *You will need to get your teacher to check your answers to this.*

D4 : Shaded fractions

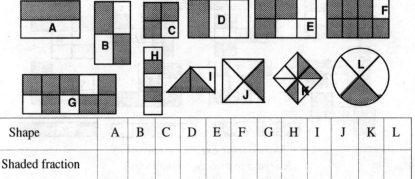

Shape	A	B	C	D	E	F	G	H	I	J	K	L
Shaded fraction												

Fill in the table for each of the shapes.

• *Check your answers. If you need any help, talk to your teacher.*

D5: Shaded and unshaded fractions

Copy this table and fill it in:

Shape	A	B	C	D	E	F	G
Shaded fraction							
Unshaded fraction							

• *STOP! Check your answers.*
If you get more than two wrong, ask your teacher to explain.

PRACTICE

P2: Shady practice

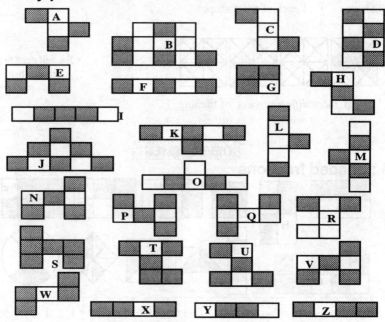

Make a table like the one below.
Extend it to include all the shapes.
Fill in the table for each shape.

Shape	A	B	C	D	E	F	...	...
Shaded fraction								
Unshaded fraction								

Check your answers.

Star Challenge 2 2

15 correct shapes = 2 stars
13-14 correct shapes = 1 star

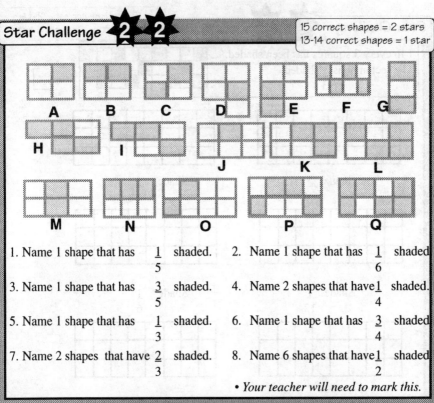

1. Name 1 shape that has $\frac{1}{5}$ shaded.
2. Name 1 shape that has $\frac{1}{6}$ shaded.
3. Name 1 shape that has $\frac{3}{5}$ shaded.
4. Name 2 shapes that have $\frac{1}{4}$ shaded.
5. Name 1 shape that has $\frac{1}{3}$ shaded.
6. Name 1 shape that has $\frac{3}{4}$ shaded.
7. Name 2 shapes that have $\frac{2}{3}$ shaded.
8. Name 6 shapes that have $\frac{1}{2}$ shaded.

• *Your teacher will need to mark this.*

Star Challenge 3 3 3

Quartering the square

12 ways = 3 stars
10 ways = 2 stars
7 ways = 1 star

These large squares have each been split into 4 identical quarters.
Each square is 4 x 4.
All lines must be straight.
All lines drawn must join corners of the smaller squares.

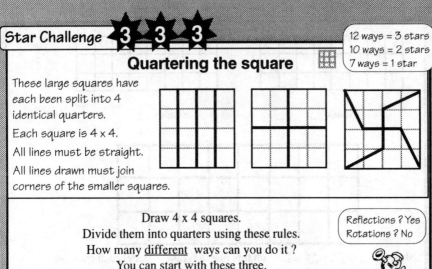

Draw 4 x 4 squares.
Divide them into quarters using these rules.
How many <u>different</u> ways can you do it ?
You can start with these three.

Reflections ? Yes
Rotations ? No

Sureshot

• *Your teacher will need to mark this.*

A BIG EDD GUIDE   *Fractions and Decimals*

Star Challenge ★ ★

12 fractions correct = 2 stars
10-11 fractions correct = 1 star

1 in every 3 squares has been shaded.
The rectangle is $\frac{1}{3}$ shaded.

Shade $\frac{5}{24}$

Shade $\frac{1}{4}$

Shade $\frac{1}{12}$

Shade $\frac{1}{6}$

Shade $\frac{1}{8}$

Shade $\frac{3}{8}$

Shade $\frac{7}{12}$

Shade $\frac{5}{6}$

Shade $\frac{1}{8}$ $\frac{7}{24}$ $\frac{5}{12}$ $\frac{1}{6}$ on this one diagram. Label each fraction.

• *Your teacher will need to mark this.*

Section 2: Equivalent fractions

In this section you will:
- meet equivalent fractions;
- work with sets of equivalent fractions;
- look for patterns in sets of equivalent fractions.

DEVELOPMENT

D1: Thinking in halves

> Fractions which are the same size are called
> **equivalent fractions**

 This diagram shows that $\dfrac{1}{2} = \dfrac{2}{4}$ — 2 shaded out of 4 is the same as 1 shaded out of 2

 This diagram shows that $\dfrac{1}{2} = \dfrac{3}{6}$ — 3 shaded out of 6 is the same as 1 shaded out of 2

What do each of these diagrams show ?

1.

2.

3.

4.

- *Check your answers.*

D2: Halves are very common fractions

Say whether each of these statements is true (T) or false (F) :

1. $\dfrac{1}{2} = \dfrac{10}{20}$
2. $\dfrac{1}{2} = \dfrac{7}{14}$
3. $\dfrac{1}{2} = \dfrac{5}{8}$
4. $\dfrac{1}{2} = \dfrac{4}{8}$
5. $\dfrac{1}{2} = \dfrac{5}{10}$
6. $\dfrac{1}{2} = \dfrac{11}{24}$
7. $\dfrac{1}{2} = \dfrac{50}{100}$
8. $\dfrac{1}{2} = \dfrac{6}{16}$

9. Make each of these fractions equivalent to a half:

$\dfrac{?}{50}$ $\dfrac{20}{?}$ $\dfrac{?}{22}$ $\dfrac{15}{?}$ $\dfrac{?}{18}$ $\dfrac{16}{?}$ $\dfrac{?}{14}$ $\dfrac{6}{?}$ $\dfrac{?}{100}$ $\dfrac{25}{?}$

- *Check your answers.*

A BIG EDD GUIDE   *Fractions and Decimals*

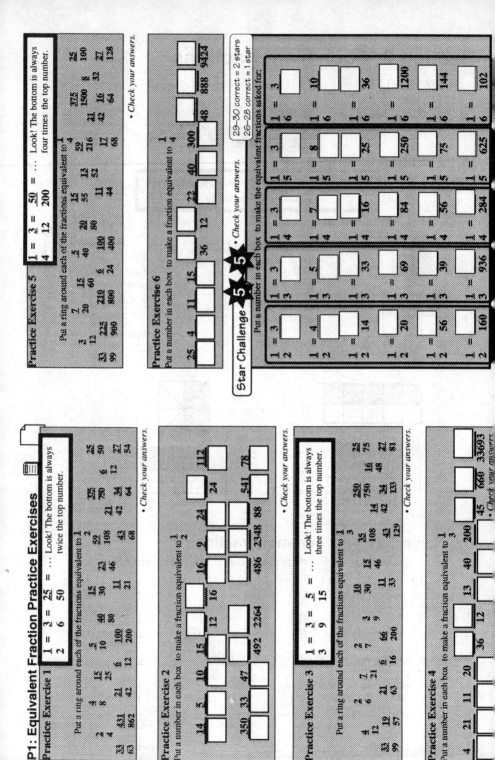

P2: Quarter masters

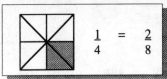

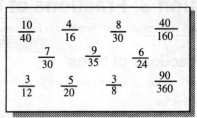

Seven of these fractions are equivalent to a quarter.
Which are they?

• *Check your answers.*

Star Challenge 6

1 star for each target achieved

Fraction searches

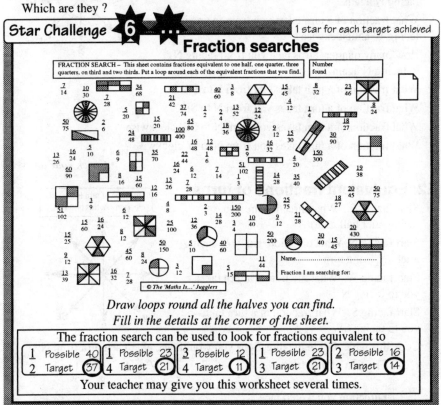

Draw loops round all the halves you can find.
Fill in the details at the corner of the sheet.

The fraction search can be used to look for fractions equivalent to

| $\frac{1}{2}$ Possible 40 Target 37 | $\frac{1}{4}$ Possible 23 Target 21 | $\frac{3}{4}$ Possible 12 Target 11 | $\frac{1}{3}$ Possible 23 Target 21 | $\frac{2}{3}$ Possible 16 Target 14 |

Your teacher may give you this worksheet several times.

P3: Fraction dominoes -- *Groups of 2-4*   a set of fraction dominoes

The rules are as for ordinary dominoes:
- Each person takes 6 dominoes.
- The person with the largest 'double' goes first.
- The next person, clockwise, puts one of his dominoes down at either end.
  The touching sides must be equivalent fractions.
- If a player cannot go then he must pick another domino from the ones left.
- The winner is the first person to get rid of all his dominoes.

A BIG EDD GUIDE   *Fractions and Decimals*

Section 3: Fractions of turns

In this section you will work with fractions of turns.

EXTENSIONS

E1: Fractions of turns

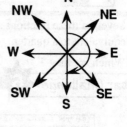

1. What fraction of a turn takes you from facing N to facing S ?
2. How many half turns take you from facing N to facing N again ?
3. What fraction of a turn takes you from facing N to facing W anticlockwise?
4. How many quarter turns take you from facing N to facing N again ?
5. What fraction of a turn takes you from S to SW ?
6. What fraction of a turn takes you from N to SE ?
7. What fraction of a turn takes you from N to SW clockwise ?
8. What fraction of a turn takes you from N to W clockwise ?

• *Check your answers.*

E2: Equivalent fractions of turns

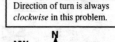
Direction of turn is always *clockwise* in this problem.

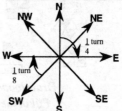

1. Start facing E. What direction are you facing after half a turn ?
2. Start facing N. What direction are you facing after $1/8$ of a turn ?
3. Start facing W. What fraction of a turn takes you to facing N ?
4. Start facing S. What fraction of a turn takes you to facing SW ?
5. Copy this table. Fill in the directions you would face after each turn from N:

Fraction of turn from N	$\frac{1}{4}$	$\frac{2}{4}$	$\frac{3}{4}$	$\frac{2}{8}$	$\frac{4}{8}$	$\frac{6}{8}$	$\frac{1}{2}$
Direction you would face							

Big Edd

$\frac{3}{4}$ of a turn is the same as $\frac{6}{8}$ of a turn

We say that $\frac{3}{4}$ is **equivalent to** $\frac{6}{8}$ and $\frac{3}{4} = \frac{6}{8}$

6. Which two fractions in the table are equivalent to $1/2$?
7. Which fraction is equivalent to $\frac{2}{8}$?

• *Check your answers.*

A BIG EDD GUIDE   *Fractions and Decimals*

Section 4: Fractions of amounts *All individual work*

In this section you will find fractions of amounts with and without a calculator.

P1: Fraction practice — PRACTICE — 25 counters

Use counters to find the answers to these.
CHECK YOUR ANSWERS AT THE END OF EACH BATCH.
Do as many batches as you need.
Then try the Star Challenge!

Batch A
1. $\frac{1}{2}$ of 8 =
2. $\frac{1}{2}$ of 6 =
3. $\frac{1}{3}$ of 6 =
4. $\frac{1}{2}$ of 12 =
5. $\frac{1}{3}$ of 12 =
6. $\frac{1}{3}$ of 15 =
7. $\frac{1}{4}$ of 16 =
8. $\frac{1}{2}$ of 20 =
9. $\frac{1}{2}$ of 2 =

Batch B
1. $\frac{1}{2}$ of 10 =
2. $\frac{1}{4}$ of 12 =
3. $\frac{1}{3}$ of 9 =
4. $\frac{1}{4}$ of 8 =
5. $\frac{1}{4}$ of 20 =
6. $\frac{1}{3}$ of 21 =
7. $\frac{1}{5}$ of 15 =
8. $\frac{1}{6}$ of 24 =
9. $\frac{1}{5}$ of 5 =

Batch C
1. $\frac{1}{2}$ of 22 =
2. $\frac{1}{10}$ of 20 =
3. $\frac{1}{2}$ of 14 =
4. $\frac{1}{5}$ of 25 =
5. $\frac{1}{6}$ of 12 =
6. $\frac{1}{7}$ of 14 =
7. $\frac{1}{6}$ of 18 =
8. $\frac{1}{7}$ of 7 =
9. $\frac{1}{3}$ of 3 =

Star Challenge 7

All correct = 1 star

Fill in the answers to each of these:

1. $\frac{1}{2}$ of 18 =
2. $\frac{1}{5}$ of 20 =
3. $\frac{1}{3}$ of 18 =
4. $\frac{1}{2}$ of 4 =
5. $\frac{1}{3}$ of 24 =
6. $\frac{1}{5}$ of 10 =
7. $\frac{1}{4}$ of 24 =
8. $\frac{1}{2}$ of 14 =
9. $\frac{1}{2}$ of 10 =

• Your teacher has the answers to these.

D1: Using a calculator to find fractions

EXAMPLE Q: Find $\frac{1}{4}$ of 512

A: *Yerwat* — What do I do?

 Big Edd — To find $\frac{1}{4}$ of something you divide it by 4!

$\frac{1}{4}$ of $512 = 512 \div 4 = 128$

CHECK YOUR ANSWERS AT THE END OF EACH BATCH.
Do as many batches as you need. **Then try the Star Challenge!**

Batch A
1. $\frac{1}{2}$ of 80 =
2. $\frac{1}{4}$ of 232 =
3. $\frac{1}{3}$ of 96 =
4. $\frac{1}{2}$ of 486 =
5. $\frac{1}{3}$ of 204 =
6. $\frac{1}{3}$ of 75 =
7. $\frac{1}{4}$ of 112 =
8. $\frac{1}{2}$ of 638 =
9. $\frac{1}{5}$ of 195 =

Batch B
1. $\frac{1}{4}$ of 396 =
2. $\frac{1}{4}$ of 316 =
3. $\frac{1}{3}$ of 498 =
4. $\frac{1}{4}$ of 876 =
5. $\frac{1}{5}$ of 265 =
6. $\frac{1}{3}$ of 219 =
7. $\frac{1}{5}$ of 155 =
8. $\frac{1}{6}$ of 246 =
9. $\frac{1}{5}$ of 540 =

Batch C
1. $\frac{1}{2}$ of 236 =
2. $\frac{1}{10}$ of 470 =
3. $\frac{1}{2}$ of 38 =
4. $\frac{1}{5}$ of 70 =
5. $\frac{1}{6}$ of 150 =
6. $\frac{1}{7}$ of 196 =
7. $\frac{1}{8}$ of 152 =
8. $\frac{1}{7}$ of 560 =
9. $\frac{1}{3}$ of 429 =

Star Challenge 8
All correct = 1 star

1. $\frac{1}{2}$ of 438 =
2. $\frac{1}{5}$ of 245 =
3. $\frac{1}{3}$ of 189 =
4. $\frac{1}{2}$ of 46 =
5. $\frac{1}{3}$ of 261 =
6. $\frac{1}{5}$ of 370 =
7. $\frac{1}{4}$ of 328 =
8. $\frac{1}{8}$ of 296 =
9. $\frac{1}{7}$ of 98 =

• *Your teacher has the answers to these.*

A BIG EDD GUIDE — *Fractions and Decimals*

D2: Fractions in action

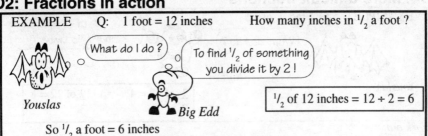

EXAMPLE Q: 1 foot = 12 inches   How many inches in $1/2$ a foot?

Youslas: What do I do?
Big Edd: To find $1/2$ of something you divide it by 2!

$1/2$ of 12 inches = 12 ÷ 2 = 6

So $1/2$ a foot = 6 inches

| 1 hour = 60 minutes |

How many minutes are there in...
1. ... $1/2$ hour
2. ... $1/4$ hour
3. ... $1/3$ hour
4. ... $1/{10}$ hour?

| 1 day = 24 hours |

How many hours are there in...
5. ... $1/2$ day
6. ... $1/4$ day
7. ... $1/3$ day
8. ... $1/6$ day?

| 1 foot = 12 inches | | 1 yard = 36 inches |

How many inches are there in...
9. ... $1/4$ foot
10. ... $1/3$ foot
11. ... $1/2$ yard
12. ... $1/4$ yard

• *Check your answers.*

D3: Using diagrams to find fractions

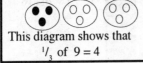
This diagram shows that $1/3$ of 9 = 4

You may find that counters will help you here.

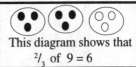
This diagram shows that $2/3$ of 9 = 6

1.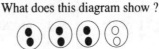

What does this diagram show?

2. What does this diagram show?

3. What does this diagram show?

4. What does this diagram show?

Draw diagrams to work out each of these:

5. $1/2$ of 6
6. $1/3$ of 15
7. $2/3$ of 15
8. $1/4$ of 12

9. $3/4$ of 12
10. $1/5$ of 10
11. $2/5$ of 10
12. $4/5$ of 10

13. $1/6$ of 12
14. $2/6$ of 12
15. $5/6$ of 12
16. $1/5$ of 15

17. $2/5$ of 15
18. $4/5$ of 15
19. $1/3$ of 18
20. $2/3$ of 18

• *Check your answers.*

A BIG EDD GUIDE   *Fractions and Decimals*

D4: More difficult fractions

EXAMPLE Q: Find $^2/_3$ of 12

Youslas: What do I do?

Ruff: $^1/_3$ of 12 = 4 and $^2/_3$ is twice $^1/_3$

$\frac{1}{3}$ of 12 = 4 so $\frac{2}{3}$ of 12 = 8

Work out:
1. $\frac{1}{8}$ of 24
2. $\frac{3}{8}$ of 24
3. $\frac{5}{8}$ of 24
4. $\frac{7}{8}$ of 24
5. $\frac{1}{2}$ of 24
6. $\frac{1}{3}$ of 24
7. $\frac{2}{3}$ of 24
8. $\frac{1}{4}$ of 24
9. $\frac{3}{4}$ of 24
10. $\frac{5}{6}$ of 24

• Check your answers.

PRACTICE
P2: More difficult fraction practice

Work out these fractions of amounts.
CHECK YOUR ANSWERS AT THE END OF EACH BATCH.
Do as many batches as you need.
Then try the Star Challenge!

Batch A
1. $\frac{1}{3}$ of 6
2. $\frac{2}{3}$ of 6
3. $\frac{1}{4}$ of 40
4. $\frac{3}{4}$ of 40
5. $\frac{1}{5}$ of 25
6. $\frac{2}{5}$ of 25
7. $\frac{3}{5}$ of 25
8. $\frac{4}{5}$ of 25
9. $\frac{2}{3}$ of £12
10. $\frac{3}{4}$ of 16 cm

Batch B
1. $\frac{1}{6}$ of 12
2. $\frac{5}{6}$ of 12
3. $\frac{1}{3}$ of 15
4. $\frac{2}{3}$ of 15
5. $\frac{1}{4}$ of 20
6. $\frac{3}{4}$ of 20
7. $\frac{1}{8}$ of 16
8. $\frac{3}{8}$ of 16
9. $\frac{3}{10}$ of 50
10. $\frac{4}{5}$ of 10

Batch C
1. $\frac{1}{8}$ of 40
2. $\frac{3}{8}$ of 40
3. $\frac{5}{8}$ of 40
4. $\frac{7}{8}$ of 40
5. $\frac{1}{6}$ of 18
6. $\frac{5}{6}$ of 18
7. $\frac{1}{4}$ of £20
8. $\frac{3}{4}$ of £20
9. $\frac{2}{3}$ of 12cm
10. $\frac{5}{6}$ of £24

Star Challenge 9
1. $\frac{1}{4}$ of 16
2. $\frac{3}{4}$ of 16
3. $\frac{1}{3}$ of 30
4. $\frac{2}{3}$ of 30
5. $\frac{1}{5}$ of 25
6. $\frac{4}{5}$ of 25
7. $\frac{3}{4}$ of 8
8. $\frac{2}{3}$ of 9
9. $\frac{2}{5}$ of £20
10. $\frac{3}{10}$ of 40 cm

All correct = 1 star

Star Challenge 10

5 correct = 2 stars
4 correct = 1 star

1. A new pair of trainers cost £40. Sarah's aunt gives her half of the money. How much does she give her?

2. My friend lives 800m from my house. I ran half the way there and walked the rest. How far did I walk?

3. A full bottle of squash contains 75 *cl*. It has one third left in it. How many *cl* does it contain?

4. Billy waited three-quarters of an hour for the bus. How many minutes did he wait?

5. Adi needed £80 to buy a bike. He saved a quarter of this. His mother gave him half of the rest. How much does he still need?

• *Your teacher has the answers to these.*

Star Challenge 11

7-8 correct = 2 stars
5-6 correct = 1 star

1. Zhaleh and Sally are paid £20 for doing odd jobs at the Youth Club. They do half the work each. They get half the pay. How much do they each get?

2. Fred and Jim painted the Youth Club. Fred did one third of the work. Jim did the rest. The rate was £30 for the job. Fred got paid one third of the money.

    (a) How much did Fred get paid?
    (b) What fraction of the work did Jim do?
    (c) How much did Jim get paid?

3. Mary and Alison dug Mrs. Brown's garden. Mary worked for 2 hours. Alison worked for 6 hours. They got paid £24 for the whole job.

    (a) What fraction of the work did Mary do?
    (b) How much should she get paid?
    (c) How much should Alison get?

4. Adi, Bob and Carl worked on a job together.
    Adi got twice as much as Bob.
    Bob got three times as much as Carl.
    Adi got £30.
    How much did Carl get?

• *Your teacher has the answers to these.*

Section 5: Common fractions & decimals

In this section you will use the most common fraction-decimal equivalents.

DEVELOPMENT

D1: Halves, quarters and three-quarters

$$0.5 = \tfrac{1}{2} \qquad 2.5 = 2\tfrac{1}{2} \qquad 7.5 = 7\tfrac{1}{2}$$

Copy and complete:

1. $3.5 = ...$ 2. $5.5 = ...$ 3. $8.5 = ...$ 4. $4.5 = ...$
5. $... = 9\tfrac{1}{2}$ 6. $10.5 = ...$ 7. $... = 6\tfrac{1}{2}$ 8. $... = 15\tfrac{1}{2}$

$$0.25 = \tfrac{1}{4} \qquad 3.25 = 3\tfrac{1}{4} \qquad 5.25 = 5\tfrac{1}{4}$$

Copy and complete:

9. $2.25 = ...$ 10. $4.25 = ...$ 11. $7.25 = ...$ 12. $9.25 = ...$
13. $... = 1\tfrac{1}{4}$ 14. $6.25 = ...$ 15. $... = 8\tfrac{1}{4}$ 16. $... = 14\tfrac{1}{4}$

$$0.75 = \tfrac{3}{4} \qquad 1.75 = 1\tfrac{3}{4} \qquad 8.75 = 8\tfrac{3}{4}$$

Copy and complete:

17. $4.75 = ...$ 18. $2.75 = ...$ 19. $9.75 = ...$ 20. $3.75 = ...$
21. $... = 6\tfrac{3}{4}$ 22. $5.75 = ...$ 23. $... = 7\tfrac{3}{4}$ 24. $... = 10\tfrac{3}{4}$
25. $6.5 = ...$ 26. $1.25 = ...$ 27. $... = 3\tfrac{1}{2}$ 28. $7.75 = ...$
29. $... = 6\tfrac{1}{4}$ 30. $2.5 = ...$ 31. $... = 2\tfrac{3}{4}$ 32. $... = 25\tfrac{1}{2}$

• *Check answers.*

PRACTICE

P1: Mixed practice

> Read 1.25 as "one point two five"

DO AS MUCH PRACTICE AS YOU NEED.
Check your answers at the end of each batch.

Batch A: *Write as decimals:*
1. $10\tfrac{1}{2}$ 2. $7\tfrac{1}{4}$ 3. $12\tfrac{1}{4}$ 4. $13\tfrac{3}{4}$ 5. $23\tfrac{1}{2}$ 6. $17\tfrac{3}{4}$ 7. $45\tfrac{1}{4}$

Write as fractions:
8. 9.75 9. 15.5 10. 16.25 11. 50.5 12. 21.75 13. 6.25 14. 13.5

Batch B: *Write as decimals:*
1. $14\tfrac{1}{4}$ 2. $11\tfrac{1}{2}$ 3. $17\tfrac{3}{4}$ 4. $26\tfrac{1}{2}$ 5. $12\tfrac{1}{4}$ 6. $99\tfrac{1}{2}$ 7. $22\tfrac{3}{4}$

Write as fractions:
8. 3.5 9. 14.75 10. 36.25 11. 21.25 12. 18.75 13. 4.5 14. 3.75

Star Challenge 12

All correct = 1 star

The Pan–Galactic Explorers never travel anywhere without their favourite snacks.
These snacks are called HANDEL BARS.
They are so popular they are often used instead of money on long trips.
At the end of one long trip, they did not have many left.
Here are the explorers with the number of bars each one has left.

Flumpf
$2\frac{1}{4}$

Dwork
7.25

Frizzbang
$1\frac{1}{4}$

Lubbly
$7\frac{1}{2}$

Glugl
$4\frac{1}{2}$

Mishrak
2.5

Zuk
1.5

Plok
$1\frac{1}{2}$

Qwerk
$4\frac{1}{4}$

Pow
0.25

Taz
4.5
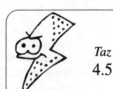

Chyps
1.25

Pesymistic
12.5

Hoblin
$2\frac{1}{2}$

Cringo
2.25

Yerwat
4.25

There are 6 pairs of explorers who have the same amount left.
List the pairs of names.

• *Your teacher will need to mark these.*

A BIG EDD GUIDE   *Fractions and Decimals*

Section 6: Equivalent decimals and fractions

In this section you will:
- change decimals into fractions;
- develop an understanding of decimals.

DEVELOPMENT

D1: Decimals and fractions

The decimal point separates the whole numbers from the bits of numbers.

Thousands T	Hundreds H	Tens T	Units U	.	tenths t	hundredths h	thousandths th	
			0	.	6			= $^6/_{10}$
			0	.	0	7		= $^7/_{100}$
			0	.	0	0	3	= $^3/_{1000}$
			1	.	9			= $1\,^9/_{10}$
			0	.	4	1		= $^{41}/_{100}$

Copy and complete this table:

Thousands T	Hundreds H	Tens T	Units U	.	tenths t	hundredths h	thousandths th	
			0	.	3			= ……
			0	.	0	8		= ……
			0	.	0	0	5	= ……
			2	.	6			= ……
			0	.	1	7		= ……
			0	.				= $^4/_{100}$
			0	.				= $^6/_{10}$
			0	.				= $^3/_{1000}$
			0	.				= $^{67}/_{100}$
			0	.				= $^{31}/_{1000}$
			…	.				= $1\,^7/_{10}$
				.				= $2^{11}/_{100}$
				.				= $4\,^{31}/_{1000}$
			0	.	0	2	7	= ……
	1	8	.	2	3	5		= ……

Just keep looking at the labels at the top of the table.

Lubbly

- *Check your answers.*

Star Challenge 13

All correct = 1 star

The Pan–Galactic Explorers' Dance Competition

The Explorers have returned from a successful mission.
To celebrate, a dance competition is organised.
Each dancer takes a numbered card from a box.

Flumpf 0.1 dances with Glugl $\frac{1}{10}$

... because the value of the numbers on their cards is the same.

The other Explorers get these numbers:

Who dances with whom?
Make a list of the pairs of dancers.

• *Your teacher has the answers to these.*

A BIG EDD GUIDE   page 141   *Fractions and Decimals*

Section 7: Changing fractions to decimals

In this section you will:
- find decimal equivalents to fractions;
- work with equivalent fractions and decimals.

DEVELOPMENT

D1: Changing fractions into decimals

We now have two ways of describing bits of whole numbers.

FRACTIONS and **DECIMALS**

To change $\frac{4}{5}$ into a decimal using a calculator

[4] [÷] [5] [=]   calculator display: 0.8

press these keys

$$\frac{4}{5} = 4 \div 5 = 0.8$$
     fraction   decimal

Big Edd

Copy and complete these fraction–decimal pairs:

1. $\frac{1}{5}$ = ...
2. $\frac{7}{10}$ = ...
3. $\frac{2}{5}$ = ...
4. $\frac{1}{8}$ = ...

5. $\frac{3}{20}$ = ...
6. $\frac{6}{50}$ = ...
7. $\frac{5}{8}$ = ...
8. $\frac{3}{8}$ = ...

• *Check your answers.*

D2: Decimal tenths

Copy and complete:

1. $\frac{1}{10}$ = ...
2. $\frac{3}{10}$ = ...
3. $\frac{5}{10}$ = ...
4. $\frac{9}{10}$ = ...

Copy these statements. Replace each ☐ with the correct number.

5. $\frac{4}{10} = 0.\square$
6. $\frac{\square}{10} = 0.2$
7. $\frac{6}{\square} = 0.6$
8. $\frac{\square}{\square} = 0.7$

• *Check answers.*

D3: Decimal hundredths

Copy and complete:

1. $\frac{1}{100}$ = ...
2. $\frac{3}{100}$ = ...
3. $\frac{5}{100}$ = ...
4. $\frac{8}{100}$ = ...

Copy these statements. Replace each ☐ with the correct number.

5. $\frac{7}{100} = 0.\square$
6. $\frac{\square}{100} = 0.06$
7. $\frac{2}{\square} = 0.02$
8. $\frac{\square}{\square} = 0.09$

• *Check answers.*

Star Challenge 14

The first fraction-decimal challenge

13 correct = 2 stars
12 correct = 1 star

$$\frac{4}{5} = 4 \div 5 = 0.8$$

Complete these tables. Each ☐ represents a whole number.

1.

Fraction	$\frac{3}{5}$	$\frac{4}{10}$	$\frac{5}{25}$	$\frac{6}{20}$	$\frac{9}{40}$	$\frac{3}{16}$	$\frac{16}{10}$
Decimal							

2.

Fraction	$\frac{\square}{5}$	$\frac{\square}{10}$	$\frac{\square}{100}$	$\frac{\square}{20}$	$\frac{\square}{25}$	$\frac{\square}{10}$
Decimal	0.8	0.9	0.05	0.15	0.32	1.4

• *Your teacher has the answers to these.*

Star Challenge 15

What a mixture !

All 6 correct = 1 star

A model maker is given a mixed box of small spanners by an uncle. A lot of the sizes are missing. These are the sizes she has:

0.45"   0.6"   0.4"   0.325"
0.3"   0.75"   0.35"   0.425"
0.275"   0.375"

1. Which spanner should she use, when she needs a spanner which is:
   (a) $\frac{3}{10}$"   (b) $\frac{3}{5}$"   (c) $\frac{3}{8}$" ?

2. Some of the sizes are missing.
What is the nearest spanner size that she has to (a) $\frac{1}{2}$"   (b) $\frac{1}{4}$"   (c) $\frac{4}{5}$" ?

• *Your teacher has the answers to these.*

Star Challenge 16

The second fraction-decimal challenge

11-12 correct = 1 star

Complete these tables. Each ☐ represents a whole number.

1.

Fraction	$\frac{9}{10}$	$\frac{13}{100}$	$\frac{27}{100}$	$\frac{19}{100}$	$\frac{43}{1000}$	$\frac{181}{1000}$	$\frac{3}{1000}$
Decimal							

2.

Fraction	$\frac{\square}{10}$	$\frac{\square}{100}$	$\frac{\square}{1000}$	$\frac{\square}{1000}$	$\frac{\square}{1000}$
Decimal	0.3	0.49	0.231	0.019	0.007

A BIG EDD GUIDE   *Fractions and Decimals*

Section 8: Decimal arithmetic

In this section you will get some practice in adding and subtracting decimals mentally or using a calculator.

All individual work

///PRACTICE///

P1: Decimal arithmogons

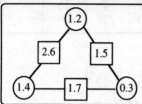

In these arithmogons, the number in each ☐ is the SUM of the numbers on either side of it.

Fill in the missing numbers:

A 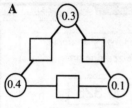   **B** 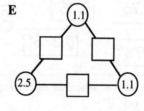   **C**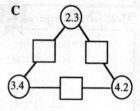

D 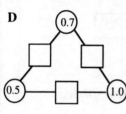   **E** 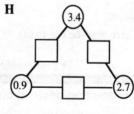 (E has top 1.1, bottom-left 2.5, bottom-right 1.1)   **F**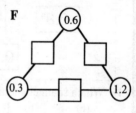

G 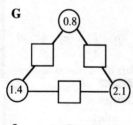   **H** 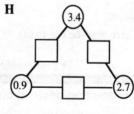   **I**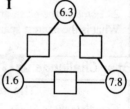

J 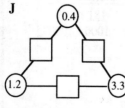   **K** 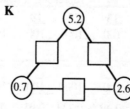   **L**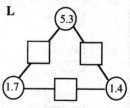

• *Check your answers.*

A BIG EDD GUIDE   *Fractions and Decimals*

P2: Harder arithmogons

The missing numbers are given below each arithmogon. Put them in the right places.

M

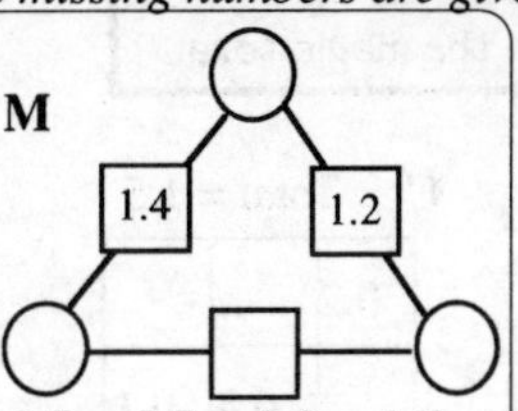

0.5 0.7 0.9 1.6

N

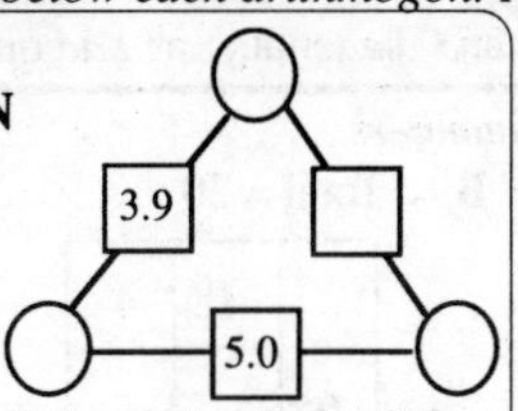

1.3 2.4 2.6 3.7

P

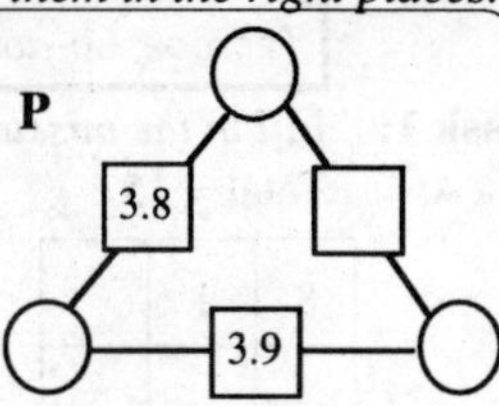

1.2 1.3 2.5 2.6

Q

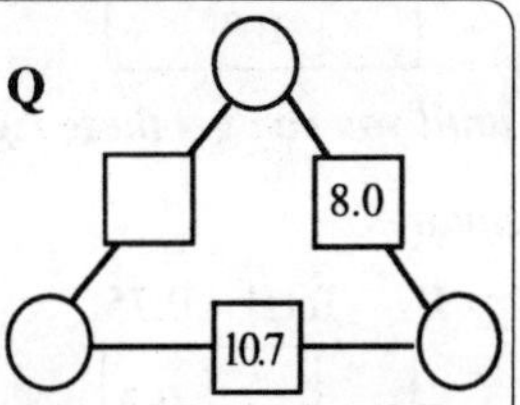

3.5 4.5 6.2 9.7

R

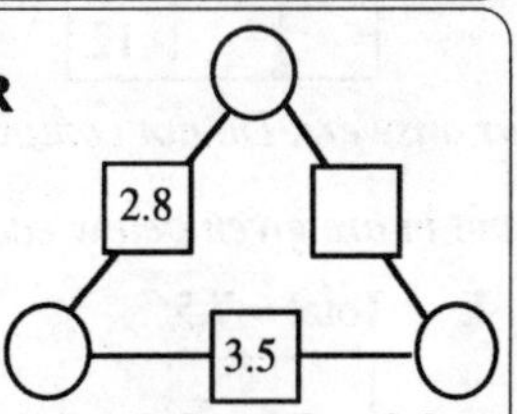

1.3 2.5 1.0 0.3

S

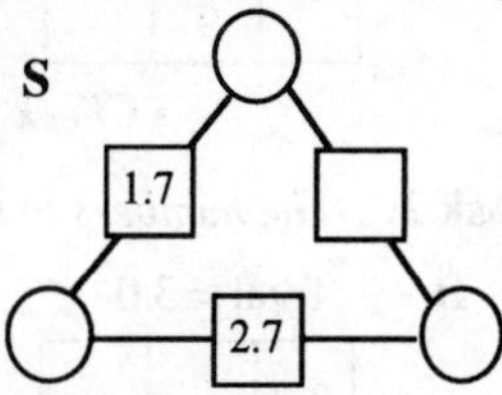

2.5 0.2 1.5 4.0

Fill in the missing numbers:

T

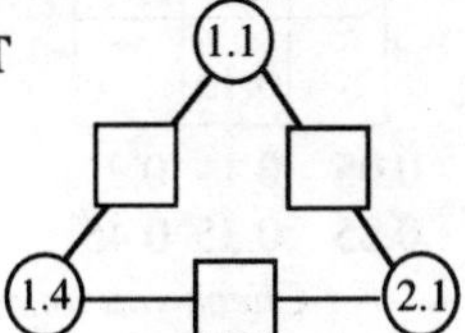

U

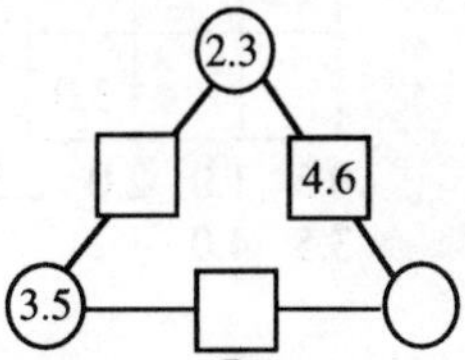

V

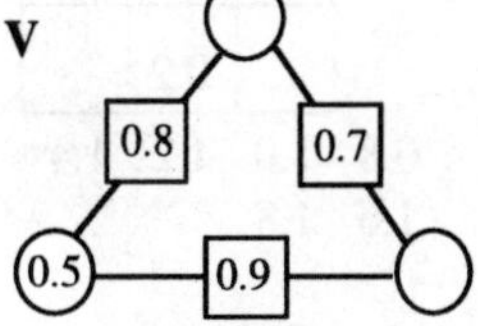

W

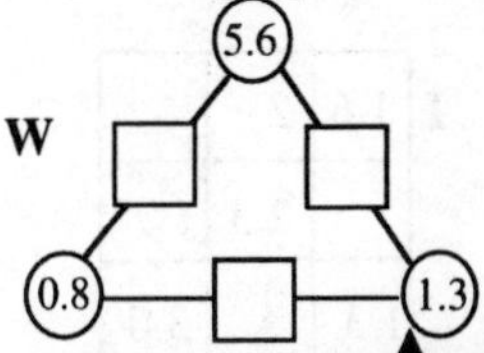

X

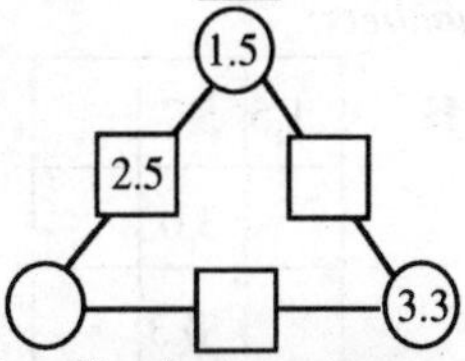

Y

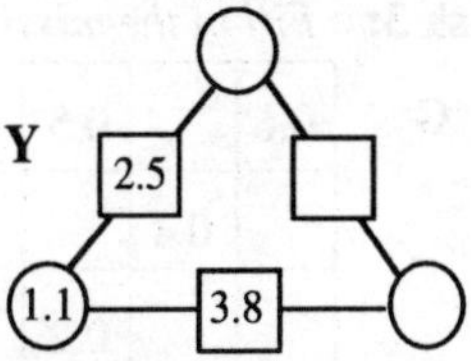

• *Check your answers.*

Star Challenge 17 17

17 correct = 2 stars
14-16 correct = 1 star

Fill in the missing numbers:

1

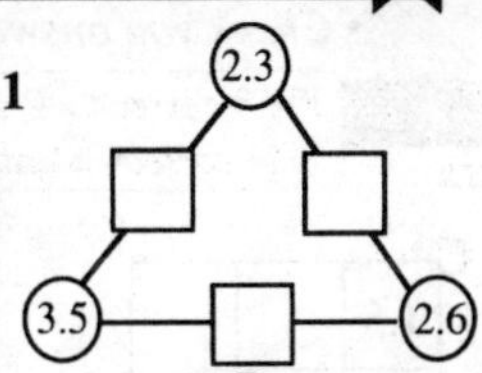

2

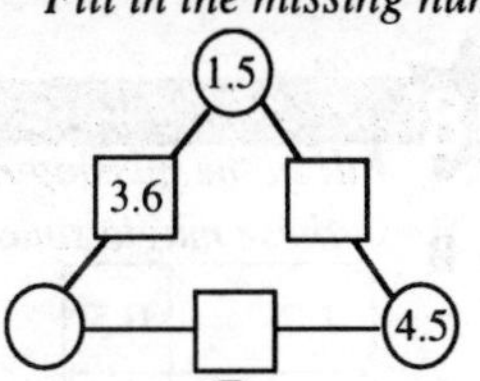

3

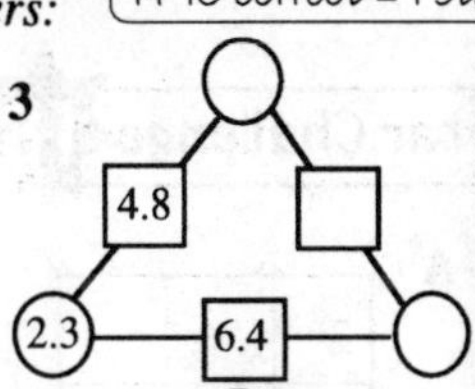

4

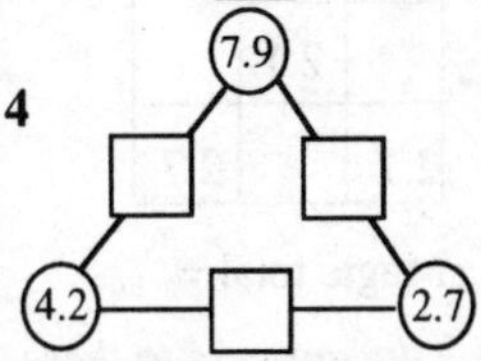

5

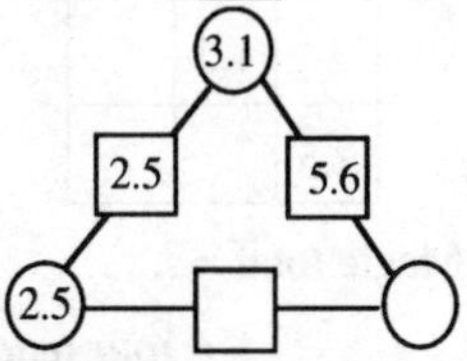

6

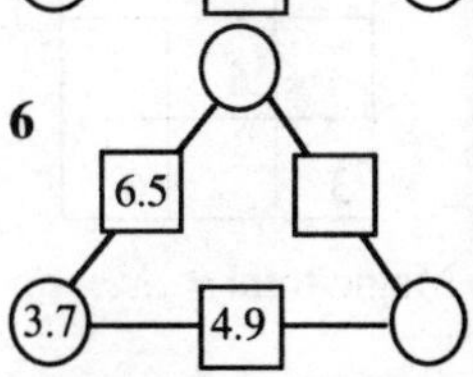

P3: Decimal magic

> In a magic square, the numbers in every line (across, up-down and diagonally) all add up to the magic total.

Task 1: *Fill in the missing numbers:*

A Total = 15

8	1	
		7
	9	

B Total = 30

	18	4
6		
		12

C Total = 1.5

0.2		
	0.5	0.1
	0.3	

• *Check your answers. Do not continue until you can get these right.*

Task 2: *The numbers to be put in are given below each square.*

D Total = 3.0

0.4		
		0.6
	0.2	

0.8 1.0 1.2 1.4
1.6 1.8

E Total = 7.5

	4.5	
1.5		
		3.0

0.5 1.0 2.0 2.5
3.5 4.0

F Total = 0.75

		0.3
0.45		
	0.15	

0.05 0.1   0.2
0.25 0.35 0.45

• *Check you answers.*

Task 3: *Fill in the missing numbers:*

G

0.6		0.5
	0.4	
		0.2

Magic total = ……

H

1.5	5.7	
	3.0	
	0.3	

Magic total = ……

I

1.6	2	
	2.3	
1.3		3.0

Magic total = ……

• *Check you answers.*

Star Challenge

15-18 correct = 2 stars
11-14 correct = 1 star

Fill in the missing numbers in these magic squares:

A

2		
	4	
3		6

Magic total = ……

B

1.2		0.5
	1.5	
2.5		

Magic total = ……

C

1.5		
	2.1	
2.1		2.7

Magic total = ……

• *Your teacher has the answers to these.*

Section 9: Money matters

In this section you will:
- practice some techniques for working with money;
- work with bills.

D1: The Money Battle   *Class discussion or individual work*

The problem: What is £2.31 + 4p ?

£2.31 + 4p = £6.31
My calculator says so !
Driller

£2.31 + 4p = £2.35
My calculator is always right !

Who is right ?
How do you know ?

Who got it wrong ?
Why did the calculator give the wrong answer ?

Sureshot

- *Check your answers.*

D2: Pounds and parts of pounds   *Individual work*

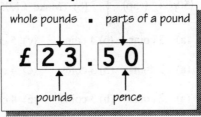

Write down what goes in each of the empty boxes:

1. (50p) = £0.50   ⇒   (20p) + (20p) + (20p) = £ ☐
2. (5p) = £0.05   ⇒   (5p) + (2p) + (1p) = £ ☐
3. (50p) + (2p) = £0.52   ⇒   (20p) + (10p) + (1p) = £ ☐
4. **£0.05 = 5p**

Write in pence: (a) £0.25 (b) £0.12 (c) £0.80 (d) £0.08

5. *Write in pounds:*   (a) 75p (b) 20p (c) 9p (d) 82p

- *Check your answers.*

A BIG EDD GUIDE   *Fractions and Decimals*

D3: Change

You go to the shop.
You have a £1 coin.
£1
The till shows £0.60
You get 40p change.

1. How much change would you get, if the till showed £0.75

2. How much change would you get, if the till showed

   (a) £0.90   (b) £0.55   (c) £0.20   (d) £0.35   (e) £0.96

3. One day you have 75p change. What did the till show?

• *Check your answers*

EXTENSION

E1: Changing coins

Coins: £1 50p 20p 10p 5p 2p 1p

1. £1.05 can be made with 3 coins   (a) Make £1.05 with 2 coins
   £1.05 = 50p + 50p + 5p   (b) Make £1.05 with 5 coins

2. Make £0.75 with   (a) 3 coins   (b) 4 coins   (c) 5 coins

3. Make £0.60 with   (a) 2 coins   (b) 3 coins   (c) 4 coins

4. Make £1.10 with   (a) 2 coins   (b) 3 coins   (c) 4 coins   (d) 5 coins

5. Make £0.24 in 5 different ways.

• *Check answers.*

Star Challenge 19 19

Targets: 20 ways 1 star
          25 ways 2 stars

Coins: £1 50p 20p 10p 5p 2p 1p

You have 5 of each coin.

Make £0.45 in as many different ways as you can.

Targets: 20 ways 1 star
          25 ways 2 stars

• *Show your answers to your teacher.*

DEVELOPMENT

D4: Bill totals

Task 1: Work out the total cost of each bill:

1. **Alice's Cafe**
   Fish and chips   £2.56
   Bread & butter   35p
   Tea   40p
   Total

2. **The Firs**
   Bed & Breakfast   £8.75
   Paper   £0.65
   Morning tea   £0.50
   Total

Task 2: Which bill was easier to work out ? ....

Explain why it was easier ....

• *Check your answers.*

D5: Checking your bill

You are less likely to make mistakes in bills if you:
- write all amounts in £ (£0.60 instead of 60p);
- stack the figures in a column;
- stack the figures with the decimal points below each other.

The second bill (The Firs) was written this way. It is easier to work out like this.

Each of these bills is written badly.
Write a new bill beside each old one. Use the hints given above.
Work out the total cost of each bill.

1. **Wang Ling's Takeaway**

		New bill
Chow Mein	£2.45	....
Noodles	90p	....
Sweet & sour veg	£1.30	....
Total		

2. **It's A Snip**

		New bill
Cut and Blow	£6.40	....
Conditioner	95p	....
Coffee	30p	....
Total		

3. **Pete's Pet Shop**

		New bill
Gerbil food	£1.65	....
Fish pellets (large)	£2.68	....
Fish pellets (small)	84p	....
Total		

4. **Patel's Papers**

		New bill
Newspapers	£3.45	....
Sweets (Sunday)	£1.23	....
Sweets (Saturday)	52p	....
Total		

• *Check your answers.*

D6: Meet the @ symbol

| 2 pens @ 12p | means | "2 pens at 12p each" |
| 3pkts nails @ 25p | means | "3 packets of nails at 25p per packet" |

Find the cost of:

1. 3 pencils @ 10p   ....
2. 4pkts nails @ 25p   ....
3. 3 cakes @ 40p   ....
4. 2 loaves @ 60p   ....
5. 3 tins beans @ 16p   ....
6. 6 roses @ £2   ....

Complete each of these bills:

7. BODGER'S DIY (very) Ltd.

4 shelves @ £2.45	....
8 brackets @ 42p	....
5 packs brass screws @ £1.06	....
Wood glue @ 48p	£0.48
TOTAL	

8. The Retreat Restaurant

4 Table D'Hote @ £11.95	....
2 bottles House Wine @ £5.24	....
4 coffees @ 60p	....
Service charge @ £1 per person	....
TOTAL	

9. Gossips' Newspaper Shop

6 copies Daily Muckraker @ 65p	....
5 copies Evening Chat @ 25p	....
1 magazine @ 48p	....
2 comics @ 35p	....
Delivery charge 25p	
TOTAL	

10. PHONEY PHONE CO.

System Rental @ £15.95	....
255 units @ 5.4p per unit	....
Phone rental @ £3.95	....
Extension charge @ £1.57	....
TOTAL	

• *Check your answers*

Star Challenge ⭐ ⭐

10 correct = 1 star

Find the mistakes

The total of each of these bills is wrong. Write each bill correctly and find the total.

1. Tommo`s Toys

Big Chance game	£4.25	......
5 packets caps	80p	......
Bang-bang cap pistol	£1.90	......
Total	£6.59	......

2. Benno`s Books

Racer's Annual	£3.95	......
Modeller's monthly	£1.40	......
Puzzla	65p	......
Total	£11.85	......

3. The total of this bill is correct, but there are two mistakes in the entries. Find them and correct them.

2 loaves	£1.60
6 cakes @ 30p	£1.08
4 packets of crisps	£6.40
1 swiss roll	£0.75
Total	£4.79

A BIG EDD GUIDE *Fractions and Decimals*

Section 10: Related fractions

In this section you will:
- explain some common errors;
- look at the relationships within some sets of fractions.

DEVELOPMENT

D1: Some common errors

1. At the end of a battle, the three winning princes make their demands.
   "I want half the kingdom" says Richard.
   "I want half as well" says Henry.
   "I want half too" says John

   Explain why they can't have what they want.

2. Mary says " I want the bigger half of the cake."

   Explain why Mary is wrong.

> The rest of this section must be done using only
> the information given in the boxes.

D2: Halves, quarters and eighths

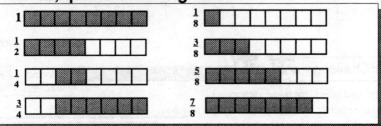

Copy and complete these statements.
Replace each ☐ with one of the fractions from the list above.
You may use a fraction more than once.

1. one quarter = ☐

2. three eighths = ☐

3. 2 × ☐ = 1

4. 3 × $\frac{1}{4}$ = ☐

5. $\frac{1}{2}$ of $\frac{1}{2}$ = ☐

6. $\frac{1}{2}$ of $\frac{1}{4}$ = ☐

7. 3 × ☐ = $\frac{3}{8}$

8. $\frac{1}{2}$ of $\frac{3}{4}$ = ☐

9. $\frac{1}{2}$ + ☐ = 1

10. $\frac{1}{2}$ + $\frac{1}{4}$ = ☐

• *Check your answers.*

A BIG EDD GUIDE   *Fractions and Decimals*

D3: Halves, thirds and sixths

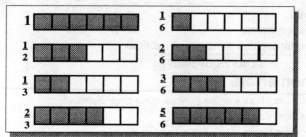

$\frac{1}{2} \times \frac{1}{3}$ means the same as $\frac{1}{2}$ of $\frac{1}{3}$

Copy and complete these statements.
Replace each ▢ with one of the fractions from the list above.
You may use a fraction more than once.

1. two thirds = ▢

2. five sixths = ▢

3. $3 \times ▢ = 1$

4. $\frac{1}{3} + ▢ = 1$

5. $\frac{1}{2}$ of $\frac{1}{3} = ▢$

6. $\frac{1}{2} \times \frac{1}{3} = ▢$

7. $\frac{1}{3} \times \frac{1}{2} = ▢$

8. $\frac{1}{2} \times \frac{2}{3} = ▢$

9. $\frac{2}{6} + \frac{3}{6} = ▢$

10. $\frac{1}{3} \times \frac{3}{6} = ▢$

11. $\frac{3}{6} = ▢$

12. $\frac{2}{6} = ▢$

• *Check your answers.*

Star Challenge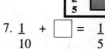

10 correct = 2 stars
9 correct = 1 star

Copy and complete these statements.
Replace each ▢ with a fraction from this box.
You may use a fraction more than once.

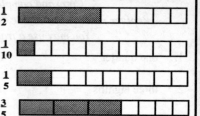

1. $5 \times ▢ = 1$

2. $\frac{1}{2} \times \frac{1}{5} = ▢$

3. $2 \times ▢ = \frac{1}{5}$

4. $3 \times \frac{1}{5} = ▢$

5. $2 \times \frac{1}{10} = ▢$

6. $5 \times \frac{1}{10} = ▢$

7. $\frac{1}{10} + ▢ = \frac{1}{5}$

8. $\frac{1}{5} + \frac{1}{5} + \frac{1}{10} = ▢$

9. $6 \times ▢ = \frac{3}{5}$

10. $\frac{1}{10} + ▢ = \frac{3}{5}$

• *Check your answers.*

High Level Challenge Section
EXTENSIONS
YOUR TEACHER HAS THE ANSWERS TO THESE.

Ch 1: Half or not a half ?

SECTION 1 — 12 correct = 2 stars / 10-11 correct = 1 star

In each case, state whether the square is half shaded or not.

Take care !

This is not as easy as it looks.

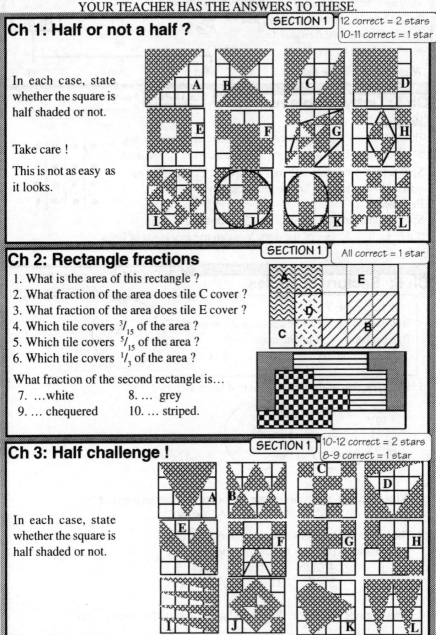

Ch 2: Rectangle fractions

SECTION 1 — All correct = 1 star

1. What is the area of this rectangle ?
2. What fraction of the area does tile C cover ?
3. What fraction of the area does tile E cover ?
4. Which tile covers $3/15$ of the area ?
5. Which tile covers $5/15$ of the area ?
6. Which tile covers $1/3$ of the area ?

What fraction of the second rectangle is…

7. …white
8. … grey
9. … chequered
10. … striped.

Ch 3: Half challenge !

SECTION 1 — 10-12 correct = 2 stars / 8-9 correct = 1 star

In each case, state whether the square is half shaded or not.

A BIG EDD GUIDE   *Fractions and Decimals*

Ch 4: Achilles and the Tortoise **SECTION 1** All correct = 1 star

Achilles the rabbit and Ben the tortoise entered the Animalympics.
They were both in the 100 m sprint.
Achilles could run twice as fast as Ben.
To make things fair, Ben was to
start half way to the finish.

Who should win the race?

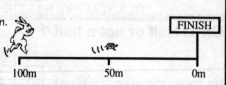

Ch 5: Dotty problems **SECTION 1** 4 correct diagrams = 2 stars / 3 correct diagrams = 1 star

Problem 1
This set of 4 x 4 dots has been split into four groups using straight lines. Each group contains one quarter of the dots.

Split sets of 4 x 4 dots into four groups each containing one quarter of the dots, in 3 more different ways.

Problem 2
Split another set of 4 x 4 dots into 5 groups that contain
$\frac{1}{8}$, $\frac{1}{4}$, $\frac{1}{16}$, $\frac{3}{16}$, $\frac{3}{8}$ of the dots. You can use any kinds of lines.

Ch 6: Sectors of circles **SECTION 1** 13 correct = 2 stars / 10-12 correct = 1 star

1 full turn = 360°
This sector of the circle contains an angle of 10°.
This sector is $\frac{1}{36}$ of the circle.

1. What fraction of the circle is each of these sectors?

   (a) 36°   (b) 60°

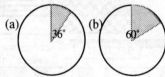

2. What fractions of the circles are sectors containing an angle of:
   (a) 45° (b) 120° (c) 270° (d) 40° (e) 30°

3. The following fractions refer to sectors of circles.
   What angles do each of the sectors contain?
   (a) $\frac{1}{5}$ (b) $\frac{4}{5}$ (c) $\frac{2}{3}$ (d) $\frac{3}{10}$ (e) $\frac{5}{18}$

4. Draw a circle and shade $\frac{5}{6}$ of it. What angle is in the shaded sector?

Ch 7: The magic cake conumdrum   SECTION 1   All correct = 1 star

1. The king has a magic cake. He has been told that, provided the cake is shared out equally, everyone who eats it will have perfect health for a year.
   The magic knife P which he must use will make only three straight cuts before it vanishes.

   How should he make the three cuts in the cake so that he and his seven sons, a total of eight people, all get exactly one eighth of the cake?

2. His wizard offers him a better magic knife P which makes seven cuts before it vanishes. He does this on condition that the king cuts the cake into thirty two equal pieces. These will be shared between the king and his seven sons, and the wizard and his 23 daughters. How can this be done?

Ch 8: In a fraction of the time   SECTION 1   10 correct = 2 stars / 8-9 correct = 1 star

Between 3.00 pm and 3.20 pm, the minute hand turns through one third of a turn.

3.00 p.m.   3.20 p.m.

What fraction of a turn does the minute hand turn through when the time goes from:

1. 10.15 am to 10.45 am
2. 9.10 pm to 9.40 pm
3. 11.35 pm to 11.50 pm
4. 8.05 am to 8.50 pm
5. 9.50 am to 10.35 am
6. 7.15 pm to 7.35 pm
7. 5.40 am to 6.20 am
8. 10.50 pm to 10.55 pm
9. 3.45 am to 4.10 am
10. 7.43 am to 7.46 pm

Ch 9: Cooking figures   SECTION 1   All correct = 1 star

1. A recipe for a dish for 4 people needs:

200 grams of flour	100 grams of cheese
400 grams of butter	80 ml of milk

   How much of each of these ingredients will you need to make the same dish for:
   (a) 2 people   (b) 3 people

2. Another recipe is for six people and it needs:

9 ounces of mushrooms	12 ounces of onions
15 ounces of potatoes	

   How much of each of these ingredients will you need to make the same dish for:
   (a) 2 people   (b) 4 people

3. How much of each of the ingredients in question 2 would you need to make the same dish for 5 people?

Ch 10: Wheel of fortune

SECTION 1 — All correct = 1 star

1. In this game, the wheel is spun and allowed to come to rest. The money that is paid out is the amount that the pointer faces when the wheel stops.

   You can assume that the wheel is equally likely to stop at each of the sectors.

   What fraction of spins do you think would win you
   (a) £10 (b) £1 (c) 10p ?

2. A game of 'Join Up the Dots' was played by three players. At the end, the position was as shown. Player A has won all the squares with A in them, player B has won all the squares with B in them and player C has won all the squares with C in them.

   Which player had won

   (a) $3/8$ of the squares   (b) $9/32$ of the squares ?

Ch 11: A variety of equivalent fractions

SECTION 2 — All correct = 1 star

Find the equivalent fractions in each of these cases:

1.

   $\dfrac{1}{4} = \dfrac{2}{?}$

2.

   $\dfrac{3}{?} = \dfrac{6}{?}$

3.

   $\dfrac{2}{?} = \dfrac{?}{12}$

4.

   $\dfrac{3}{?} = \dfrac{1}{?}$

5.

   $\dfrac{3}{?} = \dfrac{12}{?}$

6.

   $\dfrac{?}{10} = \dfrac{?}{2}$

7.

   $\dfrac{?}{100} = \dfrac{?}{10}$

8.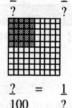

   $\dfrac{?}{100} = \dfrac{1}{?}$

Ch 12: Sets of equivalent fractions

All 22 correct = 2 stars
18-21 correct = 1 star

SECTION 2

$$\frac{26}{39} \quad \frac{45}{60} \quad \frac{6}{10} \quad \frac{3}{5} \quad \frac{3}{4} \quad \frac{9}{15} \quad \frac{36}{48} \quad \frac{2}{3} \quad \frac{9}{12}$$

$$\frac{27}{36} \quad \frac{6}{9} \quad \frac{60}{80} \quad \frac{8}{12} \quad \quad \frac{15}{25} \quad \frac{40}{60}$$

$$\frac{4}{6} \quad \frac{12}{20} \quad \frac{36}{60} \quad \frac{30}{45} \quad \frac{30}{50} \quad \frac{60}{100} \quad \frac{6}{8}$$

There are three sets of equivalent fractions here.
Sort them into the three sets.

Ch 13: Have you spotted the pattern ?

All correct = 1 star
SECTION 2

Complete these sets of equivalent fractions:

1. $\dfrac{16}{20} = \dfrac{?}{5}$

2. $\dfrac{8}{18} = \dfrac{?}{9} = \dfrac{?}{27}$

3. $\dfrac{30}{50} = \dfrac{15}{?} = \dfrac{?}{10} = \dfrac{?}{5}$

4. $\dfrac{49}{98} = \dfrac{7}{?} = \dfrac{1}{?} = \dfrac{?}{12}$

5. $\dfrac{75}{125} = \dfrac{?}{5} = \dfrac{?}{100}$

6. $\dfrac{21}{84} = \dfrac{3}{?} = \dfrac{?}{4}$

7. $\dfrac{74}{111} = \dfrac{2}{?} = \dfrac{?}{117}$

SECTION 2   10-12 correct = 1 star

Ch 14: Replacing the labels

In a workshop, there is a small rack which holds drill bits. The bits fit on the rack in order of size. The smallest bit goes on the left and the largest on the right. The size labels had faded so that they could no longer be read. The foreman gave an apprentice a new set of labels to go on the rack.

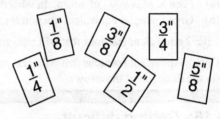

The symbol for an inch is " so a half inch drill bit has the label $\dfrac{1"}{2}$

1. Put the drill bit labels in order of size with the smallest first.

2. How many eighths are there in a quarter ?
   Put each of these sizes in terms of eighths.
   Now put the labels in order of size.
   Do you get the same order as in question 1 ?   (6 marks)

3. Another rack already has two labels in place:

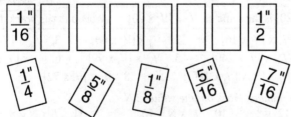

One of the labels lying on the table does not belong on this rack.
Two of the labels for this rack have been lost.

Put *all* the correct labels onto this rack.   (6 marks)

Ch 15: A Pan-Galactic compass

SECTION 3 — All correct = 1 star

The Pan-Galactic Explorers use a special compass on their ground buggies. It only has six points. S = 'Ship' (direction back to ship); SR = 'Ship right' (right of ship); A = 'Away'

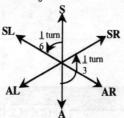

All directions in this problem are measured *anticlockwise*.

1. (a) Face S. Make $3/6$ of a turn. In what direction are you facing?
   (b) Give a simpler equivalent fraction for the same turn.

2. Give 2 equivalent fractions that will take you from A to SR.

3. Give 2 equivalent fractions that will take you from SL to SR (in the direction of the arrow).

Ch 16: Getting difficult

SECTION 4 — 23-24 correct = 2 stars; 20-22 correct = 1 star

Evaluate:

1. $2/3$ of £12
2. $3/4$ of 16 cm
3. $3/8$ of 80 l
4. $3/10$ of 20 p
5. $4/9$ of £18
6. $7/10$ of 30p
7. $3/11$ of 44 km
8. $3/5$ of 10p
9. $4/5$ of £20
10. $5/7$ x 21p
11. $2/3$ of 18 sweets
12. $3/5$ of 20 mm
13. $5/6$ of 30p
14. $5/8$ of £40
15. $2/9$ of 99p
16. $4/3$ of £30
17. $2/3$ of £297
18. $3/5$ x £4355
19. $7/10$ of £3690
20. $4/13$ of £65
21. $2/7$ of £392
22. $3/8$ x £7192
23. $2/11$ of £6193
24. $4/13$ of £4823

Ch 17: Fractions of fractions

SECTION 4 — 18 correct = 3 stars; 14-17 correct = 2 stars; 10-13 correct = 1 star

$1/2$ of [$1/4$ of 20] is the same as $1/2$ x [$1/4$ x 20]   Work out the bracket first

Evaluate:
1. $1/2$ x [$1/4$ x 16]
2. $1/3$ x [$1/5$ x 60]
3. $1/10$ x [$1/3$ x 90]
4. $1/20$ x [$1/2$ x 240]
5. $1/11$ x [$1/3$ x 99]
6. $2/3$ x [$1/4$ x 24]
7. $1/5$ x [$1/3$ x [$1/4$ x 180]]
8. $3/4$ x [$2/3$ x 72]

N is an unknown number. Work out the value of N.

9. $1/3$ x N = 12
10. $1/5$ x N = 10
11. $2/3$ x N = 8
12. $1/2$ x [$1/3$ of N] = 12
13. $1/3$ x [$1/5$ of N] = 3
14. $1/4$ x [$1/10$ of N] = 4
15. $2/3$ x [$1/4$ of N] = 4
16. $4/5$ x [$3/4$ of N] = 12
17. $3/4$ x [$2/3$ of N] = 3
18. $3/7$ x [$3/10$ of N] = 9

Ch 18: How many

SECTION 8 — 14-15 marks = 2 stars / 12-13 marks = 1 star

A school ski party stayed at a Youth Hostel in Austria.
At one point on a Tuesday evening, the party leader noted that:
There were 2 people making coffee $\frac{1}{4}$ of the group were sitting chatting
0.2 were playing pool   0.3 of them were playing table-tennis
$\frac{1}{5}$ of them were playing board games/cards; $\frac{1}{20}$ were making coffee

1. How many people were there in the group?   (1 mark)
2. How many were doing each activity?   (4 marks)

A tutor arrives to register his class at 8.55. There are 30 in his class.
He is keeping a record of who is late. One day he finds that:
one third of the class were on time
one sixth were less than one minute late
0.2 of the class were between 1 and 2 minutes late
0.1 were more than 2 minutes late.

3. How many pupils were absent? Show clearly how you work it out.
(2 marks for answer & 2 marks for clear working out)

At the end of April, Tom classified the lengths of the 160 fish in his pond.
He discovered that: $\frac{3}{8}$ of the fish were less than 4 cm long
a quarter of them were between 4 and 6 cm long
$\frac{3}{16}$ of them were between 6 and 8 cm long
one eighth of them were between 8 and 10 cm long

4. How many of the fish were in each of his four classifications?   (4 marks)
5. What fraction of the fish were more than 10 cm long?   (2 marks)

Ch 19: Seki Kowa's magic circle

SECTION 8 — All correct = 1 star

In this magic circle there are two magic totals.
Investigate this circle.

What are the two magic totals?

Where do they occur?

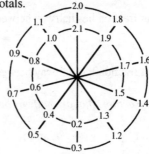

A BIG EDD GUIDE   *Fractions and Decimals*

Ch 20: The first fraction challenge

SECTION 10 — 9-10 correct = 1 star

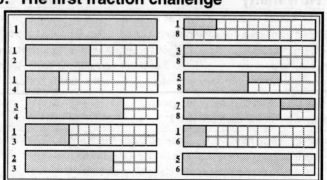

Copy and complete these statements using the information given above:

1. $\frac{1}{2} + \frac{1}{4} = \ldots\ldots$
2. $\frac{1}{3} + \frac{1}{6} = \ldots\ldots$
3. $1 - \frac{1}{6} = \ldots\ldots$
4. $\frac{1}{2} + \frac{1}{3} = \ldots$
5. $1 - \frac{2}{3} = \ldots\ldots$
6. $\frac{1}{8} + \frac{3}{8} = \ldots\ldots$
7. $1 - \frac{1}{8} = \ldots\ldots$
8. $\frac{1}{2} + \frac{1}{8} = \ldots$
9. $\frac{1}{4} + \frac{1}{8} = \ldots\ldots$
10. $\frac{1}{2} + \frac{3}{8} = \ldots\ldots$

Ch 21: The second fraction challenge

15-16 correct = 2 stars
12-14 correct = 1 star

Copy and complete these statements :

SECTION 10

1. $\frac{2}{3} - \frac{1}{6} = \ldots\ldots$
2. $\frac{2}{3} + \frac{1}{6} = \ldots\ldots$
3. $\frac{5}{8} - \frac{1}{2} = \ldots\ldots$
4. $\frac{5}{6} - \frac{2}{3} = \ldots$
5. $\frac{3}{4} + \frac{1}{8} = \ldots\ldots$
6. $\frac{3}{4} - \frac{1}{8} = \ldots\ldots$
7. $\frac{2}{3} + \frac{1}{6} - \frac{1}{2} = \ldots\ldots$
8. $\frac{1}{6} + \frac{1}{2} + \frac{1}{3} = \ldots$
9. $\frac{1}{4} + \frac{1}{4} + \frac{1}{8} = \ldots$
10. $\frac{3}{8} + \frac{1}{4} + \frac{1}{8} = \ldots$
11. $\frac{3}{5} - \frac{1}{10} = \ldots\ldots$
12. $\frac{4}{5} + \frac{1}{10} = \ldots\ldots$
13. $\frac{1}{2} + \frac{1}{5} + \frac{1}{10} = \ldots\ldots$
14. $\frac{1}{3} + \frac{1}{9} = \ldots$
15. $\frac{5}{9} + \frac{1}{3} - \frac{2}{3} = \ldots$
16. $\frac{1}{6} + \frac{4}{9} = \ldots$

Ch 22: Halfway fractions

SECTION 10
10 correct = 3 stars
8-9 correct = 2 stars
6-7 correct = 1 star

1. What fraction lies halfway between $\frac{1}{4}$ and $\frac{1}{2}$?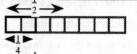

2. What fraction lies halfway between $\frac{1}{3}$ and $\frac{1}{2}$?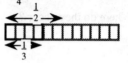

Find the fractions that are halfway between :

3. $\frac{1}{2}$ and $\frac{3}{4}$
4. $\frac{3}{4}$ and 1
5. $\frac{1}{8}$ and $\frac{1}{4}$
6. $\frac{1}{4}$ and $\frac{3}{8}$
7. $\frac{1}{2}$ and $\frac{2}{3}$
8. $\frac{1}{2}$ and $\frac{3}{5}$
9. $\frac{1}{3}$ and $\frac{1}{5}$
10. $\frac{1}{10}$ and $\frac{2}{5}$

THE NATIONAL CURRICULUM ...
... AND BEYOND ...

Big Edd

Handling
Data

> By the end of this topic you should be able to:
> Level 3
> • extract information from lists and tables
> • extract information from pictographs and bar charts
> • construct pictographs and bar charts
>
> Level 4
> • construct frequency tables
>
> Level 5
> • interpret pie charts
>
> Level 6
> • construct pie charts

A BIG EDD GUIDE TO THE NATIONAL CURRICULUM

Handling Data
Section 1 : Pictographs

In this section you will extract information from pictographs.

D1: Traffic Survey

Number of Vehicles Passing the School on Friday – 12 noon until 1 pm	
Bicycles	🚲 🚲 🚲 🚲
Motorbikes	🏍 🏍
Motor Cars	🚗 🚗 🚗 🚗 🚗 🚗
Buses	🚌 🚌 🚌
Vans	🚐 🚐 🚐 🚐 🚐
Lorries	🚚 🚚 🚚 🚚
One symbol = 2 vehicles.	

1. How much time did the survey take ?
2. *Copy and complete this table:*

Vehicle	Bicycle	Motorbike	Motor Car	Bus	Van	Lorry
Number						

3. How many vehicles went by altogether ?
4. How many two-wheeled vehicles went by during the survey ?

• *Check your answers.*

D2 : Teachers

1. *Copy and complete this table:*

Class	Number of teachers
1A	
1B	
1C	
1D	
1E	

Class	Number of teachers for each Y7 class
1A	👤👤👤👤👤👤👤👤👤
1B	👤👤👤👤👤👤👤
1C	👤👤👤👤👤👤
1D	👤👤👤👤👤👤👤
1E	👤👤👤👤👤👤👤👤
👤 or 👤 = 1 Teacher	

2. What is the usual number of teachers for a class?
3. What is the largest number of teachers that any first year class has?
4. Give a reason why one class might have more teachers than the others.

• *Check your answers.*

D3: Chips with Everything!

1. What date was this survey done?
2. 30 people have Fish and Chips. How many meals does 1 symbol stand for?
3. *Copy and complete this table:*

Meal type	Number served
Beefburger & chips	
Egg & chips	
Curry sauce & chips	
Pizza & chips	
Fish & chips	
Chips only	
Total meals	

Number of Meals Served in the Canteen on Friday the 13th.

Beefburger and Chips	🍛🍛🍛🍛🍛🍛🍛
Egg and Chips	🍛🍛🍛🍛🍛
Curry Sauce and Chips	🍛🍛🍛
Pizza and Chips	🍛🍛🍛🍛🍛
Fish and Chips	🍛🍛🍛🍛🍛🍛
Chips only	🍛🍛🍛🍛

1 symbol, 🍛 = curry sauce meals

4. How many people ate in the canteen on Friday 13th?

• *Check your answers.*

Star Challenge 1 1

11 correct = 2 stars
9-10 correct = 1 star

Number of Toads Squished on the A5 during the First Week of June

Saturday June 1st	🐸🐸🐸🐸🐸🐸🐸🐸🐸🐸🐸
Sunday June 2nd	🐸🐸🐸🐸🐸🐸🐸🐸🐸🐸🐸🐸½
Monday June 3rd	🐸🐸🐸🐸🐸½
Tuesday June 4th	🐸🐸🐸
Wednesday June 5th	🐸🐸🐸🐸½
Thursday June 6th	🐸🐸🐸
Friday June 7th	🐸🐸🐸🐸🐸🐸🐸🐸½

🐸 represents ⬭ squished toads

1. Six toads were killed on Thursday. How many were killed on Monday?
2. How many toads does the full symbol stand for?
3. How many toads does the half-symbol stand for?
4. *Copy and complete this table:*

Date in June	1st	2nd	3rd	4th	5th	6th	7th
Number of toads squished						6	

5. (a) Is it true to say that more toads were killed at the weekend?
   (b) Why do you think this is so? • *Your teacher has the answers to this*

Section 2 : Bar charts

In this section you will extract information from a variety of bar charts.

PRACTICE

P1: Lotta bottle

1. On which day is most milk delivered?
2. How much is delivered on the Friday?
3. How much is delivered on the Tuesday?
4. *Copy and complete this table:*

Day	Mon	Tues	Wed	Thurs	Fri
No. of pints					

5. Milk costs the school 30p a pint. What is the canteen's milk bill for this week?
6. Why do you think a lot more milk is delivered on Monday than Friday?

• *Check your answers.*

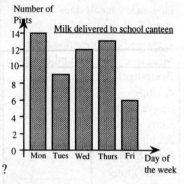

P2 : The Return of the Pan-Galactic Explorers!

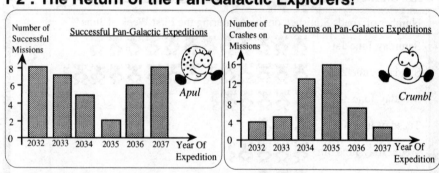

1. In which year were there five successful expeditions ?
2. How many successful expeditions were there in 2033?
3. How many crashes were there in 2033?
4. What was the total number of expeditions in 2033?
5. *Copy and complete this table:*

Year	2032	2033	2034	2035	2036	2037
Successful missions						
Crashed missions						
Total number of missions						

6. In which year was there the least number of crashes?
7. Why were there so few successful expeditions in 2035?
8. In which year was there the largest total number of missions? • *Check your answers.*

P3: Technology Classes in Year 9

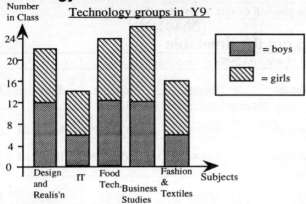

1. Design and Realisation is taken by 22 pupils. There are 12 boys. How many girls take Design and Realisation?

2. *Copy and complete:*

Subject	Design & Real'n	IT	Food Tech.	Bus. Studies	Fashion & Tex
Boys	12				
Girls					
Pupils	22	14			

3. Which subject is done by equal numbers of boys and girls?
4. How many boys are there in all these classes?
5. How many girls are there in all these classes?   • *Check your answers.*

Star Challenge

18 correct = 2 stars
16-17 correct = 1 star

1. *Copy and complete this table for the bar chart:*

Subject	English	Maths	Science	Music	French	PE
Lessons	5					
Homeworks	2					

2. English, Maths and Science are called the Core subjects. How many lessons do each of the core subjects have ? (3 answers)

3. How many pieces of homework do each of the core subjects have ? (3 answers)

4. Which subject has no homework set? Why do you think this is so ?

• *Your teacher has the answers to this.*

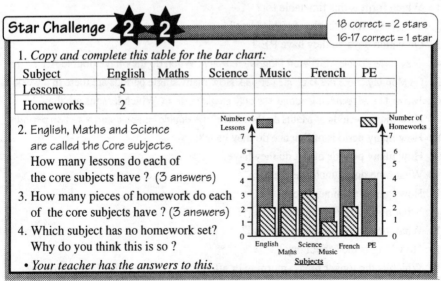

Section 3 : Information from tables

In this section you will extract information from tables.

PRACTICE

P1: Sorting out the timetable

FORM 7W		FORM TEACHER : Mr. Bennett				
Time	Day / Period	Monday	Tuesday	Wednesday	Thursday	Friday
8.55	FT	Form Time and Assembly Period				
9.20	1	MATHS	FRENCH	GEOGRAPHY	ENGLISH	CRAFT
9.55	2	MATHS	FRENCH	GEOGRAPHY	ENGLISH	CRAFT
10.30		Morning Break				
10.50	3	P.E.	SCIENCE	MATHS	FRENCH	FRENCH
11.25	4	P.E.	SCIENCE	ENGLISH	MUSIC	ART
12.00		Lunch Time				
1.15	5	SCIENCE	HISTORY	FRENCH	SCIENCE	MATHS
1.50	6	SCIENCE	HISTORY	FRENCH	SCIENCE	MATHS
2.25		Afternoon Break				
2.40	7	ENGLISH	ART	CRAFT	FORM PERIOD	P.E.
3.15	8	ENGLISH	ART	CRAFT	LIBRARY SKILLS	P.E.
3.50						

1. Which form is this timetable for?
2. Who is the form teacher for this class?
3. On which days do they have P.E.?
4. They have double Maths on Monday morning. When do they have double Art ?
5. On Monday there are 8 single periods. How many single periods are there in a week ?
6. Two of the afternoon lessons are only single periods. Which lessons are they ?
7. How many periods of Maths do they have? (A double lesson counts as two periods)
8. How many periods of Science do they have?
9. How many periods of Art do they have?
10. What time does lunchtime start?
11. How long is the lunch break ?
12. What time does the school day start?
13. What time does the school day end?
14. How long is the school day?
15. Which is the longer break, morning or afternoon?   • *Check your answers.*

A BIG EDD GUIDE   Handling Data

P2: May Days

May						
M	T	W	Th	F	S	Su
	1	2	3	4	5	6
7	8	9	10	11	12	13
14	15	16	17	18	19	20
21	22	23	24	25	26	27
28	29	30	31			

1. What day is the 9th of May ?
2. Ahmed gets his pocket money on Saturdays.
   How many times will he get his pocket money during this month ?
3. What is the date of the third Monday of the month ?
4. What day will the 11th of June be ?
5. May the 7th is a school holiday. Half term is the week marked with a box.
   How many days will you go to school on in this month ?
6. Sunday is the first day of the week.
   How many complete weeks are there in this May ?
7. What is the date on the second Saturday after May the 26th ?
8. Mary pays £40 rent every Wednesday.
   How much rent does she pay this May ?

• *Check your answers.*

P3: Luxury household goods

	Own a TV	Rent a TV	Video Recorder	Microwave Cooker	Dishwasher
Smith	2		1		
Brown		1			
Kuri	1		1	1	1
Green	2	1	2		
Ono	1	1			1

1. How many of these families own a dishwasher ?
2. How many of these families own a video recorder ?
3. Which family has the least number of these luxury goods ?
4. How many of these luxury goods has the Kuri family ?
5. How many families own a TV ?
6. How many of these families rent or own a TV ?
7. How many TVs do these families have altogether between them ?

• *Check your answers.*

Star Challenge 3

9 correct = 2 stars
7-8 correct = 1 star

Make Year	Vauxhall Astra	VW Golf	Ford Escort	Mazda 323	Renault 12
1990 G – H	3600	3125	3375	3125	2500
1991 H – J	4125	3825	3600	4150	3025
1992 J – K	4725	4350	4500	4825	4205
1993 K – L	5375	5150	5350	5850	4750
1994 L – M	6025	5525	5975	6350	5175

1. How much would you pay for a 1992 Mazda?
2. How much would you pay for a 1993 Golf?
3. Linda has £4000 to spend. What year is the newest Ford Escort that she can buy?
4. Which of these cars has the most expensive 1990 model?
5. Which of these cars has the most expensive 1994 model?
6. Which, of all these cars, is the cheapest car?
7. What are the letters underneath the years used for?
8. What letters would go under 1989?
9. Is an "L" car younger or older than a "K" car?

• *Your teacher has the answers to these.*

Star Challenge 4

All correct = 1 star

The car I bought in 1995 had all the following features:
- it was less than 3 years old;
- it cost more than £4000;
- it was not French;
- it was neither a J nor a K registration car;
- it was the second cheapest model of its year.

Which car did I buy ?
In what year was it registered ?
What was its registration letter?

• *Your teacher has the answers to these.*

Section 4 : Pie charts

In this section you will:
- extract information from pie charts;
- find out how pie charts are constructed.

DEVELOPMENT

D1: Reading simple pie charts   DO NOT MEASURE!

1. 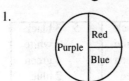 40 students chose their favourite colour.

   How many chose purple ? ....

   How many chose blue ?   ....

   How many chose red ?   ....

2. 15 girls were asked a question.

   How many said "Yes" ?   ....

   How many said "No" ?   ....

   How many said "Maybe" ? ....

3. 12 girls chose their favourite pop group

   How many chose Pulp ?   ....

   How many chose Blur ?   ....

   How many chose Oasis ?   ....

4. 24 boys were asked a question.

   How many said "Never" ?   ....

   How many said "Sometimes" ? ....

   How many said "Get lost" ?   ....

5. I have 300 stamps in my collection.

   What fraction of my collection is ☐ stamps ....

   How many ☐ stamps do I have ?   ....

   How many △ stamps do I have ?   ....

   How many ▭ stamps do I have ?   ....

   My stamp collection

6. In March 1996, three teams were out in front of the Premier Football League. 180 people were asked who they thought would win it in 1996.

   How many said "Liverpool" ?   ....

   How many said "Manchester United" ? ....

   How many said "Newcastle" ?   ....

   Check your answers.

A BIG EDD GUIDE — page 169 — *Handling Data*

D2: Recognising pie charts

Say which pie chart could show each set of information:

| 1. 3 black
3 white
3 green

pie chart ... | 2. 2 black
3 white
3 green

pie chart ... | 3. 6 black
3 white
3 green

pie chart ... | 4. 3 black
3 white
1 green
1 blue
pie chart ... | 5. 3 black
3 white
4 green
2 blue
pie chart ... |

• *Check your answers.*

D3: Working out simple angles

| EXAMPLE | 3 red and 1 green
What are the angles for
each colour on the pie chart ? | | Full circle
= 360° |

Work out the angle for each colour: DO NOT MEASURE !

1.
Colour	Number	Angle
Red	1	......
Green	1	......
Blue	1	......

2.
Colour	Number	Angle
Red	1	......
Green	1	......
Blue	1	......
Yellow	1	......

3.
Colour	Number	Angle
Red	1	......
Green	1	......
Blue	2	......

4.
Colour	Number	Angle
Red	1	......
Green	1	......
Blue	2	......
Yellow	4	......

5.
Colour	Number	Angle
Red	3	......
Green	3	......
Blue	6	......

6.
Colour	Number	Angle
Red	3	......
Green	3	......
Blue	3	......
Yellow	3	......

For Q5&6 you should also sketch the pie chart.

• *Check your answers.*

D4: Working out more difficult angles

EXAMPLE Work out the angles in the pie chart.

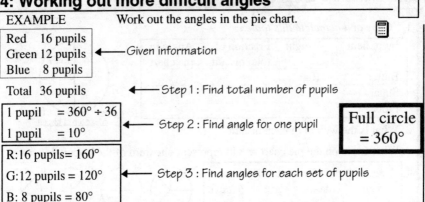

Red 16 pupils
Green 12 pupils ← Given information
Blue 8 pupils

Total 36 pupils ← Step 1: Find total number of pupils

1 pupil = 360° ÷ 36
1 pupil = 10° ← Step 2: Find angle for one pupil

R: 16 pupils = 160°
G: 12 pupils = 120° ← Step 3: Find angles for each set of pupils
B: 8 pupils = 80°

Full circle = 360°

Work out the angles in each pie chart. Fill in the gaps.

1. Red 20 pupils
Black 10 pupils
Orange 6 pupils

Total ...... pupils
1 pupil = 360° ÷ ...
        = ...
R: 20 pupils = ...
B: 10 pupils = ...
O: 6 pupils = ...

2. Purple 10 pupils
Yellow 8 pupils

Total ...... pupils
1 pupil = 360° ÷ ...
        = ...
P: 10 pupils = ...
Y: 8 pupils = ...

3. Pink 15 pupils
Green 3 pupils

Total ...... pupils
1 pupil = ... ÷ ...
        = ...
P: 15 pupils = ...
G: 3 pupils = ...

4. Green 3 pupils
Red 3 pupils
White 4 pupils

Total ...... pupils
1 pupil = ... ÷ ...
        = ...

G: 3 pupils = ...
R: 3 pupils = ...
W: 4 pupils = ...

5. Orange 3 pupils
Brown 2 pupils
Yellow 1 pupil

Total ...... pupils
1 pupil = ... ÷ ...
        = ...

O: 3 pupils = ...
B: 2 pupils = ...
Y: 1 pupil = ...

6. Blue 7 pupils
Pink 5 pupils
Green 8 pupils
Purple 4 pupils

B: = ...
Pi: = ...
G: = ...
Pu: = ...

• *Check your answers.*

Star Challenge 5

19-20 marks = 2 stars
15-18 marks = 1 star

1. *Copy and complete this table:*

Ingredient	Weight	Fraction of total biscuit	Angle in pie chart
Butter	10g		
Sugar			
Flour			

(8 marks)

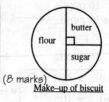

Make-up of biscuit

2. What is the weight of each biscuit ? (1 mark)

3. What angle on the pie chart would represent one third of the biscuit ? (1 mark)

4. A second kind of biscuit is made of :
$\frac{1}{8}$ flour $\frac{1}{4}$ butter $\frac{1}{4}$ syrup $\frac{3}{8}$ oats

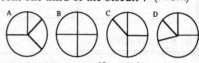

Which two of these pie charts could represent this biscuit ? (2 marks)

5. Copy the two pie charts for the second kind of biscuit and label them correctly.

(8 marks)

• *Your teacher has the answers to these.*

Star Challenge 6

12 correct = 2 stars
10-11 correct = 1 star

1. There are 10 blue cars in the car park.

(a) How many cars are white ?

(b) How many cars are red ?

(c) How many cars are there altogether ?

(d) What angle is the red sector ?

(e) What angle is the "others" sector ?

(f) How many "others" are there ?

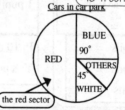

Cars in car park

2.

Icee

The Pan-Galactic Leisure Company did a survey of the holidays taken by Pan-Galactic Explorers in 2392. 30 Explorers went to Earth.

Copy and complete this table using the information given in the pie chart :

Holiday Destinations

Holiday destinations	Number of PGEs	Angle on pie chart
Earth	30	60°
Mars		
Venus		
Saturn		

• *Your teacher has the answers to these.*

Section 5 : Displaying information

In this section you will display information using bar charts, pictographs and pie charts. This is preparation for the project at the end of the topic.

DEVELOPMENT

It is better if the whole class starts this section together!

D1: Animal shivers

36 Y7 pupils were asked which animals they would not like to meet.
Here is what they said.

My worst animal	Number of pupils
Snake	8
Tiger	3
Shark	6
Bear	2
Spider	10
Wolf	7

Task 1: Draw a bar chart to display this information.
Label it clearly and give it a title.

Task 2: Draw a pictograph to display this information.
Use simple shape(s).

Task 3: You are going to make a pie chart to display this information.

(a) *Copy and complete this table:*

Animal	Snake	Tiger	Shark	Bear	Spider	Wolf
Angle						

(b) Draw a pie chart.
Put the name of the animal in each sector.
Put the angle size in each sector.
Give it a title.

- *Your teacher must check these diagrams to make sure you have put everything in.*

Star Challenge 7 7

6 correct = 2 stars
5 correct = 1 star

Another 33 Y7 pupils were asked which animals they would not like to meet.
Here is what they said.

My worst animal	Number of pupils
Snake	9
Tiger	3
Shark	5
Bear	2
Spider	7
Wolf	7

Work out what the angles would be if you wanted to put this information onto a pie chart. (6 marks)

The answers are difficult because they are not whole numbers.

Give each angle to the nearest degree.

This is very difficult. If you can't do it now, you will be able to try again next year.
- *Your teacher will need to mark this!*

A BIG EDD GUIDE   Handling Data

Section 6 : Collecting your own information

(In this section you will work with frequency tables (tally charts))

DEVELOPMENT

D1: Tally charts   *Class discussion*

The whole class must start this section together!

Did you know ...
... the "tallyman" was the man who used to tally (keep count of) the number of sheep, the bags of grain, ... brought to market.

He had "tally sticks" on which he made a notch (cut) for every animal or sack that he counted.

Tally-stick

1. What did 𝆲𝆭𝆬𝆬𝆬 mean on his stick ? How many animals has he tallied here ?

We use **a tally chart** to help us collect and sort information.
It can also be called **a frequency table.**

2. In this frequency table:
   - how many bags of barley were sold ?
   - how many bags of wheat were sold ?
   - how many bags of oats were sold ?

Bags of grain	Tally	Frequency
wheat	༜༜༜ ΙΙ	
maize	༜༜༜ ༜༜༜ ΙΙ	12
barley	༜༜༜ ༜༜༜ Ι ༜༜༜ ༜༜༜	
oats	༜༜༜ ༜༜༜	

D2 : Who tells the worst jokes ?   *Class activity*

Put this tally chart/frequency table onto the classroom board.

Fill in the names of five teachers in your school.

Ask each member of the class who they think tells the worst jokes.

Tally the results on the tally chart.

Teacher	Tally	Frequency
....		
....		
....		
....		
....		
|ΙΙΙΙΙΙΙΙΙΙΙΙΙ| Total	

D3: Royal death   *Small groups*

King Charles the First died in 1643.

Make a survey of how each person in the class thinks he died.

Copy this Tally Chart into your book and fill it in.

Draw and label a bar chart to show your results.

• *Show your teacher.*

HOW DID HE DIE ?	Tally	Frequency
In his sleep		
Heart attack		
Bubonic plague		
Run over by a coach		
Killed in battle		
Beheaded		
Hung, drawn & quartered		

Section 7 : The project

In this section you will use the skills you have developed in this booklet to collect, organise and display data.

EXTENSIONS

The whole class must start this section together!

You will work in small groups.   *Groups of 3 – 4*
You may do the project on this page or choose from one of the ideas in E2.
Decide which project you will do.
Share the tasks out amongst the members of the group.

E1: Vampire blood

Task 1 : Collecting and sorting the data

A firm is going to market a new soft drink aimed at 10-12 year olds.
One name they have suggested is "Vampire Blood".
Choose four names that you think are better than this.
Ask each member of your class which name they like best.
Record the results of your survey in a frequency table (tally chart).

Task 2 : Displaying data

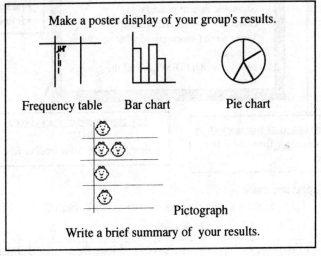

Make a poster display of your group's results.

Frequency table   Bar chart   Pie chart

Pictograph

Write a brief summary of your results.

Your teacher will give marks for your display.
Marks will be awarded for:
- accuracy of results
- correctly drawing <u>and labelling</u> frequency table, bar chart, pie chart and pictograph
- good display
- good summary

YOUR TEACHER WILL AWARD STARS FOR GOOD MARKS !

E2: Your project

Task 1 : Collecting and sorting the data

Choose a topic.

It can be one of those suggested in the chart below – or one of your own.

Collect the data for your topic.

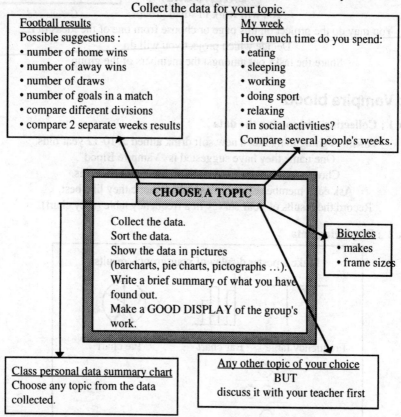

Football results
Possible suggestions :
- number of home wins
- number of away wins
- number of draws
- number of goals in a match
- compare different divisions
- compare 2 separate weeks results

My week
How much time do you spend:
- eating
- sleeping
- working
- doing sport
- relaxing
- in social activities?

Compare several people's weeks.

CHOOSE A TOPIC

Collect the data.
Sort the data.
Show the data in pictures
(barcharts, pie charts, pictographs ...).
Write a brief summary of what you have found out.
Make a GOOD DISPLAY of the group's work.

Bicycles
- makes
- frame sizes

Class personal data summary chart
Choose any topic from the data collected.

Any other topic of your choice
BUT
discuss it with your teacher first

Task 2 : Displaying data

Make a poster display of your group's results.

It should include:

| Frequency table | Bar chart | Pictograph | Pie chart |

A brief summary of your results.

Your teacher will give marks for your display.
Marks will be awarded for:
- accuracy of results
- correctly drawing <u>and labelling</u> frequency table, bar chart, pie chart and pictograph
- good display
- good summary

YOUR TEACHER WILL AWARD STARS FOR GOOD MARKS !

High Level Challenge Section

EXTENSIONS
YOUR TEACHER HAS THE ANSWERS TO THESE.

Ch 1: Brothers and sisters — SECTION 1

All correct = 1 star

Number of brothers and sisters of children in 7W

- None: 🙂 🙂 🙂
- One: 🙂 🙂 🙂 🙂
- Two: 🙂 🙂 🙂 ☺
- Three: 🙂 🙂 ☺
- Four: 🙂 ☺
- Five: ☺

🙂 = 2 children

1. *Copy and complete this table:*

Number of brother & sisters	0	1	2	3	4	5
Number of pupils						

2. How many children in 7W have no brothers or sisters ?
3. How many children have more than 3 brothers and sisters ?
4. How many children have less than 4 brothers and sisters ?
5. How many children are there in the class ?
6. How many brothers and sisters do the children in 7W have altogether ?

Ch 2: How 'green' is my valley ? — SECTION 2

All correct = 1 star

1. How many tonnes of waste paper does the Rhondda valley recycle in a year ?

2. What percentage of glass bottles is recycled in the Ogwen valley ?

3. Which is the best at recycling bottles ?

4. Which is the worst at recycling waste paper ?

5. What was the total amount of land reclaimed during the year ?

Bottles recycled by bottle banks (Percentage recycled)

R = Rhondda Valley
O = Ogwen Valley
D = Dyffryn Valley
L = Lleyn Peninsula
C = Coed Valley

Waste paper recycled (Number of thousand tons reclaimed)

Area of land reclaimed (Number of sq. km reclaimed)

A BIG EDD GUIDE — Handling Data

Ch 3: Teaching all ages in Wessex! SECTION 2 (All correct = 1 star)

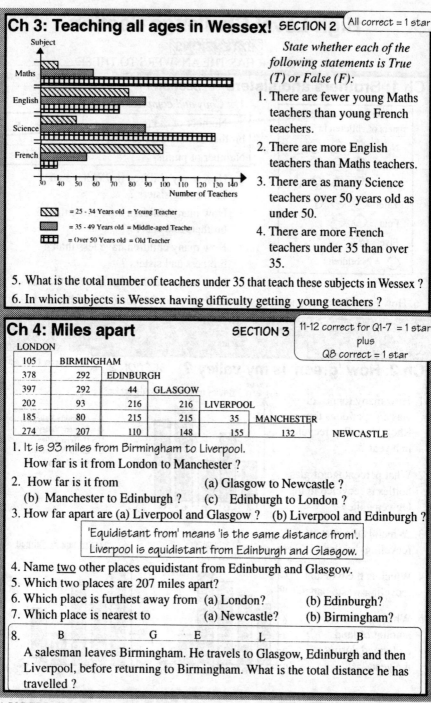

= 25 - 34 Years old = Young Teacher
= 35 - 49 Years old = Middle-aged Teacher
= Over 50 Years old = Old Teacher

State whether each of the following statements is True (T) or False (F):

1. There are fewer young Maths teachers than young French teachers.
2. There are more English teachers than Maths teachers.
3. There are as many Science teachers over 50 years old as under 50.
4. There are more French teachers under 35 than over 35.
5. What is the total number of teachers under 35 that teach these subjects in Wessex?
6. In which subjects is Wessex having difficulty getting young teachers?

Ch 4: Miles apart   SECTION 3   11-12 correct for Q1-7 = 1 star plus Q8 correct = 1 star

LONDON						
105	BIRMINGHAM					
378	292	EDINBURGH				
397	292	44	GLASGOW			
202	93	216	216	LIVERPOOL		
185	80	215	215	35	MANCHESTER	
274	207	110	148	155	132	NEWCASTLE

1. It is 93 miles from Birmingham to Liverpool.
   How far is it from London to Manchester?
2. How far is it from   (a) Glasgow to Newcastle?
   (b) Manchester to Edinburgh?   (c) Edinburgh to London?
3. How far apart are (a) Liverpool and Glasgow?   (b) Liverpool and Edinburgh?

   'Equidistant from' means 'is the same distance from'.
   Liverpool is equidistant from Edinburgh and Glasgow.

4. Name <u>two</u> other places equidistant from Edinburgh and Glasgow.
5. Which two places are 207 miles apart?
6. Which place is furthest away from   (a) London?   (b) Edinburgh?
7. Which place is nearest to   (a) Newcastle?   (b) Birmingham?

8.   B_____G____E_____L_____B

   A salesman leaves Birmingham. He travels to Glasgow, Edinburgh and then Liverpool, before returning to Birmingham. What is the total distance he has travelled?

A BIG EDD GUIDE   page 178   *Handling Data*

Ch 5 : Bus timetable for Route 58   SECTION 3

Q1-6 correct = 1 star
Q7-9 correct = 1 star

MONDAYS TO SATURDAYS	am @NS	am $	am	am	pm	pm
MARYPORT (Station Street)	7.20	8.20	9.53	11.53	1.53	3.53
Dearham (Commercial)	7.35	8.30	10.03	12.03	2.03	4.03
Dovenby (Ship)	7.44	8.39	10.12	12.12	2.12	4.12
Papcastle (PO Corner)	7.49	8.44	10.17	12.17	2.17	4.17
COCKERMOUTH (Main Street)	7.55	8.47	10.20	12.20	2.20	4.20

	am +NS	am	am	pm	pm	pm *NS	pm S
COCKERMOUTH (Main Street)	7.58	9.23	10.23	12.23	2.23	4.40	4.40
Papcastle (PO Corner)	8.00	9.25	10.23	12.25	2.25	4.42	4.42
Dovenby (Ship)	8.06	9.31	10.31	12.31	2.31	4.48	4.48
Dearham (Commercial)	8.15	9.40	10.40	12.40	2.40	4.57	4.57
MARYPORT (Station Street)	8.25	9.50	10.50	12.50	2.50	5.12	5.07

```
Key: @   Operates via Grasslot, Ewanrigg and Fairfield Car Park
     NS  Not Saturdays
     S   Saturdays only
     $   On schooldays operates to Cockermouth Upper School
     +   On schooldays operates via Towncroft & Netherall School
     *   Operates via Ewanrigg and Grasslot
```

1. (a) Which two places does the bus travel between ?
   (b) Which places does it go through on the way ?

2. Mr Cooper has to be in work in Cockermouth by 9.00am.
   What is the time of the bus he should catch from Maryport ?

3. Mrs Hamilton has a dental appointment in Maryport at 2.20pm.
   What is the time of the latest bus she can get from Dovenby?

4. Where does the 58 bus stop at in Papcastle?

5. How long is the usual journey from Maryport to Cockermouth?

6. What is the earliest bus I can catch from Dearham to Cockermouth on Saturday ?

7. I get the 12.03 bus from Dearham. Where should I be 14 minutes later?

8. The 12.23 from Cockermouth is 20 minutes late.
   What time do you think it will probably get to Dovenby ?

9. What two extra places does the 4.40 from Cockermouth visit (except on Saturdays) ?

Ch 6: The Last Post   SECTION 3

Q2-8 correct = 1 star
Q9-11 correct = 1 star

LETTER POST - RATES FOR LETTERS

Weight not over	First Class	Second Class	Weight not over	First Class	Second Class
60g	25p	19p	500g	£1.25	98p
100g	38p	29p	600g	£1.55	£1.20
150g	47p	36p	700g	£1.90	£1.40
200g	57p	43p	750g	£2.05	£1.45
250g	67p	52p	800g	£2.15	Not admissible over 750g
300g	77p	61p	900g	£2.35	
350g	88p	70p	1000g	£2.50	
400g	£1.00	79p	Each extra 250g or part thereof 65p		
450g	£1.13	89p			

1. Jack wanted to post a letter weighing 65g. He thought that by first class post it would cost 25p. It cost him 38p. Explain why.

> IF YOU DO NOT UNDERSTAND WHY – FIND OUT
> – OR YOU WILL NOT BE ABLE TO DO THE REST OF THE QUESTIONS !

2. How much will it cost Freda to send a 180g letter by first class post ?
3. Marcus only has 75p. His letter weighs 290g. Can he afford to send it first class?
4. Linford has £1.30. What is the heaviest letter he can send by second class post ?
5. Marsha has a 1500g letter.
   (a) How much will it cost her to send it first class ?
   (b) Why can she not send it second class ?

PARCEL POST RATES

Weight not over	Cost	Weight not over	Cost
1 kg	£2.70	8 kg	£6.10
2 kg	£3.30	10 kg	£7.10
4 kg	£4.70	30 kg	£8.40
6 kg	£5.25		

Please note that parcels over 10 kg and up to 30 kg are accepted at most Post Offices but <u>cannot</u> be accepted for addresses in Jersey.

6. What is the heaviest <u>letter</u> that can be sent by 2nd class post ?
7. How much does it cost Zhaleh to send a 4.6 kg parcel to Harif?
8. It cost Leroy £6.10 to send a parcel to his family.
   What is the heaviest this parcel could have been?
9. What is the heaviest parcel Shadiq could send to Mark for £4.70?
10. What is the cheapest way of sending a packet by post that weighs:
    (a) 740g   (b) 850g   (c) 960g ?
    In each case, give the price and state whether it goes 1st class, 2nd class or parcel rate.
11. (a) Can I send a 20kg parcel to Jersey by parcel post?
    (b) Give a reason for your answer.

Ch 7: Sur le Pont d'Avignon ...   SECTION 3

10 marks = 3 stars
9 marks = 2 stars
8 marks = 1 star

ROUTE INFORMATION	OUTWARD			HOMEWARD		
Route	Day	Date	Time	Day	Date	Time
BOULOGNE – AVIGNON	Fri	11/5–19/10	D20.25	Sat	12/5–20/10	D17.45
	Sun/Tues	27/5–9/9	D20.25 A08.00	Mon/Wed	28/5–10/9	D17.45 A08.00
	Sat/Thurs	30/6–1/9	D20.25 A08.00	Sun/Fri	1/7–2/9	D17.45 A08.00

CABIN CHARGES – Single journey			Price per berth		
Cabin	2nd class	1st class	Cabin	2nd class	1st class
Single sleeper	–	£90	4 bed sleeper	–	£12
2 bed sleeper	–	£41	6 bed sleeper	£9	–
3 bed sleeper	£28	–			

	MOTORAIL SUPPLEMENTS					
	2nd class			1st class		
	Car	Adult (12yr+)	Child (4-11)	Car	Adult (12yr+)	Child (4-11)
SINGLE	£108	£42	£21	£108	£66	£33
RETURN	£216	£68	£34	£216	£102	£51

CHILDREN: ANY CHILD 12 OR OVER HAS TO PAY THE ADULT FARE
An infant (0–3yr) who occupies a berth is charged the child fare and cabin supplement.

- The family consists of Mr and Mrs Khan and their children Zhilah aged 2 and Kazem aged 9.
- They live in Newcastle, 345 miles from the ferry port of Dover.
- Their petrol cost is 8p per mile travelled.
- They will catch the ferry from Dover to Boulogne and the total single fare for this journey will be £72.50.
- They will travel 2nd class on the Motorail from Boulogne to Avignon, leaving on a Tuesday and returning on a Wednesday.
- They take a 3-bed sleeper both ways – Zhilah does not occupy a berth.
- They estimate that they will travel 1000 miles in their car while they are in Avignon.
- They will return by ferry from Boulogne to Dover and then drive back to Newcastle.

Your task: Work out the total travel costs for the Khan family holiday in Avignon, France. Show how you work it all out.

Marks: 1 mark for *ferry fares total*;   2 marks for *cost of petrol*;
2 marks for *cost of motorail travel*;   1 mark for *overall total*;
4 marks for *clearly setting out how you worked it all out*.

A BIG EDD GUIDE   *Handling Data*

Ch 8: The Royal Birthday Cake SECTION 4

23-24 marks = 2 stars
20-22 marks = 1 star

ROYAL PROCLAMATION
Next Sunday
King Zog's 50th Birthday
Share his birthday cake.
All subjects in the Palace Courtyard at midday
will get equal shares in his birthday cake.

11.00 King Zog opened his curtains. There were 36 people in the courtyard.
11.15 He went out onto the balcony. There were 60 people in the courtyard.
11.30 King Zog, now wearing the Royal Robes, looked out. There were 90 people.
11.45 He put on his crown and went out again onto the balcony. Now there were 120.
12.00 He went down into the courtyard. There were 180 people waiting for the cake.

1. *Copy and complete this table:*   angle of slice

Time	Number of subjects in courtyard	Angle of slice of cake
11.00		10°
11.15		
11.30		
11.45		
12.00		

(5 marks)

2. At 11.00 o'clock, there were 36 people in the courtyard.
   Each person is represented by 10° on this pie chart.
Copy and complete this table :

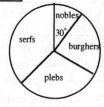

Zog's subjects	Number of each	Angle in pie chart
Nobles	3	30°
Burghers	8	
Plebs	10	
Serfs	15	
	36	360°

(3 marks)

3. At 11.30, there were 90 people.
   (a) What angle, on a pie chart for these 90, represents each person ?
   (b) *Copy and complete this table:*

Zog's subjects	Number	Angle in pie chart
Nobles	5	
Burghers	20	
Plebs	30	
Serfs	35	
	90	360°

(4 marks)

4. At 11.45 there were 120 people. There were 10 nobles, 30 burghers, 40 plebs & 40 serfs.
Draw an accurate pie chart to represent the nobles, burghers, plebs and serfs at 11.45.
Explain how you calculate each of the angles on the pie chart. (8 marks)

5. At 12.00 noon, the pie chart showing the different types of people would look
exactly the same as the one showing the people at 11.45.
How many nobles, burghers, plebs and serfs were there at 12.00 ? (4 marks)

Ch 9 : Hypothesis testing

12 marks = 2 stars
10-11 marks = 1 star

A **hypothesis** is a statement which you have not yet proved true or false.

Choose one, or more, of these hypotheses.

Collect data to test this hypothesis. (4 marks)

Organise the data and display it clearly. (4 marks)

Interpret the data. (2 marks)

Explain whether the data shows that the hypothesis is true or false. (2 marks)

Hypothesis 1: One third of all car number plates carry a number which is divisible by 3.

Hypothesis 2: More boys than girls write with their left hand.

Hypothesis 3: The girls in Y7 are taller than the boys.

Hypothesis 4: Most pupils in Y7 are less than 165 cm tall.

Hypothesis 5: The most popular sport amongst the pupils in Y7 is football.

Hypothesis 6: In Y7, more girls than boys play regularly for school or sports club teams.

Hypothesis 7: Football teams in the Second Division score more goals in a year than teams in the First Division.

Hypothesis 8: In Y7, the boys get higher marks than the girls in maths tests.

Ch 9 : Hypothesis testing

A hypothesis is a statement which we have to try to prove or disprove.

To test one, or more, of these, you can:
* collect data relating to the hypothesis
* organise the data into tables, graphs, formulae
* interpret your results, the data

Example: imagine the boys show that, she girls' maths test score is below the boys'.

Hypothesis 1: One third of all class senior pupils carry a number which is divisible by five.

Hypothesis 2: More boys than girls read with their feet rigid.

Hypothesis 3: The girls in Y2 are taller than the boys.

Hypothesis 4: More pupils in Y2 wear glasses than can read.

Hypothesis 5: The most popular ice cream at the pupils in Y2 is vanilla.

Hypothesis 6: In Y2, more girls than boys play regularly for school or sports club teams.

Hypothesis 7: Football teams in the second Division score more goals in a year than teams in the First Division.

Hypothesis 8: In Y2, the boys get higher marks than the girls in maths tests.

Hukka

A BIG EDD GUIDE — Handling Data

THE NATIONAL CURRICULUM ...
... AND BEYOND ...

Big Edd

Angle

> By the end of this topic you should be able to:
>
> Level 3
> - use compass bearings
> - understand the terms clockwise and anti-clockwise
>
> Level 4
> - calculate fractions of turns
> - calculate angles on a clock
>
> Level 5
> - recognise parallel, perpendicular, horizontal and vertical lines
> - classify angles
> - measure and draw angles accurately
> - estimate angles
>
> Level 6
> - calculate angles on a staright line, at a point and in a triangle
> - calculate angles in equilateral and isosceles triangles

Angle
Section 1: Turning

In this section you will:
- work with turns and fractions of turns;
- follow turning instructions.

DEVELOPMENT

D1: Teacher doesn't know which way to turn *Class activity*

This kind of activity is sometimes called "people maths". People are used instead of equipment. You are going to use your teacher as a 'turning machine'. The class must decide what instructions to give the teacher. Join in with the discussion and help decide what instructions to give. Do not write any answers down.

1. Tell your teacher (nicely) to stand facing the class.
   You want your teacher to face in the opposite direction.
   Give an instruction, *using two words only*, to tell your
   teacher to do this.   Did this work ? If not, try again.

2. Tell your teacher to face the side of the classroom.
   You want your teacher to face the class again.
   Give an instruction, *as a fraction of a turn*, to tell
   your teacher to do this.   Did this work ? If not, try again.

3. What words can you use to tell your teacher the direction of turn ?

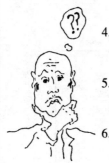

Now, give your teacher instructions how to move, so that you can find the answers to each of these questions.

4. Your teacher is facing the class and then makes a half turn.
   What turn will make the teacher face the class again ?
   Find two different answers.

5. Your teacher is facing the class and then makes a quarter turn.
   What turn will make the teacher face the class again ?
   Find two different answers.

6. Your teacher: • is facing the class;
   • is only allowed to turn *clockwise*;
   • makes a quarter turn .
   What turn will make your teacher face the class again ?

7. Your teacher makes a quarter turn *clockwise*, then another quarter turn *clockwise*.
   What single turn would have the same effect ?

8. Your teacher makes a half turn *anti–clockwise*, then a quarter turn *anti–clockwise*.
   What single turn would have the same effect ? Find two different answers.

9. Your teacher makes a half turn *anti–clockwise*, then a quarter turn *clockwise*.
   What single turn would have the same effect ?

10. Your teacher makes a three–quarter turn *clockwise*, then a half turn *clockwise*.
    What single turn would have the same effect ?

P1: Combining turns

$\frac{1}{4}$ ↻ + $\frac{1}{4}$ ↻ = $\frac{1}{2}$ ↻

↻ means a clockwise turn

↺ means an anti-clockwise turn

Give a single turn which is the same as:

1. $\frac{1}{2}$ ↻ + $\frac{1}{4}$ ↻
2. $\frac{1}{4}$ ↻ + $\frac{1}{2}$ ↻
3. $\frac{1}{2}$ ↻ + $\frac{1}{4}$ ↺
4. $\frac{1}{4}$ ↺ + $\frac{1}{2}$ ↻
5. $\frac{1}{4}$ ↻ + $\frac{1}{2}$ ↺
6. $\frac{1}{2}$ ↻ + $\frac{1}{2}$ ↻
7. $\frac{3}{4}$ ↻ + $\frac{1}{2}$ ↻
8. $\frac{1}{4}$ ↻ + $\frac{3}{4}$ ↺
9. $\frac{3}{4}$ ↻ + $\frac{3}{4}$ ↻
10. $\frac{1}{2}$ ↻ + $\frac{3}{4}$ ↻ + $\frac{1}{2}$ ↺

• Check your answers.

D2: Recognising fractions of turns

On a clock the numbers are equally spaced.

The minute hand has turned through $\frac{1}{12}$ of a turn, between these two times.

What fraction of a turn does *the minute hand* make between each pair of times?

1.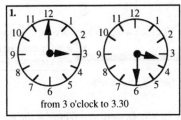
   from 3 o'clock to 3.30

2.
   from 2 o'clock to 2.15

3.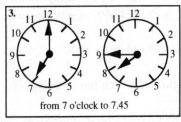
   from 7 o'clock to 7.45

4.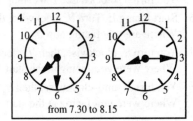
   from 7.30 to 8.15

A BIG EDD GUIDE   Angle

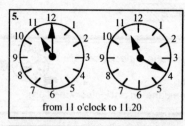
from 11 o'clock to 11.20

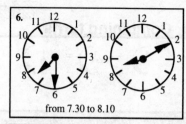
from 7.30 to 8.10

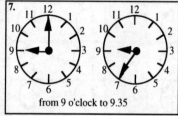
from 9 o'clock to 9.35

from 4.05 to 5 o'clock

• *Check your answers.*

PRACTICE
P2: Following turning instructions

The arms of this compass rose are equally spaced.
From NE to N is $1/8$ of a turn
From S to E is $1/4$ of a turn

1. Start facing North. Turn $1/8$ clockwise. Where are you facing?
2. Start facing SW. Turn $3/8$ clockwise. Where are you facing?
3. Start facing S.
   Turn $1/8$ clockwise, then $1/2$ clockwise, then $1/8$ clockwise. Where are you facing?

• *Check your answers.*

Star Challenge 1
4-5 correct = 1 star

4. Start facing NE. Turn $1/8$ anti-clockwise, then $3/8$ clockwise. Where are you facing now?
5. You turn $3/8$ clockwise. You end up facing E. Where were you facing at the start?
6. Start facing E. Turn $5/8$ clockwise, then $1/2$ anti-clockwise, then $1/4$ clockwise. Where are you facing now?
7. You turn $1/8$ clockwise, then $1/4$ clockwise. You end up facing W. Where were you facing at the start?
8. You turn $1/8$ anti-clockwise, then $1/4$ anti-clockwise. You end up facing NW. Where were you facing at the start?

• *Your teacher has the answers to these.*

A BIG EDD GUIDE   Angle

Section 2: Describing angles

In this section you will:
- meet a definition of an angle;
- describe angles in three different ways.

DEVELOPMENT

D1: Angles and how you describe them

The **angle** between two directions (or between two lines) is the amount of turn needed to move from the first direction to the second direction

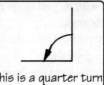

This is a quarter turn
This is a right angle
This is 90°

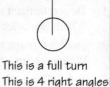

This is a full turn
This is 4 right angles
This is 360°

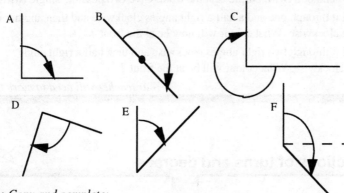

Task 1: *Copy and complete:*

Angle	A	B	C	D	E	F
Fraction of a turn						

Task 2: *Copy and complete:*

Angle	A	B	C	D	E	F
Number of right angles						

Task 3: *Copy and complete:*

Angle	A	B	C	D	E	F
Angle in degrees						

• *Check your answers.*

Did you know ...

... a long time ago, mathematicians, thought that the sun moved round the earth once every year. They thought that a year had 360 days. They said that the sun moved on degree every day.   **1 revolution = 360°**

Star Challenge 2

5-6 correct = 1 star

This is a coloured golf umbrella looked down on from above.

Give it a twirl

> A quarter turn can also be called **a right angle**

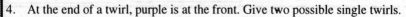

For each question start with the red at the front.

1. Twirl it through a right angle.
   Which two colours could now be at the front ?
2. Twirl it through half a right angle.
   Which colours could now be at the front ?
3. Twirl it through one and a half a right angles.
   Which colours could be at the front ?
4. At the end of a twirl, purple is at the front. Give two possible single twirls.
5. Twirl it through one and a half a right angles clockwise and then another right angle clockwise. What colour will now be at the front ?
6. Twirl it through two right angles clockwise and then half a right angle anti–clockwise. What colour will be at the front ?

  • *Your teacher will need to mark these.*

D2: Fractions of turns and degrees

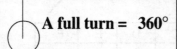

A full turn = 360°   **A right angle = 90°**

Copy and complete:

1. A half turn = ...°
2. A quarter turn = ...°
3. $1/3$ of a turn = ...°
4. $1/10$ of a turn = ...°
5. Two full turns = ...°
6. $1/4$ of a turn = ...°
7. $1/8$ of a turn = ...°
8. $3/4$ of a turn = ...°
9. 2 right angles = ...°
10. $1/2$ a right angle = ...°
11. 3 right angles = ...°
12. $1/3$ of a right angle = ...°
13. $1/10$ of a right angle = ...°
14. $1\frac{1}{2}$ right angles = ...°

  • *Check your answers.*

D3: Tracing paper turn meter

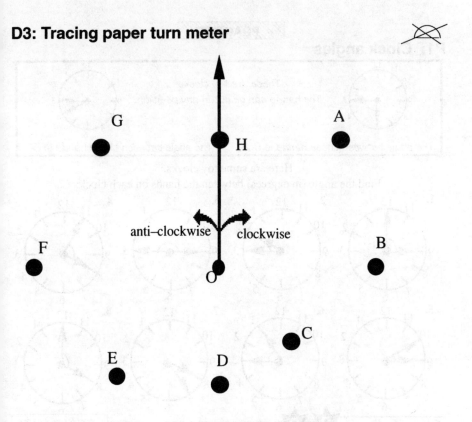

Put tracing paper over the diagram.
Draw the arrow on the tracing paper and the centre dot – but not the other dots.
Put the point of pencil at O. Turn the tracing paper until the arrow reaches each letter.

Copy and complete these two tables:

Point	A	B	C	D	F	H
Fraction of turn *clockwise*						
Degrees of turn *clockwise*						

Point	G	F	D	B	E	C
Fraction of turn *anti–clockwise*						
Degrees of turn *anti–clockwise*						

• *Check your answers.*

P1: Clock angles

  These are toy clocks.
The hands can be put in any position.

The angle between these hands is 90°.   The angle between these hands is 30°.

Here are some toy clocks.
Find the angle (in degrees) between the hands on each clock:

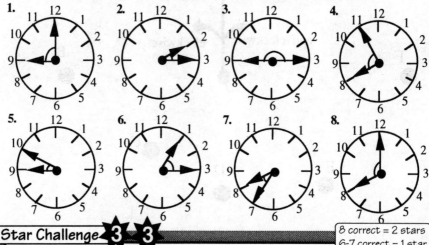

Star Challenge

8 correct = 2 stars
6-7 correct = 1 star

Find the marked angle between the hands on each toy clock.
Give your answers in degrees.

• *Your teacher has the answers to these.*

P2: Compass turns

Copy and complete this table:

Start	Finish	Direction	Angle turned through
E	S	c	90°
NE	E	c	...
SW	W	...	45°
NW	NE	c	...
NW	NE	a–c	...
N	...	c	135°
W	E	c	...
W	SE	c	...
E	SW	c	...
NW	S	a–c	...

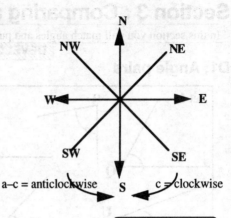

a–c = anticlockwise   c = clockwise

• *Check your answers.*

Did you realise... ...that to sail north is to travel *towards* the north, but the north wind blows *from* the north?

5–6 correct = 1 star

Star Challenge 4

Copy and complete this table:

Start	Finish	Direction	Angle
W	...	a–c	225°
...	NE	c	180°
...	SW	a–c	135°
...	E	c	225°
...	N	a–c	315°
...	SW	c	225°

Did you know... ...that a sou'wester is a strong oilskin coat worn to keep sailors dry in storms? ...that it got its name from the wind that brings the storms, the sou'wester.

• *Your teacher has the answers.*

Star Challenge 5

15-16 marks = 2 stars
11-14 marks = 1 star

Compass angles

The direction between N and NE is called NNE (north of north east).
The direction between E and NE is called ENE (east of north east).

1. Copy the compass rose and label the other six unmarked directions in the same way. (6 marks)

What are the angles between:

2. N and E?
3. S and SW?
4. SE and SW?
5. N and NNE?
6. S and SSE?
7. NNE and ENE?
8. SSE and NNE?
9. WSW and ENE?
10. WNW and NE?
11. ESE and WSW?

(Q2-11 one mark each)

• *Your teacher has the answers.*

A BIG EDD GUIDE   Angle

Section 3 : Comparing angles — *All individual work*

In this section you will match angles and put angles in order of size.

DEVELOPMENT

D1: Angle pairs

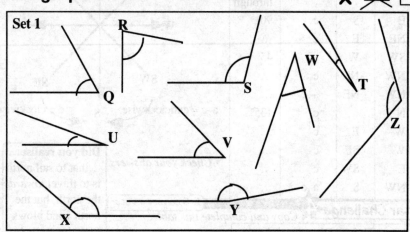

For each angle in the Set 1, there is an equal angle in the Set 2.

Task 1: Guess which pairs are equal. Write down your guesses as pairs.
Write $\hat{Q} = \hat{A}$ if you think angle Q is the same size as angle A (– it isn't).

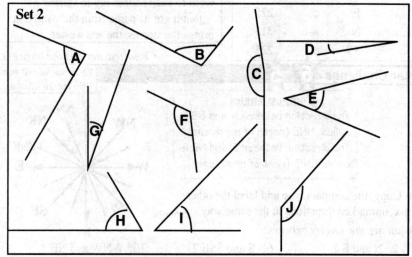

Task 2: Cut out each angle in Set 2 from the worksheet.
Match each angle with its equal angle in Set 1.
How many of your guesses were right ?

• *Check your answers.*

A BIG EDD GUIDE   page 194   *Angle*

D2: Ordering angles

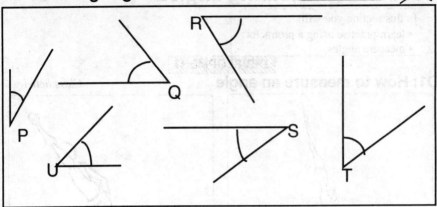

Trace each angle. Put the angles in order of size.

• *Check your answers.*

All correct = 1 star

Star Challenge 6

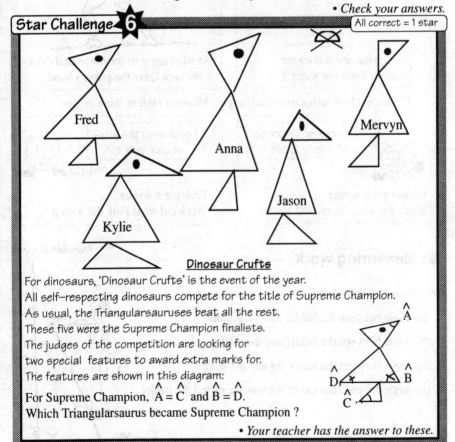

Dinosaur Crufts

For dinosaurs, 'Dinosaur Crufts' is the event of the year.
All self-respecting dinosaurs compete for the title of Supreme Champion.
As usual, the Triangularsauruses beat all the rest.
These five were the Supreme Champion finalists.
The judges of the competition are looking for
two special features to award extra marks for.
The features are shown in this diagram:
For Supreme Champion, $\hat{A} = \hat{C}$ and $\hat{B} = \hat{D}$.
Which Triangularsaurus became Supreme Champion ?

• *Your teacher has the answer to these.*

Section 4: Measuring angles

In this section you will:
- learn/practise using a protractor;
- measure angles.

D1: How to measure an angle   *Class activity*

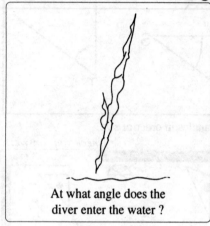

At what angle does the diver enter the water?

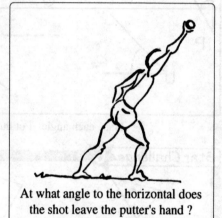

At what angle to the horizontal does the shot leave the putter's hand?

1. Discuss how to measure each angle. Measure each of these angles.

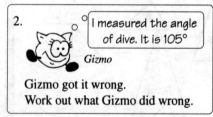

2. Gizmo: "I measured the angle of dive. It is 105°"

Gizmo got it wrong.
Work out what Gizmo did wrong.

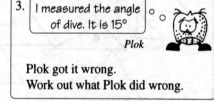

3. Plok: "I measured the angle of dive. It is 15°"

Plok got it wrong.
Work out what Plok did wrong.

D2: Measuring work   *Individual work*

Measure each of these angles:

1. the angle between the ladder and the ground
2. the angle between the ladder and the wall
3. the angle between the man's leg and the ladder
4. the angle between the top of the man's arm and the ladder

- Check your answers.

A BIG EDD GUIDE   page 196   Angle

D3: Measuring and labelling angles
Individual work

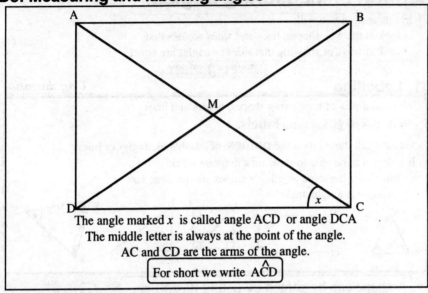

The angle marked x is called angle ACD or angle DCA
The middle letter is always at the point of the angle.
AC and CD are the arms of the angle.

For short we write $A\hat{C}D$

Measure each of these angles. Copy and complete each of these statements:

$A\hat{C}D$ = ... $A\hat{C}B$ = ... $A\hat{B}D$ = ... $B\hat{M}A$ = ... $C\hat{M}B$ = ...

Star Challenge

• *Check your answers.*
8 correct = 2 stars
6-7 correct = 1 star

Asil made a camp, deep in the forest. He made a map to show his favourite places.

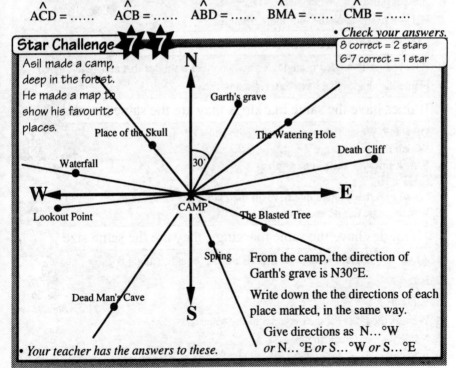

From the camp, the direction of Garth's grave is N30°E.

Write down the the directions of each place marked, in the same way.

Give directions as N...°W or N...°E or S...°W or S...°E

• *Your teacher has the answers to these.*

A BIG EDD GUIDE   *Angle*

Section 5: Measuring angles

In this section you will:
- look at the way shapes, lines and sides are labelled;
- look at ways of showing that sides or angles are equal.

DEVELOPMENT

D1: Labelling
Class discussion

We need a way of identifying shapes, angles and lines.

We do this by giving them **labels.**

We also call these labels the **names** of the shapes, angles or lines.

It is useful to be able to show on a diagram when:
- lines have the same length • angles are the same size
- an angle is a right angle

A shape can be named by listing its corners   *Yerwat*

1. ABC is a triangle. What shape is DEFG ?
2. HIJ is a triangle. Name four more triangles.

Right angles are marked with small squares   *Chyps*

3. HJK is a right-angled triangle. Name two other triangles that are right-angled.
4. Name the shapes that have four right angles.

If lines have the same markings they are the same length   *Idea*

5. DE = GF. Which line is the same length as DG ?
6. Which line is the same length as AC ?
7. Which lines are the same length as XY ?
8. Is HJ = HK ?
9. Name two shapes here that have all their sides the same length.
10. Which shape has no equal sides ?

If angles have the same markings, they are the same size

11. Angle X = angle Y = angle Z. Which angle is equal to angle B ?
12. Is $\hat{L} = \hat{N}$?
13. Is $\hat{D} = \hat{F}$?

Big Edd

14. What is the label for the diagonal of the square ?
15. Name two identical triangles.
16. Which lines could you draw to split DEFG into two identical triangles ?

D2: Classifying angles
Individual work

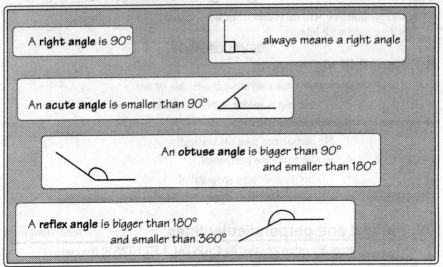

For each angle below, say whether it is **acute, obtuse, reflex** or **a right angle**.

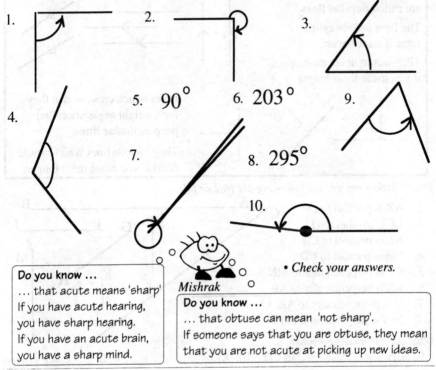

Do you know ...
... that acute means 'sharp'
If you have acute hearing, you have sharp hearing.
If you have an acute brain, you have a sharp mind.

Mishrak

• Check your answers.

Do you know ...
... that obtuse can mean 'not sharp'.
If someone says that you are obtuse, they mean that you are not acute at picking up new ideas.

Section 6: The language of lines

In this section you will meet and work with some common words and labelling used with lines.

DEVELOPMENT

D1: Sensible statements   *Class discussion*

Discuss whether each statement is sensible or not.

1. A table top is meant to be horizontal.
2. All walls are vertical.
3. No aeroplanes take off vertically.
4. House roofs are horizontal.
5. All horizontal lines are parallel.
6. Any horizontal line is perpendicular to any vertical line.

D2: Parallel and perpendicular lines   *Individual work*

Lines in a diagram are often labelled by CAPITAL LETTERS at the ends.
A_____B is called the line AB.

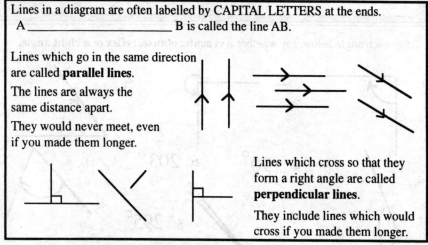

Lines which go in the same direction are called **parallel lines**.

The lines are always the same distance apart.

They would never meet, even if you made them longer.

Lines which cross so that they form a right angle are called **perpendicular lines**.

They include lines which would cross if you made them longer.

State whether each of the following are true or false:

1. AB is parallel to OP
2. EF is parallel to IJ
3. KL is parallel to CD
4. GH is parallel to CD
5. OP is perpendicular to MN
6. KL is perpendicular to AB
7. IJ is perpendicular to AB
8. MN is perpendicular to EF

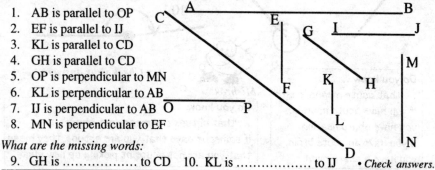

What are the missing words:

9. GH is .... to CD
10. KL is .... to IJ   • *Check answers.*

A BIG EDD GUIDE   *page 200*   *Angle*

Star Challenge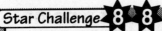

12 correct = 2 stars
9-11 correct = 1 star

Angle Word Search

P	A	R	A	T	U	R	F	L	E	X	M	A	S	T	P	O	L
A	W	M	L	T	E	E	A	T	I	H	L	G	N	R	E	R	Y
R	E	A	I	H	R	M	D	C	B	A	N	O	R	I	F	U	L
A	L	C	N	O	M	A	E	I	N	L	F	T	U	X	H	E	X
L	E	C	E	T	C	M	S	W	A	N	G	E	R	E	C	T	A
L	A	H	S	U	T	E	E	O	R	G	O	N	S	E	L	G	N
E	S	T	E	R	A	S	L	E	C	D	O	S	E	H	O	L	I
L	R	R	N	F	U	P	F	U	T	I	O	N	A	R	C	A	D
I	S	U	T	L	L	U	O	N	E	L	T	E	A	H	Y	X	P
R	P	E	N	T	E	Z	W	L	Z	R	E	E	I	L	G	H	T
A	I	Q	U	A	R	T	G	E	I	A	N	G	L	D	R	I	L
G	O	G	H	E	N	N	T	P	E	N	D	I	C	U	L	A	R
O	N	T	H	V	A	I	R	R	M	A	R	S	A	R	A	L	L
R	B	S	E	T	F	V	I	E	L	E	F	P	A	T	E	E	R
L	I	T	U	S	E	P	G	P	R	H	S	T	W	O	L	A	L
P	R	G	H	P	E	R	L	I	P	M	A	R	G	O	O	N	E

Find these words and phrases hidden here.
Each word, or phrase, makes its own shape.

For example: O
        B
          T U S E

Put a loop around each word or phrase that you can find.

The words and phrases are:

ACUTE	OBTUSE	REFLEX
DIAGONAL	PERPENDICULAR	PARALLEL
RIGHT ANGLE	RECTANGLES	TRIANGLE
PARALLELOGRAMS	HALF TURN	FULL TURN

• *Your teacher has the answers to these.*

Section 7: Angles on a line and at a point

In this section you will investigate the relationships between some sets of angles.

DEVELOPMENT

D1: Investigating angles on a straight line

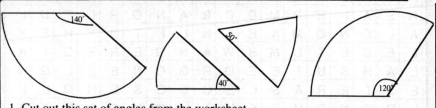

1. Cut out this set of angles from the worksheet.
   Fit *two of them* together to make a semicircle. Stick the semicircle in your book.

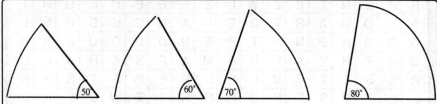

2. Cut out this set of angles.
   Fit *three of them* together to make a semicircle. Stick the semicircle in your book.

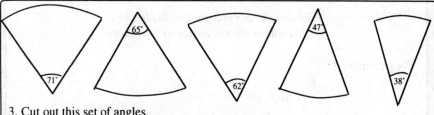

3. Cut out this set of angles.
   Fit *three of them* together to make a semicircle. Stick the semicircle in your book.

4. Copy and complete this sentence:

   > The angles on a straight line add up to ....°

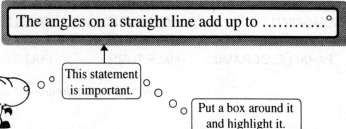

Big Edd

• *Check your answers.*

D2: Calculating angles on a straight line

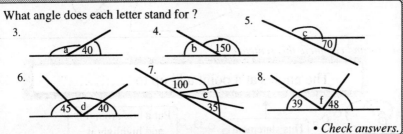

1. What is the angle hidden under the spilt ink?
2. What is the value of x?

What angle does each letter stand for?
3. 4. 5. 6. 7. 8.

• Check answers.

PRACTICE
P1: Angles on a straight line practice

Batch A: What angle does each letter stand for?

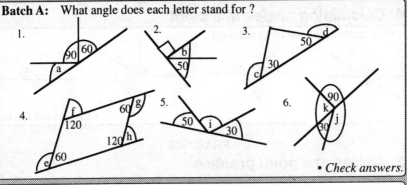

• Check answers.

Batch B: What angle does each letter stand for?

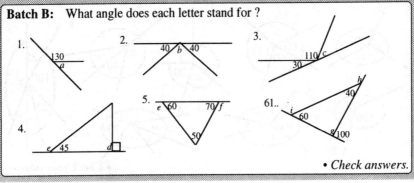

• Check answers.

A BIG EDD GUIDE — Angle

D3: Investigating angles at a point   P ✂ 📄

1. Cut out this set of angles. Fit *three of them* together to make <u>a full circle</u>.

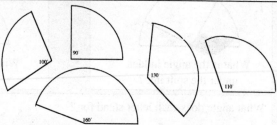

2. *Copy and complete this sentence:*

> The angles at a point add up to ....°

Big Edd: This statement is important. Put a box around it and highlight it.

• *Check your answers.*

D4: Calculating angles at a point

What angle does each letter stand for?

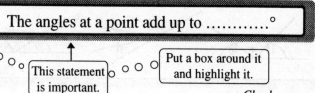

1. 140, 40, p, 140
2. 45, 135, 70, q
3. 90, 75, r, 72
4. 45, s, 40, 180

• *Check your answers.*

PRACTICE

P2: Angles at a point practice

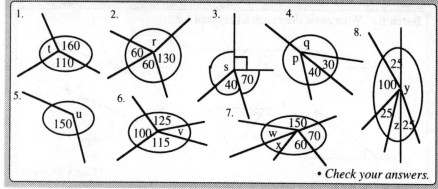

1. t, 160, 110
2. r, 60, 60, 130
3. s, 40, 70
4. q, p, 40, 30
5. 150, u
6. 125, v, 100, 115
7. 150, w, x, 70, 60
8. 25, 100, y, 25, z, 25

• *Check your answers.*

A BIG EDD GUIDE — *Angle*

Section 8: Angles on crossed lines

In this section you will work with angles on crossed lines.

DEVELOPMENT   *Individual work*

D1: Opposite angles

Opposite angles are equal

Copy each diagram. Replace each letter with the correct angle.

1. (40, b, a, c)
2. (d, e, 60, f)
3. (110, h, i, g)
4. (45, j, l, k)
5. (120, p, m, n)
6. (140, s, r, q)
7. (125, u, t, v)
8. (y, 84, x, w, 30)
9. (b, 111, a, c, 42)

• *Check your answers.*
11-12 correct = 2 stars
7-10 correct = 1 star

Star Challenge 9 9

| Opposite angles are equal | Angles on a straight line add up to 180° | Angles at a point add up to 360° |

Copy each diagram. Replace each letter with the correct angle.

1. (45, a, 45)
2. (40, b, 60)
3. (45, 75, 20, c)
4. (145, d, e, 15)
5. (58, g, 60, f, 60)
6. (60, 65, j, i, h)
7. (50, k, 85, 115)
8. (23, l, 141, 117)

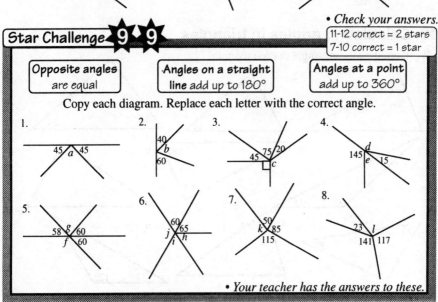

• *Your teacher has the answers to these.*

A BIG EDD GUIDE   page 205   *Angle*

Section 9: Angles in triangles

In this section you will work with angles in triangles.

DEVELOPMENT

D1: Investigating triangles   *Class activity / individual work*

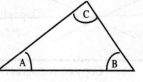

1. Draw a large triangle on a piece of paper. The angles can be any size.
2. Label the angles A, B and C, *inside* the triangle.
3. Cut out the triangle. Tear it into three pieces. Each piece must contain one angle.

4. Put the three angles together in any order. What do you notice?

5. Put the three angles together in a different order. Does the same thing happen?

6. *Copy and complete this sentence:*

   The angles in a triangle add up to ....°

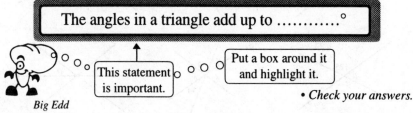

• Check your answers.

D2: Calculating angles in triangles   *Individual work*

Work out the missing angle in each triangle.

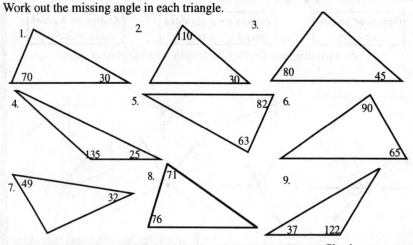

• Check your answers.

A BIG EDD GUIDE   page 206   Angle

P1: Angles in triangles practice

Copy each diagram. Replace each letter with the correct angle size.

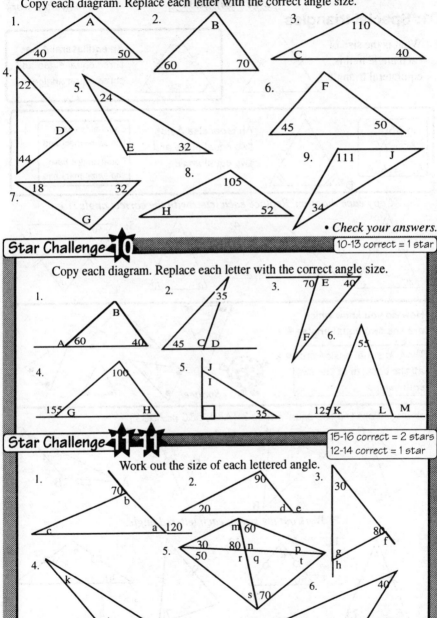

• *Check your answers.*

Section 10: Special triangles

In this section you will work with equilateral triangles and isosceles triangles.

DEVELOPMENT — *All individual work*

D1: Special triangles

1. What is the size of each angle in this equilateral triangle?

An **equilateral** △ has three equal sides and three equal angles

In △ABC
AB = AC
$A\hat{B}C = A\hat{C}B$

An **isosceles** △ has two equal sides and two equal angles

Equal sides have the same markings.

Equal angles have the same markings.

Copy each diagram. Replace each letter with the correct angle size.

2.

3.

4.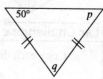

5.

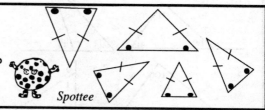

How do you know which are the two equal angles?

The two equal angles are at the bottom of the two equal sides.

Spottee

Which angles are the two equal angles? [A&B, B&C or A&C?]

6.

7.

8.

9.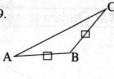

Work out the size of each lettered angle.

10.

11.

12.

13.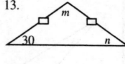

• *Check your answers.*

D4: Working out the base angles (the equal angles)

1. The equal angles are also called the 'base angles'.

Work out the size of each of the base angles.
• *If you cannot do this, talk to your teacher.*

Work out the size of the base angles in each triangle:

1.
2.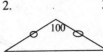
3.
4.

• *Check your answers.*

PRACTICE
P1: A mixture of isosceles triangles

Copy each diagram. Replace the letters with the correct angle sizes.

1.
2.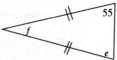
3.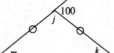
4.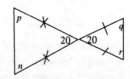
5.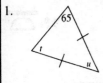
6.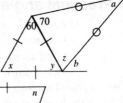

• *Check your answers.*

Star Challenge 12

20 correct = 2 stars
17-19 correct = 1 star

Copy each diagram. Replace the letters with the correct angle sizes.

1.
2.
3.
4.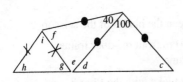
5.

• *Your teacher has the answers to these.*

A BIG EDD GUIDE page 209 Angle

Section 11: Estimating angles

In this section you will estimate the size of some angles.

DEVELOPMENT

D1: Estimating angles
Small groups leading back to class discussion

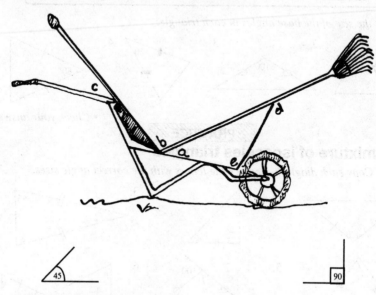

Estimate the size of each of these angles:
- a = angle between rake and bottom of barrow
- b = angle between the rake and the shovel
- c = angle between the shovel and the barrow handle
- d = angle between the rake and the outside of the barrow
- e = angle between the front and the bottom of the barrow

D2: Practical angles

In each of the following cases:
- estimate the angle and write down your estimate;
- find a way of measuring the angle;
- write down the angle and explain how you measured it.

1. Open a pair of scissors.
   What is the largest angle you can get between the blades of the scissors?

2. When the edge of the classroom door is 30 cm from the door frame, what angle does the door make with the frame?

3. What angle does the back leg of your chair make with the floor?

• *You will need to get your teacher to mark this.*

A BIG EDD GUIDE   *page 210*   *Angle*

Small group / individual work

Section 12: Drawing angles

In this section you will draw angles as accurately as you can.

DEVELOPMENT

D1:A: Constructing triangles

> There are six pieces of information for any triangle –
> 3 side lengths and 3 angle sizes.
> A triangle can be drawn accurately if you are given one side length plus any two other pieces of information.

Task 1: Draw each of these triangles as accurately as possible.
Put the information you were given onto your drawing.
Measure the lines/angles asked for.
Give lengths of lines to the nearest 0.1 cm and angles to the nearest degree.

1.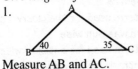
Measure AB and AC.

2.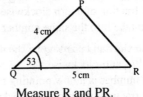
Measure R and PR.

3.
```
      X
  5cm/ \6cm
    /   \
   Y-----Z
     7cm
```
Measure Y.
(Hint: you'll need a pair of compasses.)

4.
```
        L
       /90\
      /    \
     /      \
    /60      \
   M----------N
       6 cm
```
Measure LN.
• Check answers.

Star Challenge ⭐⭐⭐

39 marks = 3 stars
35-38 marks = 2 stars
30-34 marks = 1 star

For each of the triangles in the table that it is possible to draw:
• make a rough sketch and put the given information onto it; (1 mark)
• make an accurate drawing of the triangle; (3 marks)
• fill in the missing information in the table. (3 marks)

35 marks in total

Just to make things a little more difficult – two of these triangles are impossible to draw. Say which two they are and explain why each one cannot be drawn. (4 marks)

Δ No.	Side AB	Side BC	Side CA	angle A	angle B	angle C
1	4 cm	5 cm	......	......	40°	......
2	6 cm	......	......	65°	50°	......
3	7 cm	5.2 cm	4.5 cm	......	......	......
4	6 cm	2.1 cm	3.5 cm	......	......	......
5	......	5 cm	......	......	60°	40°
6	......	......	10cm	110°	......	75°
7	......	......	5.2 cm	......	56°	64°

• *Your teacher will need to mark these.*

High Level Challenge Section
EXTENSIONS
YOUR TEACHER HAS THE ANSWERS TO THESE.

Ch 1: Equivalent turns   SECTION 1   All correct = 1 star

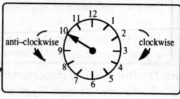

1. Start with the hand pointing to the 10.
   (a) Turn $7/12$ clockwise.
       What number is it now pointing to?
   (b) What fraction of a turn in the opposite direction is the same as $7/12$ clockwise?

2. Start with the hand pointing to the 8.
   (a) Turn $5/12$ anti-clockwise.
       What number is it now pointing to?
   (b) What fraction of a turn clockwise would take it to the same number?

   Did you know that before clocks were invented ...
   ... the term used for the clockwise direction was **sun wise**
   ... the term used for anticlockwise was **contrariwise** or **widdershins**

3. Start with the hand pointing to the 4.
   (a) Turn $11/12$ anti-clockwise.
       What number is it now pointing to?
   (b) What fraction of a turn anti-clockwise would take it to the same number?

4. Start with the hand pointing to the 1.
   (a) Turn $7/12$ clockwise then $5/12$ anticlockwise.
       What number is it now pointing to?
   (b) What single turn would take it to this number?

Ch 2: Headscratcher – where am I?   SECTION 1   All correct = 1 star

I go 10 km North, 10 km East and then 10 km South.
I end up back where I started. Where am I?

Ch 3: Bicycle gearing   SECTION 1   All correct = 1 star

1. The chain wheel of this bicycle is a cog with 42 teeth. The cog on the back wheel has 21 teeth. When the chain wheel makes one turn, how many turns does the back wheel make?

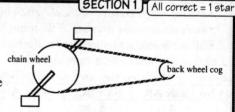

2. When the cyclist changes gear, the chain moves to another cog on the back wheel that has 14 teeth. When the chain wheel makes one turn, how many turns does the back wheel now make?

3. If another chain wheel has 48 teeth, how many teeth must the back wheel cog have, if it is to turn 4 times for every one turn of the chain wheel?

Ch 4: Real clocks

SECTION 2 — Q1-5 correct = 1 star ; Q6 correct = 1 star

1. At 6.30, the hour hand is midway between the 6 and the 7. What is the angle between the hands ?

What is the angle between the hands of a real clock at :

2. 8.30   3. 2.20   4. 12.40   5. 10.10

6. Find a time when the angle between the hands of a clock is exactly 45°.

Ch 5: Old and new compasses

SECTION 2 — 14-16 correct = 2 stars ; 10-13 correct = 1 star

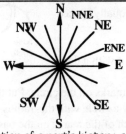
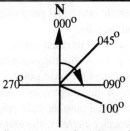

In a celebration of a port's history, ships of all ages are sailing down the river. The ships travel in convoys of eight vessels. The convoy leader gives the navigational instructions by radio to each ship. The "Silver Lady" is a very old ship and she only has a Mariner's 16–point compass on board. All instructions are given on 3–figure bearings (as on a modern compass). Each 3–figure bearing is the number of degrees turned through from the North in a clockwise direction.

> If the steersman is given the bearing 090°, he steers East.

What direction should he steer for each of these bearings :
1. 045°   2. 180°   3. 225°   4. 315°

What bearings would he be given to steer in each of these directions:
5. W   6. SE   7. NNE   8. ESE   9. SSE   10. WSW

For each of these bearings, *between which two directions* should he steer:
11. 080°   12. 260°   13. 275°   14. 318°   15. 48°   16. 226°

Ch 6: Drawing envelope curves

SECTION 2 — 3 stars : one for each correct curve

1. **The Cardioid (Heart–Shaped Curve)**
   Draw a circle with radius 7 cm.
   Draw and label a 36 point circle.
   Join each point on the circle with the point
   that is double its size.

   [For example, 10° is joined to 20° and 50° to 100°.
   Note: 210° cannot be joined to 420°, because there
   is no 420°. It is joined to 60°. Why ?]

   continued on next page

2. **The Nephroid (Kidney–Shaped Curve]**
   Draw and label a 36–point circle of radius 7 cm.
   Join each point on the circle with the point that is three times its size.
3. **The Epicycloid of Cremona**
   This is made by joining each point with the point that is four times its size.
   It is even better if you draw it on a 72–point circle.

Ch 7: Circle envelopes

SECTION 2 — 3 stars: one for each investigation – results and evidence

You will need at least A4 paper for this.

Draw a circle with radius 4 cm in the centre of a sheet of paper.
Divide the circle into equal parts using 150 equally spaced marks round the edge.
This circle is called the **base circle**.
Choose any point within the circle and mark it with a dot.
This point is called the **base point.**
Put the point of the compass onto one of the marks on the circle. Put the point of the compass pencil onto the base point. Draw a circle with this radius.
Draw all the other circles with centres on each of the marks on the base circle.
Each circle must pass through the base point.

Investigate:
1. Do you get the same kind of shape for each base point <u>inside</u> the base circle ?
2. What happens if the base point is <u>on</u> the base circle ?
3. What happens if the base point is <u>outside</u> the circle ?

Ch 8: Match pairs

SECTION 3 — All correct = 1 star

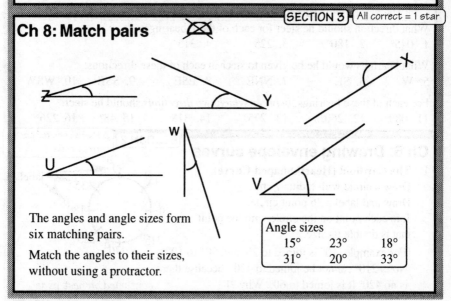

The angles and angle sizes form six matching pairs.

Match the angles to their sizes, without using a protractor.

Angle sizes
15°   23°   18°
31°   20°   33°

A BIG EDD GUIDE   page 214   *Angle*

Ch 9: Matching angles

SECTION 4 8-10 correct = 2 stars / 6-7 correct = 1 star

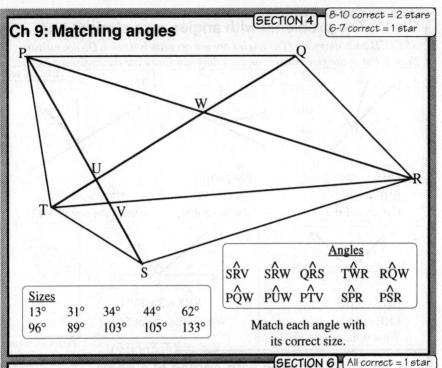

Angles
SR̂V   SR̂W   QR̂S   TŴR   RQ̂W
PQ̂W   PÛW   PT̂V   SP̂R   PŜR

Sizes
13°   31°   34°   44°   62°
96°   89°   103°   105°   133°

Match each angle with its correct size.

Ch 10: The Mystic HexaCircaRectangle

SECTION 6 All correct = 1 star

The ancient religion of Mathestopheles relies on a perfect knowledge of which lines in the Mystic HexaCircaRectangle are parallel and which are perpendicular. Here is the Mystic HexaCircaRectangle.

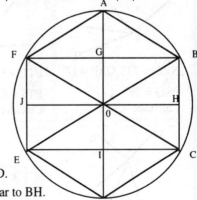

Unfortunately, Trainee High Priest Hamilton's mathestophelic knowledge is weak and he needs your help to answer these questions:

1. Is AB parallel to OC ?
2. Is AF parallel to IE ?
3. Is AG perpendicular to CI ?
4. Is FJ perpendicular to BH ?
5. Name two lines which are parallel to CD.
6. Name three lines which are perpendicular to BH.
7. The secret path HI is not shown. Name a line which is parallel to it.
8. Another secret path is parallel to CD and goes through the point G. Name one other point that it goes through.

Ch 11: The problems with angles on a straight line...

SKETCH each diagram. (The angles are not accurately drawn. Do not measure them.) Put in the given angles on each diagram. Calculate the angles asked for.

SECTION 7

1.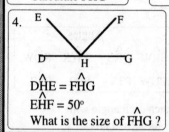
$D\hat{H}E = 30°$
$E\hat{H}F = 42°$
Calculate $F\hat{H}G$

2.
$P\hat{N}Q = 61°$
$R\hat{N}M = 58°$
Calculate $R\hat{N}Q$

3.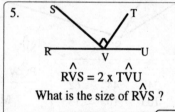
$U\hat{Y}V = 38°$
What is the size of $V\hat{Y}W$?

4.
$D\hat{H}E = F\hat{H}G$
$E\hat{H}F = 50°$
What is the size of $F\hat{H}G$?

5.
$R\hat{V}S = 2 \times T\hat{V}U$
What is the size of $R\hat{V}S$?

SECTION 7 — 10-11 correct = 2 stars, 6-9 correct = 1 star

Ch 12: The problems with angles at a point ...

SKETCH each diagram. (The angles are not accurately drawn. Do not measure them.) Put in the given angles on each diagram. Calculate the angles asked for.

1.
$N\hat{R}O = 73°$ $O\hat{R}P = 47°$
$P\hat{R}Q = 39°$
Calculate $Q\hat{R}N$

2.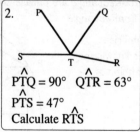
$P\hat{T}Q = 90°$ $Q\hat{T}R = 63°$
$P\hat{T}S = 47°$
Calculate $R\hat{T}S$

3.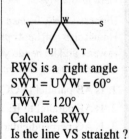
$R\hat{W}S$ is a right angle
$S\hat{W}T = U\hat{V}W = 60°$
$T\hat{W}V = 120°$
Calculate $R\hat{W}V$
Is the line VS straight ?
Explain your answer.

4.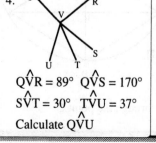
$Q\hat{V}R = 89°$ $Q\hat{V}S = 170°$
$S\hat{V}T = 30°$ $T\hat{V}U = 37°$
Calculate $Q\hat{V}U$

5.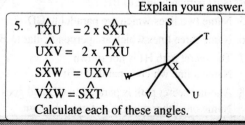
$T\hat{X}U = 2 \times S\hat{X}T$
$U\hat{X}V = 2 \times T\hat{X}U$
$S\hat{X}W = U\hat{X}V$
$V\hat{X}W = S\hat{X}T$
Calculate each of these angles.

A BIG EDD GUIDE   *Angle*

Ch 13: Polygon Challenge 1

SECTION 9 — 7-9 marks = 1 star

1. What is the sum of the angles of a triangle. (1 mark)
2. A quadrilateral can be split into two triangles like this:
   What is the sum of the angles of a quadrilateral? (1 mark)
3.

   What is the sum of the angles of a pentagon?
   (1 mark)

> A **polygon** is a flat shape with straight sides.
> A **regular polygon** has all sides and all angles equal.

Sketch as many of these shapes as you can: (1 mark for each reasonable sketch)

4. a regular triangle
5. a regular quadrilateral
6. a regular pentagon (5 sides)
7. a regular hexagon (6 sides)
8. a regular heptagon (7 sides)
9. a regular octagon (8 sides)

Ch 14: Polygon Challenge 2

SECTION 9 — All correct = 1 star

In Polygon Challenge 1, you probably found the regular heptagon the most difficult, if not impossible, to draw. It would have been much easier if you had known what size the angles of a heptagon are. The next part of the problem will be to find the angles of regular polygons.

10. *Use the techniques you developed at Level 1 to fill in this table as far as the octagon. THEN, use the patterns in the table to fill in the entries for the decagon and icosagon.*

Regular shape	Number of sides	Number of triangles	Sum of angles	Size of each angle
Triangle	3	1	180	60
Quadrilateral	4			
Pentagon	5			
Hexagon	6			
Heptagon	7			
Octagon	8			
Decagon	10		Use the pattern to work out these.	
Icosagon	20			

Ch 15: Polygon Challenge 3

SECTION 9 — Correct answer = 1 star

11. Find the number of sides of any one regular polygon that has angles greater than or equal to 179°.

Ch 16: Parallel lines

SECTION 9 — 34-35 marks = 2 stars / 29-33 marks = 1 star

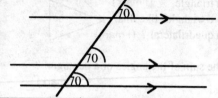

Lines marked → are parallel.
Angles crossing parallel lines make the same angle with each line.

1. (16 marks)

2. (6 marks)

Copy this diagram into your book. Replace each letter in the diagram with the size of the angle.

Find the lettered angles in this diagram. To find all of these angles, you will probably have to find other angles as well.

Copy each of the following diagrams. Find all the lettered angles.

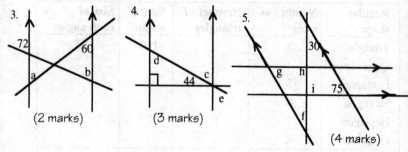

3. (2 marks)
4. (3 marks)
5. (4 marks)

Find the values of x and y.

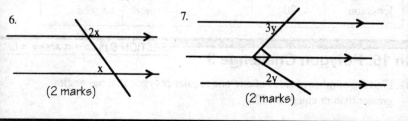

6. (2 marks)
7. (2 marks)

A BIG EDD GUIDE

SECTION 9 All correct = 1 star

Ch 17: Angles on a line and in triangles

1. 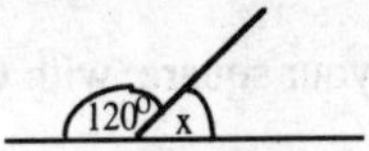 What is the value of x ? (120°, x)

2. 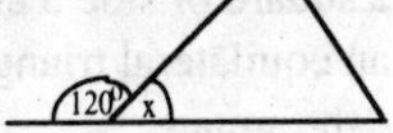 What is the value of x now ? (120°, x)

3. 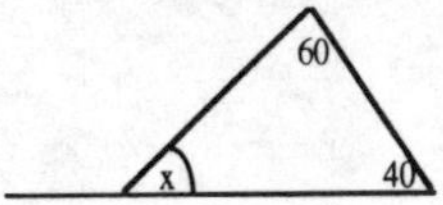 What is the value of x ? (60, x, 40)

4. 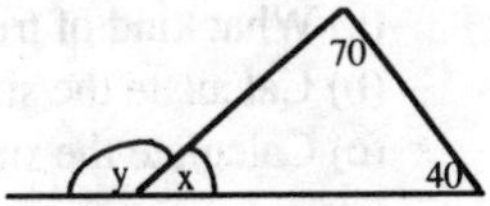 What is the value of y ? (70, y, x, 40)

5. 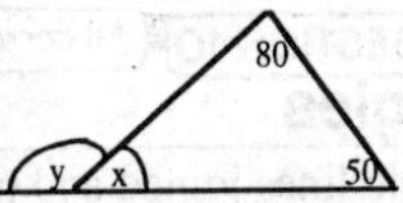 Calculate the value of x and y. (80, y, x, 50)

6. 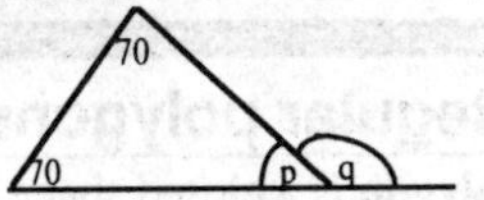 Calculate the value of p and q. (70, 70, p, q)

7. What is the value of t? (85, 50, t)

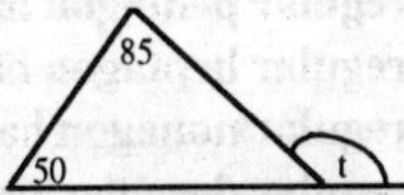

SECTION 10 All **A** correct = 1 star / All **B** correct = 1 star / All **C** correct = 1 star

Ch 18: Angle challenge

- *Copy each diagram.*
- *Calculate each lettered angle – do **not** measure.*
- *Replace each letter in the diagram with the size of the angle.*

A: (square with diagonals, letters d, e, a, b, c, f, g; second diagram with x, p, q, v, w, t, 70, r, s, u)

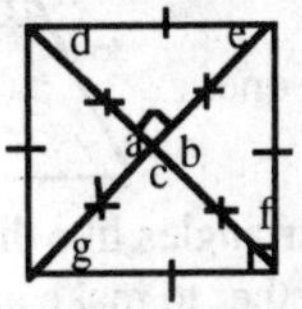

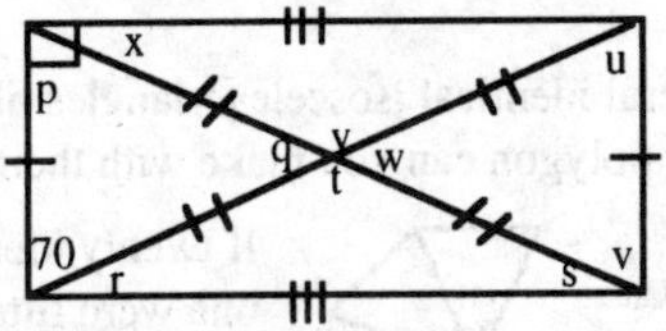

B: 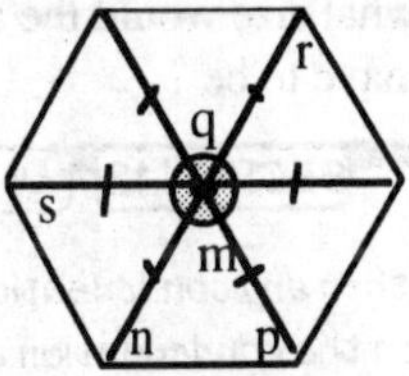 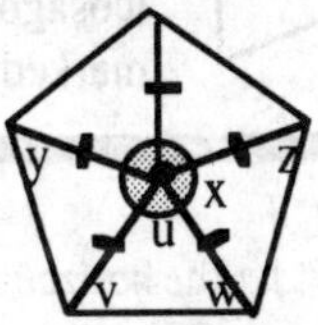 Regular hexagon (letters s, q, r, m, n, p) Regular pentagon (letters y, x, z, u, v, w)

C: A regular octagon is made from 8 congruent (identical) triangles.

Calculate the size of (a) $A\hat{H}O$ (b) $B\hat{O}D$ (c) $F\hat{E}D$

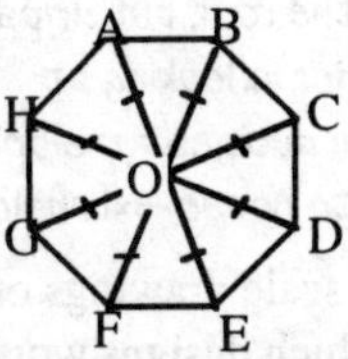

A BIG EDD GUIDE   page 219   *Angle*

Ch 19: Some wordy problems

SECTION 10 — All correct = 1 star

A: Draw a square of side 3 cm. Label it ABCD.
Draw an equilateral triangle COD on the side of your square, with O outside the square.
Draw the line BO.
    (a) What kind of triangle is BCO ?
    (b) Calculate the size of angle BCO.
    (c) Calculate the size of angle COB.

B: The top angle of an isosceles triangle is x degrees.
Express each of the other angles in terms of x.

Ch 20: Regular polygons from triangles

SECTION 10 — All correct = 1 star

A **polygon** is a closed shape made from straight lines joined end to end.
A **regular polygon** is a polygon where all the sides and angles are equal.

A **regular pentagon** has 5 equal sides.
A **regular heptagon** has 7 equal sides.
A **regular nonagon** has 9 equal sides.
A **regular decagon** has 10 equal sides.
A **regular icosagon** has 20 equal sides.

regular octagon   regular hexagon

1. Construct six equilateral triangles with sides 5 cm long. Cut them out.
   Which regular polygon can you make with these triangles?
   Stick the polygon in your book.

2. Construct several identical isosceles triangles like this one.
   Which regular polygon can you make with them ?

3. If twenty identical triangles like this one were fitted together to make an icosagon, what size would the angle marked $x°$ have to be ?

Ch 21: Angle of drip

SECTION 12 — All correct = 1 star

If a roof slopes at more than 27° to the horizontal, then any condensation runs down the inside of the roof. If the slope is 27° or less, then the condensation does not run down the roof, but drips from the roof. In these cases a vent must be fitted.

A builder is looking at several designs for sloping roofs to house-extensions.

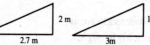

Make scale drawings of each roof and measure the angle.
For which designs would he need to fit a vent ?

A BIG EDD GUIDE   *Angle*

Ch 22: The garden plan

SECTION 12

Stage 2 = 2 stars
Stage 3 = 1 star

Mary Beth wants to draw an accurate plan of her garden. As her aunt is a professional surveyor, she borrows a theodolite to measure the angles accurately.

THEODOLITE
vertical angle scale (not needed in this problem)

Stage 1: She wants to show exactly where the willow tree is.

Willow tree

45   65
L — back wall of house — R
← 10m →

look in here

+ horizontal angle scale to measure horizontal angles

This is very rough sketch of the position of the willow tree.

Draw a line to represent the back wall of the house. **Use a scale of 1 cm to 1 m**.
Draw an angle of 45° at the left end of the house (L).
Draw an angle of 65° at the right end of the house (R).
Show the position of the tree.
What is the actual distance of the tree from L ?
What is the actual distance of the tree from R ?

• *If your answers are approximately 9.5 m and 7.6 m, then you are correct and can go on to Stage 2. If not, talk to your teacher.*

Stage 2: On the next page is Mary Beth's rough sketch of the garden. It is not very accurate. The angles she has measured for each point are given in this table.

Point	W	P1	Y	X	Z	C	O	P4	M	V1	V2
L angle	45°	125°	100°	94°	39°	55°	65°	97°	52°	93°	67°
R angle	65°	10°	36°	35°	100°	95°	85°	50°	52°	52°	78°

Make an accurate scale drawing of the garden.
Use a scale of 1 cm to 1m.
Use a whole page in your book.
Draw all construction lines lightly in pencil.

Mary Beth's rough sketch is on the next page. Use it and the table to make the scale drawing in Stage 2.

Do not rub them out. Ink in the actual lines of the drawing of the garden.

Stage 3: Use your diagram (not this sketch) to find the answers to these questions. Give all your answers to the neares 0.1m.

1. How far is the centre of the pond from the house ?
2. How far is the oak tree from Z ?   3. What are the angles for Q from L and R ?
4. What are the angles for V4 from L and R ?
5. There are four fence posts, P1, P2, P3, P4.
   They are all the same distance apart.
   P2 and P3 are between P1 and P4. Draw in P2 and P3.
   How far are P2 and P3 from L?

A BIG EDD GUIDE   page 221   Angle

Mary Beth's sketch (to be used for Ch: 22

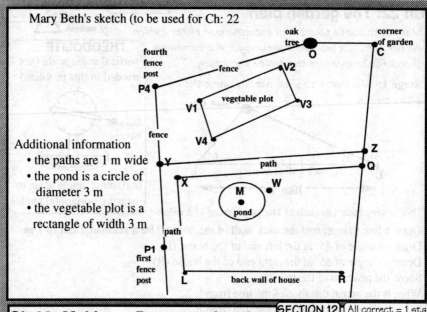

Additional information
- the paths are 1 m wide
- the pond is a circle of diameter 3 m
- the vegetable plot is a rectangle of width 3 m

Ch 23: Making a Penrose triangle

SECTION 12 | All correct = 1 star

1. Construct an equilateral triangle in pencil.
   Make its sides 10cm long.

2.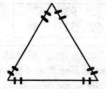

   Make pencil marks 1 cm and 2 cm from each corner, on all three sides of the triangle.

3. Join the points to make this pattern.

4.

   Colour in the lines shown in this diagram.
   Rub out the other lines.

5. Shade the diagram with three different colours to make this 3–D shape stand out clearly.

6. What is odd about this shape ?

A BIG EDD GUIDE   *Angle*

Ch 24: Goal–shooting and goal–keeping problems
SECTION 12

1 star for each correct Task

The goal mouth is 8 m wide.
The goal keeper stands on the centre spot.
He can stop shots within 2.5 m on either side of him.
The forward can take his shot at goal anywhere along AG, but he must not be less than 3m from G.   angle of clear shot   angle of clear shot
                                                                                                     12 m line

Task 1:
1. Predict the point that will give the largest angles of clear shot.
   Write down your prediction.
2. Make an accurate scale drawing of the problem.
   Measure and show the angles of clear shot for several points along AG.
3. Where is the best point to shoot from ?

Task 2:
The goalkeeper stands at the centre of an 8 m goal.
He can stop shots within 2.5 m on either side of him.
The shot is taken from A, 12 m directly in front of the centre of the goal.

4. What is the shortest distance the goal keeper must come out (along AG) to completely block any shot ? Explain how you work it out.

Task 3:
In a goal–shooting competition, the goalkeeper stands at the centre of an 8 m goal.
He can stop shots within 2.5 m on either side of him.
The shot at goal can be taken anywhere on the 12 m line.

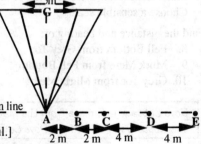

5. Make an accurate scale drawing.
   Measure both angles of clear shot for the points A – E (and any other points you feel would be helpful.]
   List the angles for each point in the form of a table.
   Where is the best point to take it from ?
   Explain why you think it is the best point.

A BIG EDD GUIDE   page 223   Angle

Ch 25: Bearings and scale drawings

SECTION 12 — 17-22 marks = 2 stars / 12-16 marks = 1 star

> The **bearing** is the angle turned though from the North *clockwise*.

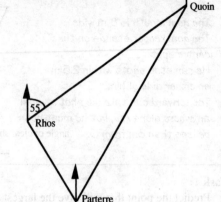

Measure the bearing of:
1. Quoin from Rhos
2. Parterre from Rhos
3. Parterre from Quoin.
4. Rhos from Quoin
5. Quoin from Parterre
6. Rhos from Parterre
   (6 marks)

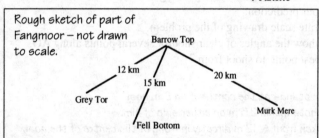

Rough sketch of part of Fangmoor – not drawn to scale.

Murk Mere is 20 km from Barrow Top on a bearing of 130°
Fell Bottom is 15 km from Barrow Top on a bearing of 191°
Grey Tor is 12 km from Barrow Top on a bearing of 244°

7. Make an accurate scale drawing of the positions of these four places. Choose a sensible scale. (6 marks)

Find the distance and bearing of:
8. Fell Bottom from Grey Tor
9. Murk Mere from Fell Bottom
10. Grey Tor from Murk Mere
11. Grey Tor from Fell Bottom
12. Barrow Top from Fell Bottom
    (5 marks)

> Dove Cottage is 3 miles from the Manor House on a bearing of 203°
> The Rectory is 7 miles from Dove Cottage on a bearing of 054°

Work out the distance and bearing of:
13. The Manor House from Dove Cottage (5 marks)
14. Dove Cottage from the Rectory

THE NATIONAL CURRICULUM ...
... AND BEYOND ...

Big Edd

Number Patterns

By the end of this topic you should be able to:

Level 3
- know whether a number is divisible by 2, 5, 10

Level 4
- recognise multiples of a number
- find factors of a number
- explain number patterns and predict terms
- recognise square numbers and cube numbers

Level 5
- work out powers of numbers
- use index notation for powers

Level 6
- recognise number patterns in patterns of shapes
- find triangle numbers

Number Patterns
Section 1: Square Numbers

> In this section you will:
> • investigate square numbers;
> • do some puzzles that use square numbers.

DEVELOPMENT
D1: Investigating square numbers   *Pairs or individual work*

1. The smallest square you can make is using one block. ☐
   Make the next smallest square.
   You will need 4 blocks.

2. Make the next three squares.
   When you have made the first five squares, show them to your teacher.

3. | The first square is made from **1** block. | The first square number is **1**. |
   | The second square is made from **4** blocks. | The second square number is **4**. |

   Write down the next three square numbers.

4. *Copy and complete :* $1 \times 1 = 1$
   $2 \times 2 = 4$
   $3 \times 3 = ...$
   $4 \times 4 = ...$
   $5 \times 5 = ...$

   > Square numbers are also called squares.

5. The first 5 square numbers are 1, 4, 9, 16, 25
   Work out the next two square numbers.

Big Edd

6. *Copy and complete:*
   The first ten square numbers are 1, 4, ... , ... , ... , ... , ... , ... , ... , ...

7. | The second square number is 4. |
   | The fourth square number is 16. |

   Write down:
   (a) the sixth square number   (b) the tenth square number
   Work out:
   (c) the eleventh square number   (c) the 20th square number

   • *Check your answers to questions 5, 6, 7..*

D2: Squaring numbers — *Individual work*

This is a table of numbers and their squares..
Fill in the gaps.

Numbers	2	3	7	9		12	0			4	6			11
Squares	4	9	49		25			1	64			4	100	

• *Check your answers.*

PRACTICE

P1: Calculator squares search

Fill in the missing numbers :

1. ...... x ...... = 16   2. ...... x ...... = 64   3. ...... x ...... = 144
4. ...... x ...... = 169   5. ...... x ...... = 225   6. ...... x ...... = 484
7. ...... squared = 25   8. ...... squared = 841
9. **Challenge !** n squared = 7921 What is the value of n ? ....

• *Check your answers.*

P2 : Sum squares

| Squares are | 0 | 1 | 4 | 9 | 16 | 25 | 36 | 49 | 64 | 81 | 100 | 121 | 144 | . |

2 = 1 + 1	17 = ... + ...	20 = ... + ...	106 = ... + ...	10 = ... + ...
5 = 1 + 4	50 = ... + ...	25 = ... + ...	145 = ... + ...	104 = ... + ...
13 = 4 + 9	80 = ... + ...	125 = ... + ...	26 = ... + ...	169 = ... + ...
18 = 9 + 9	65 = ... + ...	85 = ... + ...	52 = ... + ...	313 = ... + ...
8 = ... + ...	74 = ... + ...	61 = ... + ...	202 = ... + ...	

2, 5, 13, 18 have been written as the sum of two squares.
Write each of the other numbers as the *sum of two squares only*.

• *Check your answers.*

Star Challenge

18-19 correct = 2 stars
15-17 correct = 1 star

1 = 1 − 0	7 = ... − ...	13 = ... − ...	19 = ... − ...	25 = ... − ...
2 = No	8 = ... − ...	14 = No	20 = ... − ...	26 = ... − ...
3 = 4 − 1	9 = ... − ...	15 = ... − ...	21 = ... − ...	27 = ... − ...
4 = ... − ...	10 = No	16 = ... − ...	22 = No	28 = ... − ...
5 = 9 − 4	11 = ... − ...	17 = ... − ...	23 = ... − ...	29 = 225 − 196
6 = No	12 = ... − ...	18 = No	24 = ... − ...	30 = No

22 of these numbers can be written as the difference of two squares.
How many more of these can you write as the difference of two squares ?

• *Your teacher has the answers.*

Star Challenge

2 2 2

11 correct sets = 3 stars 10 correct sets = 2 stars
8-9 correct sets = 1 star

Make this set of cards:

| 1 | 2 | 3 | 4 | 5 | 6 | 7 | 8 | 9 | 10 |

You can only use each card once in each question. Use as many cards as you can. You will probably not be able to use them all!

1. **1 + 3 = 4** and 4 is a square number.

   Put the cards `1` `3` together. This is a **square pair**.

   Use the rest of the cards to make more square pairs. Use as many cards as possible.
   Write down all the square pairs. [There are at least two ways of doing this!]

2. Big Edd started with `1` `8` and made this set: `1 8` `2 7` `3 6` `4 5`

   Big Edd found two other sets starting with `1` `8`

   Find Big Edd's other two sets.

   Big Edd

3. `2` `4` `10` make a **square triple**.

   Letmewin made eight different sets using square pairs and square triples.
   How many different sets can you make?
   [You can use just square triples.]

   Letmewin
   • *Show your sets to your teacher.*

Star Challenge

3 3

One star for each correct spiral

1. Start in the middle of a sheet of squared paper.
   Shade a square block of 4 squares.
   Put the number 1 in a square next to the shaded block.
   Write the numbers 2,3,4,5,6,7,...
                 in a spiral round the shaded block.
   Shade in the **square numbers** as you come to them.
   Continue shading the square numbers until a pattern appears.
   You should go up to 100 at least.

2. Try another spiral going round a shaded block of two squares.
   [Do you need to write in all the numbers, or only the square numbers?]

   • *Your teacher will need to mark this*

Section 2 : Cubes and squares

In this section you will:
- investigate cube numbers;
- do some puzzles that use both square and cube numbers.

DEVELOPMENT

D1: Investigating cube numbers   *In pairs or individual work*

      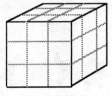

1 cube   This cube is made up of ? small cubes   This cube is made up of ? small cubes

1. (a) Make these three cubes from small cubes. **Show the cubes to your teacher.**
   (b) How many small cubes are there in the second cube ?
   (c) How many small cubes are there in the third cube ?

2. Write down the first three cube numbers.

3. *Copy and complete :* $1 \times 1 \times 1 = ...$
   $2 \times 2 \times 2 = ...$
   $3 \times 3 \times 3 = ...$

4. What is the fourth cube number ?

5. *Copy and complete:*
   The first ten cube numbers are 1 , ... , ... , ... , ... , ... , ... , ... , ... , ...

• *Check your answers to question 5.*

D2: Cubing numbers   *Individual work*

This is a table of numbers and their cubes.
Copy the table and fill in the gaps.

Numbers	2	1	5	6			12	15	20
Cubes	8		125		729	1000			

• *Check your answers*

A BIG EDD GUIDE   *Number Patterns*

PRACTICE

P1: Calculator cube search

Copy each statement. Fill in the missing numbers.

| EXAMPLE $5 \times 5 \times 5 = 125$ |

1. ...... x ...... x ...... = 8
2. ...... x ...... x ...... = 27
3. ...... x ...... x ...... = 1000
4. ...... x ...... x ...... = 1331
5. ...... x ...... x ...... = 2744
6. ...... x ...... x ...... = 27000
7. ...... x ...... x ...... = 15625

• *Check your answers.*

Star Challenge ★ ★ ★

See targets for star ratings

Find some cube numbers that are also square numbers.

TARGETS:
- 1 number — fair
- 2 numbers — good [1 star]
- 3 numbers — excellent [2 stars]
- 4 numbers or more — brilliant ! [3 stars]

• *Your teacher will need to mark these.*

Star Challenge ★ ★

12 correct = 2 stars
10-11 correct = 1 star

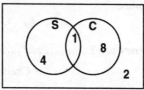

Make a copy of this diagram.

In the circle S, you are going to put square numbers.

In the circle C, you are going to put cube numbers.

1. Why is 1 in the overlapping part of S and C ?

2. Why is 2 outside the circles ?

3. *Draw the diagram. Put these numbers in their correct places:*

9   81   27   5   25   16   225   100   12   64

• *Your teacher will need to mark these.*

A BIG EDD GUIDE — *Number Patterns*

Section 3: Powers

In this section you will meet and work with powers of numbers.

DEVELOPMENT

D1: Powers

> There is a mathematical shorthand which is used when a number is multiplied by itself several times.
>
> $7 \times 7 \times 7 \times 7 \times 7 = 7^5$ read this as **"7 to the power of 5"**
>
> $2 \times 2 \times 2 \times 2 = 2^4$ read this as **"2 to the power of 4"**
>
> $4 \times 4 \times 4 = 4^3$ read this as **"4 to the power of 3"**
>   or as **"4 cubed"**   since it is a cube number
>
> $6 \times 6 = 6^2$ read this as **"6 to the power of 2"**
>   or as **"6 squared"** since it is a square number

> You read 3^6 as   **3 to the power of 6**

How would you read:

1. 4^5 2. 7^2 3. 6^4 4. 5^3 5. 9^7 6. 3^8 7. 11^2 8. 10^6

> **5 to the power of 4**   is written as 5^4

How would you write:

9. **9 to the power of 6**
10. **14 to the power of 5**
11. **6 to the power of 4**
12. **2 cubed**
13. **15 squared**
14. **27 to the power of 4**

                                                         • *Check your answers.*

D2: Calculating powers of numbers

> The calculator key sequence to find 6^2 is :
>
> $6^2 =$ [6] [x] [6] [=]   36   So we write $6^2 = 36$

Use a calculator to work out the values of these. Write your answers like this.

1. 3^2 2. 5^2 3. 10^2 4. 14^2 5. 26^2

> The calculator key sequence to find 6^3 is :
>
> $6^3 =$ [6] [x] [6] [x] [6] [=]   216

Use a calculator to work out the values of these.

6. 2^3 7. 7^3 8. 10^3 9. 5^3 10. 15^3

> $3^5 =$ [3] [x] [3] [x] [3] [x] [3] [x] [3] [=] 243

Use a calculator to work out the values of these.

11. 6^4 12. 2^5 13. 5^5 14. 7^4 15. 2^9 16. 4^6 17. 2^8 18. 8^2

                                                         • *Check your answers.*

P1: Finding the powers

Copy and complete these statements. Replace each ■ with a number.

1. $25 = 5^■$
2. $27 = 3^■$
3. $8 = 2^■$
4. $1000 = 10^■$
5. $32 = 2^■$
6. $64 = 2^■$
7. $64 = 4^■$
8. $125 = 5^■$
9. $36 = 6^■$
10. $216 = 6^■$
11. $243 = 3^■$
12. $625 = 5^■$
13. $16807 = 7^■$
14. $14641 = 11^■$
15. $279841 = 23^■$
16. $24137569 = 17^■$

• *Check your answers.*

P2: Sums of powers   *Copy and complete :*

1. $2^2 + 3^2 = 4 + 9 = ...$
2. $4^2 + 6^2 = ... + ... = ...$
3. $5^2 + 12^2 = ... + ... = ...$
4. $8^2 + 11^2 = ... + ... = ...$
5. $3^2 + 2^3 = ... + ... = ...$
6. $4^3 + 15^2 = ... + ... = ...$

• *Check your answers.*

Star Challenge 6
All correct = 1 star

Find the values of :
1. $1^2 + 2^2 + 3^2$
2. $3^2 + 4^2 + 5^2$
3. $2^2 + 8^2 + 9^2$
4. $2^2 + 2^3 + 2^4$
5. $3^2 + 3^3 + 3^4$
6. $5^2 + 7^3$
7. $2^4 + 3^5 + 6^2$
8. $6^3 + 5^2 + 4^4$
9. $13^2 + 2^2 - 5^2$
10. $10^2 - 9^2 - 1^2$

• *Show your teacher.*

Star Challenge 7

42-43 squares correct = 2 stars
36-41 squares correct = 1 star

Across
1. 2^6
2. 3^4
4. $2^4 + 4^2 - 1$
5. $5^2 + 6^2$
6. $2^2 + 2^3 + 2^4$
7. $5^4 + 10^2 + 2^2$
8. $5^2 + 2^2$
10. $2^3 + 3^3$
11. $4^3 + 3^2$
12. 4^2
14. $3^5 + 2^6$
15. $2^9 + 5^2$
17. $(3^3 + 5^2)^2$
19. 4^4

Down
1. $8^2 - 2^2 + 1^2$
2. $2^9 + 3^5 + 4^3$
3. $(2^3 + 3^2)^2$
4. $3^2 + 5^2$
5. 5^4
6. $(2^4 - 1^3)^2$
9. $3^4 - 2^3$
10. $2^2 \times 3^2$
11. $5^2 + 5^3 + 5^4$
12. $3^4 + 4^3 + 3^3$
13. $5^4 + 4^4 + 3^5 + 5^2$
14. $5^3 \times 3^1$
16. 2^5
18. $3^4 - 3^2$

• *Your teacher has the answers to these*

Section 4: Triangle Numbers

In this section you will:
- investigate triangle numbers;
- do some puzzles using triangle numbers;
- look at some other number patterns.

DEVELOPMENT *In pairs or individual work*

D1: Investigating triangle numbers

1.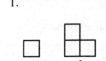

   These shapes give the first three triangle numbers.

   Make these three triangle shapes.
   Make the next three triangle shapes.
   EACH SHAPE MUST BE A DIFFERENT COLOUR.
   Show all 6 triangles to your teacher.

2. *Copy and complete:*

The first six triangle numbers are 1, 3, 6, ... , ..., ...

3. Let us call the first triangle number T_1 and the second triangle number T_2

   Copy and complete:
   $T_1 = 1$
   $T_2 = 3$
   $T_3 = 6$
   $T_4 = ...$
   $T_5 = ...$
   $T_6 = ...$

4. How many blocks do you add to the second Δ to make the third Δ?
5. How many blocks do you add to the third Δ to make the fourth Δ?
6. *Copy and complete:*
   $T_2 + 3 = T_3$
   $T_3 + ... = T_4$
   $T_4 + ... = T_5$
   $T_5 + ... = T_6$
   $T_6 + ... = T_7$

7. What number do you add to T_4 to get T_5?
8. What number do you add to T_5 to get T_6?
9. What number do you add to T_6 to get to T_7?
10. What is the value of T_7?

    • *Check your answers.*

Star Challenge 8
All correct = 1 star

1. Explain how you would work out T_8 from T_7.
2. *Copy and complete*

T_4	T_5	T_6	T_7	T_8	T_9	T_{10}	T_{11}	T_{12}
10	15	21						
5	6							

   • *Your teacher has the answers to these.*

A BIG EDD GUIDE   *Number Patterns*

EXTENSION
E1: Connecting square and triangle numbers

the Δs you made in D1

1. Take the Δs you made for T_2 & T_3.
They must be two different colours.
Put the Δs together to make a square.

This dot diagram shows that
$T_2 + T_3 = 9$
Copy this dot diagram.

2. (a) Which two Δs make the number 4.
(b) Draw a dot diagram like this to represent the square number 4. Split it into two triangles.
(c) Which two triangle numbers add up to 4 ?

• *Check your answers.*

Star Challenge 9
All correct = 1 star

1. (a) Draw a diagram to show that 16 can be split into two triangle numbers.
(b) $T_m + T_n = 16$. Find m and n.
2. What square number do T_5 and T_6 make ?
3. What square number do T_6 and T_7 make ?
4. What square number do T_{20} and T_{21} make ?

• *Your teacher has the answers to these.*

Star Challenge 10
12 correct = 2 stars
10-11 correct = 1 star

| Triangle numbers | 1 | 3 | 6 | 10 | 15 | 21 | 28 | 36 | 45 | 55 | 66 | 78 .. |

Copy these sums into your book.
Replace the Δs with triangle numbers to make each sum correct.

1. $9 = \Delta + \Delta$
2. $25 = \Delta + \Delta$
3. $18 = \Delta + \Delta$
4. $24 = \Delta + \Delta$
5. $100 = \Delta + \Delta$
6. $51 = \Delta + \Delta$
7. $27 = \Delta + \Delta$
8. $84 = \Delta + \Delta$
9. $87 = \Delta + \Delta$
10. $19 = \Delta + \Delta + \Delta$
11. $10 = \Delta + \Delta + \Delta$
12. $31 = \Delta + \Delta + \Delta$

• *Your teacher has the answers to these.*

Star Challenge 11
All correct = 1 star

1.
(a) Draw the next two V–patterns.
(b) What are the first 10 V–numbers ?

2.
(a) Draw the first five hollow-square patterns.
(b) What are the first 7 hollow-square numbers?

3.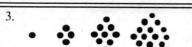
(a) Draw the first 6 diamond patterns.
(b) What are the first 7 diamond numbers ?

4.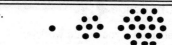
Find the first six hexagonal numbers.

• *Your teacher has the answers to these.*

A BIG EDD GUIDE — *Number Patterns*

Section 5: Divisibility

In this section you will:
- understand what is meant by "divisible by";
- find and work with divisibility rules.

DEVELOPMENT

D1: Which answers are whole numbers ?

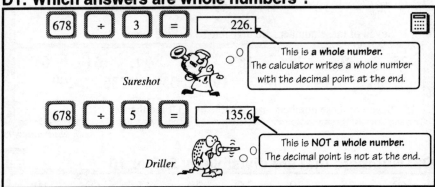

Which of these give answers which are whole numbers ?

A: $88 \div 4$ B: $90 \div 4$ C: $36 \div 3$ D: $46 \div 3$ E: $45 \div 7$

F: $582 \div 5$ G: $469 \div 7$ H: $143 \div 13$ I: $257 \div 16$ J: $222 \div 37$

• Check answers.

D2: What does "divisible by" mean ?

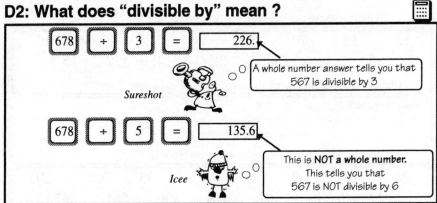

1. Is 789 divisible by 6 ?
2. Is 435 divisible by 5 ?
3. Is 435 divisible by 7 ?
4. Is 38 divisible by 3 ?
5. Is 24 divisible by 8 ?
6. Is 27 divisible by 3 ?
7. Is 18 divisible by 9 ?
8. Is 40 divisible by 6 ?
9. Is 26 divisible by 2 ?
10. Is 14 divisible by 5 ?
11. Is 44 divisible by 13 ?
12. Is 80 divisible by 16 ?

| 13 | 35 | 72 | 55 | 63 | 46 | 49 | 81 |
| 64 | 56 | 93 | 21 | 26 | 84 | 41 | |

13. Six of these numbers are divisible by 7. Find them.

| 40 | 65 | 29 | 16 | 30 | 24 | 14 | 92 |
| 95 | 12 | 47 | 49 | 108 | 52 | 26 | |

14. Seven of these numbers are divisible by 4. Find them.

| 25 | 39 | 26 | 183 | 320 | 90 | 51 | 65 |
| 117 | 79 | 142 | 195 | 351 | 336 | 299 | |

15. Seven of these numbers are divisible by 13. Find them.

• Check your answers.

D3: Numbers that are divisible by 2, 5 or 10

| 60 | 75 | 30 | 36 | 70 | 45 | 69 | 100 |
| 95 | 40 | 300 | 125 | 240 | 450 | 35 | |

1. Eight of these numbers are divisible by 10. Find them.

Possible rules
A number that is divisible by 10 ends in 0 or 5   A number that is divisible by 10 ends in 0
A number that is divisible by 10 ends in 0, 2, 4, 6 or 8

2. Which of these possible rules is the correct one ?

| 52 | 55 | 70 | 19 | 80 | 23 | 69 | 20 |
| 85 | 44 | 900 | 225 | 314 | 128 | 15 | |

3. Eight of these numbers are divisible by 5. Find them.

Possible rules
A number that is divisible by 5 ends in 0 or 5   A number that is divisible by 5 ends in 0
A number that is divisible by 5 ends in 0, 2, 4, 6 or 8

4. Which of these possible rules is the correct one ?

| 24 | 15 | 40 | 16 | 71 | 35 | 68 | 201 |
| 17 | 28 | 567 | 678 | 120 | 561 | 2472 | |

5. Eight of these numbers are divisible by 2. Find them.

Possible rules
A number that is divisible by 2 ends in 0 or 5   A number that is divisible by 2 ends in 0
A number that is divisible by 2 ends in 0, 2, 4, 6 or 8

6. Which of these possible rules is the correct one ?   • Check your answers.

D4: Using divisibility rules

> **Divisibility rules** A number that is divisible by 10 ends in 0
> A number that is divisible by 5 ends in 0 or 5
> A number that is divisible by 2 ends in 0, 2, 4, 6 or 8

Task 1:
Write down all the numbers here that are divisible by 10.

Task 2:
Write down all the numbers here that are divisible by 5.

Task 3:
Write down all the numbers here that are divisible by 2.

```
24      47      29      85
    70      38      73
95      22      452     711
    215     666     999
4545    8432    631     123
    252     170     290
205     275     746     649
    570     891     639
3390    1437    2389    542
```

• *Check your answers.*

Star Challenge 12

16380 is divisible by ... ?

All correct = 1 star

Numbers to try   2   3   4   5   6   7
                 8   9   10 11 12 13

| 16380 is divisible by | 16380 is <u>not</u> divisible by |

Try each number and put it into the correct set.

• *Your teacher has the answers to these.*

Star Challenge 13

Copy and complete this table: 17-18 correct = 1 star

number	is divisible by 2	is divisible by 10	is divisible by 5
65	No	No	Yes
90	…	…	…
36	…	…	…
57	…	…	…
435	…	…	…
390	…	…	…
7544	…	…	…

• *Your teacher has the answers to these.*

A BIG EDD GUIDE   *Number Patterns*

Section 6: Multiples

In this section you will:
- recognise the connection between 'divisible by' and 'multiple of';
- do some problems involving multiples.

DEVELOPMENT

D1: "Divisible by" and "multiples of"

> A number is a multiple of 3 if it is divisible by 3
> 3, 6, 9, 12, ...   are divisible by 3
> 3, 6, 9, 12, ...   are **multiples of 3**

1. Write down all the multiples of 10 between 14 and 52.
2. Write down all the multiples of 3 between 10 and 20.
3. Write down all the multiples of 5 between 17 and 57
4. Write down all the multiples of 7 between 20 and 30.

> 45   37   30
> 89   75   24   60

5. Four of these numbers are multiples of 3 <u>and</u> multiples of 5. Find them.

• *Check your answers.*

D2: Multiples of 3 and 9

> A number is a multiple of 3 if its final digit sum is 3, 6 or 9

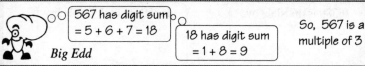

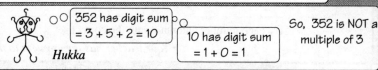

For each number, say whether it is a multiple of 3 (YES) or not (NO).

1. 87   2. 453   3. 68   4. 378   5. 459
6. 1733   7. 8647   8. 774   9. 3447   10. 5472

> A number is a multiple of 9 if its final digit sum is 9

For each number, say whether it is a multiple of 9 (YES) or not (NO).

11. 63   12. 457   13. 927   14. 1431   15. 7236

• *Check your answers.*

Star Challenge 14

All correct = 1 star

Multiples of 5 end in 5 or 0
The final digit sum of a multiple of 9 is always 9

Shade all the multiples of 9 with one colour.

Use another colour and shade all the multiples of 5

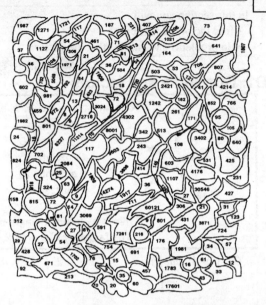

• Show it to your teacher.

All correct = 1 star

Star Challenge 15

All correct = 1 star

	June 1992					
Sun	Mon	Tues	Wed	Thur	Fri	Sat
1	2	3	4	5	6	
7	8	9	10	11	12	13
14	15	16	17	18	19	20
21	22	23	24	25	26	27
28	29	30				

1. The first part of the worksheet contains 8 copies of this calendar.
   On the first copy, shade in all the multiples of 2.
   On the second copy shade in all the multiples of 3.
   In the same way, use the other copies of the calendar to shade in multiples of 4,5,6,7,8,9

2. The second part of the worksheet is made up of eight different calendars.
   Choose any one of these calendars and shade in the multiples of 2.
   Is the pattern you get similar to the first pattern for multiples of 2 ?

3. Investigate the patterns made by the other multiples.
   For which multiples do you always get a similar pattern ?
   • Explain what you have found to your teacher.

A BIG EDD GUIDE   Number Patterns

Section 7: Factors

In this section you will :
- find factors of numbers;
- do problems and puzzles that use factors.

DEVELOPMENT

D1: Guzzintas and factors

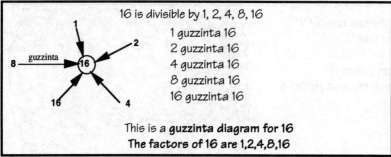

16 is divisible by 1, 2, 4, 8, 16

1 guzzinta 16
2 guzzinta 16
4 guzzinta 16
8 guzzinta 16
16 guzzinta 16

This is a **guzzinta diagram for 16**
The factors of 16 are 1,2,4,8,16

1. *Copy and complete:*

   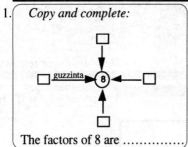

   The factors of 8 are ....

2. *Copy and complete:*

   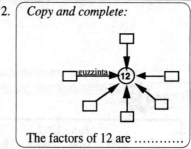

   The factors of 12 are ....

3. | 1 is a factor of every number | Is this a true statement ?

4. | Any number is a factor of itself. | Is this a true statement ?

5. 6 has four factors. Find all the factors of 6.

6. 15 has four factors. Find all the factors of 15.

7. 25 has three factors. Find all the factors of 25.

8. *Copy and complete:*

   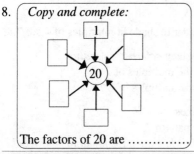

   The factors of 20 are ....

9. *Copy and complete:*

   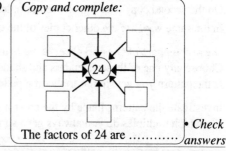

   The factors of 24 are ....

• *Check answers*

D2: Factor pairs

1. *Copy and complete:*

    $6 \div 2 = ...$ 6 is divisible by 2   ... is a factor of 6

    $6 \div 3 = ...$ 6 is divisible by ...   ... is a factor of 6

2. *Copy and complete:*

    $6 \div 1 = ...$ 6 is divisible by ...   ... is a factor of 6

    $6 \div 6 = ...$ 6 is divisible by ...   ... is a factor of 6

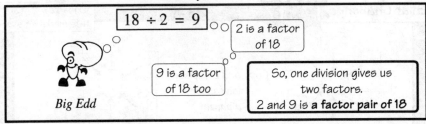

3. Find two factor pairs of 10.
4. Find three factor pairs of 18.
5. Find three factor pairs of 20.   • *Check your answers.*

D3: A systematic way of getting <u>all</u> the factors of a number

$18 \div 2 = 9$ & $18 \div 9 = 2$

because   **18 = 2 x 9**

EXAMPLE: Use factor pairs to find all the factors of 28

Calculator working	What you write down
$28 \div 1 = 28$	$28 = 1 \times 28$
$28 \div 2 = 14$	$28 = 2 \times 14$
$28 \div 3$ not possible	
$28 \div 4 = 7$	$28 = 4 \times 7$
$28 \div 5$ not possible	
$28 \div 6$ not possible	So, factors of 28 are 1, 28, 2, 14, 4, 7
$28 \div 7 = 4$	
(already have 4x7)	

Use factor pairs to find all the factors of each number.
Set your working out as in the example.

1. 15   2. 24   3. 30   4. 25

5. 36   6. 40   7. 49   8. 48

• *Check your answers.*

$9 = 1 \times 9$
$9 = 3 \times 3$
Factors of 9 are 1, 9, 3
We only write
the 3 down once.

Do–med

A BIG EDD GUIDE   *Number Patterns*

Star Challenge 16

8 correct = 2 stars
6-7 correct = 1 star

Find <u>all</u> the factors of each number :

1. 9
2. 10
3. 16
4. 27
5. 60
6. 90
7. 51
8. 84

• *Your teacher has the answers to these.*

Star Challenge 17

16 marks = 2 stars
11-15 marks = 1 star

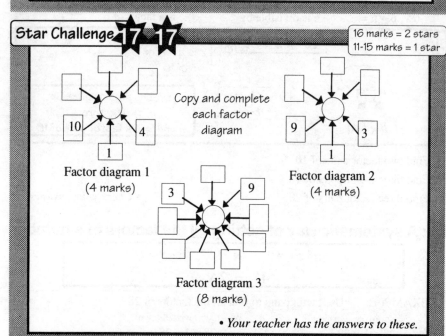

Copy and complete each factor diagram

Factor diagram 1
(4 marks)

Factor diagram 2
(4 marks)

Factor diagram 3
(8 marks)

• *Your teacher has the answers to these.*

Star Challenge 18

1 star for each correct number and its 12 factors

$60 = 1 \times 60$ $60 = 4 \times 15$
$60 = 2 \times 30$ $60 = 5 \times 12$
$60 = 3 \times 20$ $60 = 6 \times 10$

60 has 12 factors

Find three more numbers, less than 100, that have EXACTLY 12 factors.
Show all working.

• *Your teacher will need to mark these.*

Section 8: Prime numbers

In this section you will :
- meet prime numbers;
- do some puzzles that use prime numbers.

DEVELOPMENT

D1: The factor table

1. *Copy and complete this table of factors for all the numbers from 1 to 20.*

Number	Factors	Number of factors
1	1	1
2	1,2	2
3	1,3	2
4	1, 2, 4	3
5		
6		
7		
8		
9		
10		
11		
12		
13		
14		
15		
16		
17		
18		
19		
20		

2. **A prime number** has exactly two factors.

   List the prime numbers between 1 and 20.

   • *Check your answers.*

Star Challenge 19

9-10 marks = 1 star

3. List the prime numbers between 20 and 40. (4 marks)

4. Copy and complete this table:

Square numbers	Factors	Number of factors
1	1	1
4		
...		
...		
25		

(5 marks)

5. What is special about the number of factors each square number has ? (1 mark)

• *Your teacher has the answers to these.*

Star Challenge 20 20 20

See targets for star rating

An emirp is a prime number which, when reversed, is also prime.
31 and 13 is one set of emirps.

How many more can you find?
You cannot use single digit prime numbers.

• *Your teacher has the answers to these.*

emirp is prime backwards

TARGETS:
3	good	(1 star)
5	very good	(2 stars)
more than 5	superb!	(3 stars)

 Hukka

Star Challenge 21 21 21

21 2-digit primes = 3 stars
19-20 2-digit primes = 2 stars
16-18 2-digit primes = 1 star

1. A 2–digit prime number cannot end in 2. Why?
2. What other digits can it *not* end in?
3. There are twenty one 2–digit prime numbers.

Complete this table of 2–digit primes.

11	13	17	19
	23		
		37	
	53		
			89

• *Your teacher has the answers to these.*

Star Challenge 22 22

8-9 correct = 2 stars
6-7 correct = 1 star

13 is a 2–digit prime number
13 can be written as the sum of two square numbers   13 = 4 + 9

There are ten 2–digit prime numbers that
can be written as the sum of two square numbers.

Find the other nine 2–digit prime numbers.
Show all working.

• *Your teacher has the answers to these.*

A BIG EDD GUIDE   *Number Patterns*

High Level Challenge Section
EXTENSIONS
YOUR TEACHER HAS THE ANSWERS TO THESE.

Ch 1: Square headscratchers
SECTION 1 3 correct = 2 stars / 2 correct = 1 star

1. What is the largest number less than 100 that can be expressed as the sum of two squares?
2. I am a 3–digit palindromic number.
   I am even and square.
   When divided by 2, I am not palindromic.
   What number am I?
3. A number, n, is cubed and the answer is squared. The final number is **46656**. Find n.

Ch 2: Investigating last digits
SECTION 2 10 marks = 2 stars / 8-9 marks = 1 star

1. Write down the first twenty-two square numbers.
   Write down the last digits of these square numbers.
   Describe the pattern formed by the last digits of square numbers. (2 marks)
2. What is the pattern formed by the last digits of cube numbers? (2 marks)
3. Are there any digits that never appear as the last digit of a square number? (3 marks)
4. Are there any digits that never appear as the last digit of a cube number? (1 mark)
5. Two of these are square numbers. One is not.

   46225   203402   135424

   Which one is not square and how can you tell just by looking at it? (2 marks)

Ch 3: Pythagorean triples
SECTION 3

Three numbers form a **Pythagorean Triple** if the sum of the squares of two numbers equals the square of the third number.

$$3^2 + 4^2 = 25 = 5^2$$

Therefore **3, 4, 5** form a Pythagorean Triple.

Find the number that each of these letters stands for:

1. $6^2 + 8^2 = a^2$
2. $5^2 + 12^2 = b^2$
3. $c^2 + 24^2 = 25^2$
4. $d^2 + 15^2 = 17^2$
5. $e^2 + 21^2 = 29^2$
6. $f^2 + 40^2 = 41^2$
7. $g^2 + 24^2 = 26^2$
8. $h^2 + 12^2 = 15^2$

All correct = 1 star

These are all Pythagorean Triples. What is the value of each letter?

9. **3, 4, p**   10. **5, 12, q**   11. **6, r, 10**   12. **8, s, 17**

All correct = 1 star

Triple challenge! These are all Pythagorean Triples. What is the value of each letter?

13. **36, 77, x**   14. **48, y, 73**   15. **15, 112, z**

All correct = 1 star

A BIG EDD GUIDE   *Number Patterns*

Ch 4: Happy and sad numbers

SECTION 3

> A **happy number** is a positive whole number for which the sum of the squares of the digits eventually ends in 1.

1. 32 is happy because

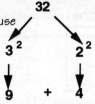

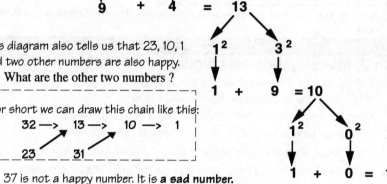

This diagram also tells us that 23, 10, 1 and two other numbers are also happy.
What are the other two numbers ?

For short we can draw this chain like this:

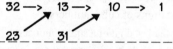

2. 37 is not a happy number. It is **a sad number.**
   Use the same method to find why 37 is sad.

3. In the chain formed for 37, you should have met the number 58.
   58 is also sad. How do you know ?
   What other sad numbers can you find from this chain ?

4. How do you know from this last chain that 85 is also sad ?

5. You are going to find all the happy numbers less than 100.
   Make a list of all the numbers from 1 to 100 and, every time you make a chain cross off all the sad numbers and circle all the happy numbers in this list.
   Make a display of all the chains of happy numbers.

If you get all the happy numbers in their correct chains, you earn 3 stars.

Ch 5: Digit sums

SECTION 6 All correct = 1 star

1. Which of the numbers **57, 93, 218, 369, 205, 924, 7773** is a multiple of 3 ?
2. Which of the numbers **47, 63, 198, 279, 405, 714, 8884** is a multiple of 9 ?
3. Which of the numbers **27, 36, 237, 372, 809, 673, 376** is a multiple of 6 ?
4. Explain how you can tell whether a number is a multiple of 6 without dividing it by 6.

A BIG EDD GUIDE   *Number Patterns*

Ch 6: Spiral multiples of 4

SECTION 6

Shade one small square in the middle of a sheet of squared paper.
Write the numbers 1,2,3,4,5.........
in a spiral which starts :

As you draw the spiral, shade in the multiples of 4.
Explain the pattern that they make.

Possible extensions :
What different patterns do you get if you vary the shape and/or size of the "shaded island" that you put in the centre of your spiral ?

> 1 star for each correct pattern and explanation – up to a maximum of 3 stars.

Ch 7: Triangular match patterns

SECTION 4

1. These triangles are made with matches :

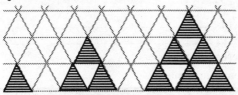

△ number 1   △ number 2   △ number 3

Continuing the same pattern, draw △ number 4, △ number 5 and △ number 6.

(3 marks)

2. Copy and complete this table :

	△ no 1	△ no 2	△ no 3	△ no 4	△ no 5	△ no 6
number of small shaded triangles	1	3				
number of small unshaded triangles	0	1				
total number of small triangles	1	4				
number of matches needed to make shape	3					

(4 marks for all correct but –1 mark for each error)

3. Explain the pattern in each row of numbers. (4 marks)

4. What connection is there between row 1 and row 2 (1 mark)

> 12 marks = 2 stars   11 marks = 1 star

Ch 8: Abundant, perfect and deficient numbers

SECTION 7

36 marks = 2 stars
30–35 marks = 1 star

> The **factors** of 8 are 1,2,4,8
> The **proper factors** of 8 are 1,2,4
> The **sum of the proper factors** of 8 is 7
>
> The sum of the proper factors of 8 is less than 8.
> So, 8 is said to be a **deficient number**.
>
> If the sum of the proper factors is more than the number, the number is an **abundant number**.
>
> If the sum of the proper factors equals the number itself, the number is a **perfect number**.

1. Show that 12 is an abundant number. (2 marks)
2. Show that 15 is a deficient number. (2 marks)
3. Why is 3 a deficient number ? (2 marks)
4. Investigate numbers up to 20 and show whether they are abundant, deficient or perfect. Put your answers in a table like this:

Abundant numbers	
Perfect numbers	
Deficient numbers	

(20 marks)

5. Find the two smallest perfect numbers. (4 marks)
6. Find the first six abundant numbers. (6 marks)

Ch 9: Multiple Headscratcher

SECTION 7

3 correct = 2 stars
2 correct = 1 star

1. N is an unknown number that you have to find from these clues :

   > 72 and 90 are both multiples of N.
   > N has six factors.
   > N has exactly three multiples between 80 and 130.

   What is the value of N ?

   > 185, 518, 851 all have a factor 37

2. Find three other digits that can be arranged in three different ways to make numbers all with a factor of 37. Give the 3 digits and the 3 numbers.
3. Repeat Q2 with another set of 3 digits.

Ch 10: Prime calculator search

SECTION 8

3 correct = 2 stars
2 correct = 1 star

1. Two prime numbers multiplied together make **4891**. What are the numbers ?
2. **6887** is also the product of two prime numbers. What are the numbers ?
3. The product of THREE prime numbers is **21199**. What are the numbers ?

A BIG EDD GUIDE   *Number Patterns*

THE NATIONAL CURRICULUM ...
... AND BEYOND ...

Big Edd

Nets, Cubes and Volumes

> By the end of this topic you should be able to:
> Level 4
> - find volumes by counting cubes
> - construct shapes from given information
>
> Level 6
> - recognise nets of a cube
> - work out dimensions from a net
> - interpret and make isometric drawings
> - calculate volumes of cuboids

A BIG EDD GUIDE TO THE NATIONAL CURRICULUM

Nets, Cubes and Volumes
Section 1: Cubes and nets of cubes

In this section you will:
- learn the meaning of the words faces, edges, vertices and nets;
- look at some of the properties of a cube;
- meet some polyominoes;
- investigate some nets of cubes.

DEVELOPMENT

D1: Examining cubes   *Small groups – one set of answers per group*

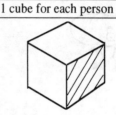

1 cube for each person

1. A **FACE** is a surface.
   How many faces does a cube have ?

2. What shape is each face?

3. Look at the cube from several angles.
   What is the largest number of faces that you can see when holding the cube still ?

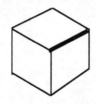

4. An **EDGE** is where two faces meet.
   How many edges does a cube have ?

5. Are all the edges the same length ?

6. Look at the cube from several angles.
   What is the largest number of edges that you can see when holding the cube still ?

7. The corner of a solid shape is called a **VERTEX**.
   The name for more than one vertex is **VERTICES** .
   How many vertices does a cube have ?

8. How many edges meet at a vertex ?   say ver-ti-sees

9. How many faces meet at a vertex ?

10.   A **NET** is flat plan of a shape.

    If a net of a cube is cut out, it will fold up to make a cube.

    A net of a cube is made from ▓ squares.

    What number is under the blot ?

• *Check your answers.*

A BIG EDD GUIDE   page 250   *Nets, Cubes and Volumes*

A choice of approach

For the rest of this section, follow one of three alternative approaches, either D2A or D2B on the next two pages, or D2C which is in the Teachers' Guide for this booklet.

> A **polyomino** is a shape made up of one, or more, squares with edges fitting side by side.
>
> is a **monomino**   is a **domino**
>
> A **tromino** is made from 3 squares.
>
> A **tetromino** is made from 4 squares.
>
> A **pentomino** is made from 5 squares.
>
> There is more than one possible tromino, tetromino and pentomino.

D2A: From hexominoes to nets   *Small groups*

> A **hexomino** is made from 6 squares fitting side by side.
>
> There are 35 different possible hexominoes.

1. Draw 12 different hexominoes.

2. Choose some hexominoes that you think will make nets for cubes.
   Draw them on 2 cm squared paper. Cut them out.
   Can you fold them into cubes?

3. Continue until the group has found 4 different nets for a cube.
   Draw the nets in your books.

• *Check your answers.*

D2B:** A systematic investigation to find *all* the nets of a cube

Individual work

1. A **tromino** is made from 3 squares.
   Draw two different trominoes.
   Can you find a third different tromino?

2. A **tetromino** is made from 4 squares.
   Draw five different tetrominoes.

3. ▭▭▭▭ is the **straight tetromino**.
   Draw it on two centimetre squared paper.
   Cut it out. Fold it to make part of a cube.
   How many faces are missing from the cube?

4. Colour the edges around one missing face red.
   Colour the edges around the other missing face blue.
   If you add one square to a red edge and one square to a blue edge, you will have a **NET OF A CUBE**.

   is one net made by this method.
   How many *different* nets can you make in this way?
   Draw them.

5. is the **skew tetronimo**.
   Draw it on centimetre squared paper. Cut it out.
   Fold it so that it makes part of a cube.
   How many faces are missing from the cube?

6. Colour the edges around one missing face red.
   Colour the edges around the other missing face blue.
   If you add one square to a red edge and one square to a blue edge, you will have a net of a cube.
   How many different nets can you make? Draw them.
   Are any of them the same as any you found in question 2?

7. There is another cube net that can be made from the skew tetromino, but not by using the rules in question 4. Can you find it?

8. Investigate the other three tetrominoes.
   Can any of these form part of the net of a cube?

9. There are 11 possible nets for a cube.
   If you have not found them all, go back and try to find the missing ones.
   If you have too many, check and see which ones have been repeated.

   • *Check your answers.*

Section 2: Nets of many shapes – *All individual work*

In this section you will:
- look at some of the properties of a cuboid;
- make some nets of cuboids;
- make nets for some other solid shapes.

DEVELOPMENT

D1: Examining cuboids

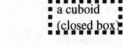

1. How many faces does the cuboid have?
2. Are all the faces the same?
3. What shapes are the faces?

4. How many edges does a cuboid have?
5. Are they all the same length?

6. How many vertices does a cuboid have?
7. How many edges meet at a vertex?
8. How many faces meet at a vertex?

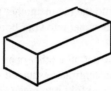

• *Check your answers.*

D2: Nets of cuboids (closed boxes)

Task 1: Look at these four shapes.
Which ones do you think will fold up to make a cuboid?

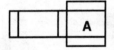 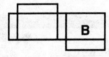 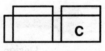

Task 2: Cut out each of the shapes from the worksheet. Fold them up.
Write down which ones make a cuboid.
Were you right in your guesses in question 1?

• *Check your answers.*

PRACTICE

P1: Making boxes

1.

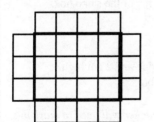

Draw this net on centimetre squared paper.

Cut it out.

Check that it folds up to make an open box.

A BIG EDD GUIDE   page 253   *Nets, Cubes and Volumes*

2. Draw this piece on centimetre squared paper.
   Cut it out.
   Check that it will fit as a lid for the box.

   Stick it on your net like this.
   Check that this new net will
   make a closed box.

3. Cut the lid off.
   Stick it onto the net in another place, so that you will get a closed box.
   Stick the new net into your book.

4. Here is the net of another open box.
   Draw it on centimetre squared paper.
   Cut it out and fold it to make an open box.
   To make a closed box you need to add this piece.

   Draw it. Cut it out. It can be stuck in four different places to make nets
   of closed boxes. Draw the four possible nets.

   • *Check your answers.*

Star Challenge 1

All correct = 1 star

Design your own nets

1. This is the net of a closed box.
   Imagine that it is cut out and folded
   up to make the box.
   What will the length of the box be?
   What will the width of the box be?
   What will the height of the box be?

   5cm

   8cm

2. On centimetre squared paper, draw a *different* net of the same box.
   Cut it out. make sure it makes the same box.
   Stick the net in your book.

3. Draw the net of a box that is 5 cm long, 2cm wide and 2 cm high.
   Cut it out. Make sure it makes the correct size box.
   Stick the net in your book.

   • *Your teacher will need to mark this.*

A BIG EDD GUIDE   *page 254*   *Nets, Cubes and Volumes*

Star Challenge 2 2 2 2

Puzzles 1,2 correct = 1 star
Puzzles 1,2,3 correct = 2 stars
Puzzles 1,2,3,4 correct = 3 stars
Puzzles 1,2,3,4,5 correct = 2 stars

Exasperating dice
5 puzzles and 5 levels of exasperation !

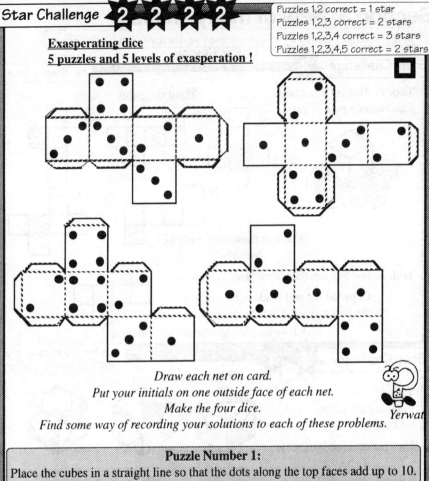

Draw each net on card.
Put your initials on one outside face of each net.
Make the four dice.
Find some way of recording your solutions to each of these problems.

Yerwat

Puzzle Number 1:
Place the cubes in a straight line so that the dots along the top faces add up to 10.

Puzzle Number 2:
Place the cubes in a straight line so that the dots along two sides add up to 10.

Puzzle Number 3:
Place the cubes in a straight line so that the dots along three sides add up to 10.

Puzzle Number 4:
Place the cubes in a straight line so that the dots along four sides add up to 10.

Puzzle Number 5 – The ultimate challenge !
Place the cubes in a straight line so that the four faces show 1,2,3,4
(in any order) along all four sides.

• *Show your solutions to your teacher.*

Section 3: Nets of many shapes

In this section you will try to solve some puzzles involving nets of boxes.

Star Challenge 3

EXTENSION

All correct = 1 star

Task 1: This cube has been standing in a pool of paint.

Mind the paint

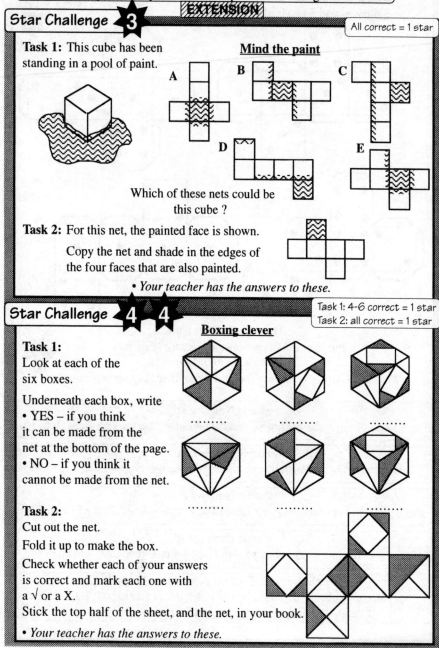

Which of these nets could be this cube?

Task 2: For this net, the painted face is shown.

Copy the net and shade in the edges of the four faces that are also painted.

• *Your teacher has the answers to these.*

Star Challenge 4

Task 1: 4-6 correct = 1 star
Task 2: all correct = 1 star

Boxing clever

Task 1:
Look at each of the six boxes.

Underneath each box, write
• YES – if you think it can be made from the net at the bottom of the page.
• NO – if you think it cannot be made from the net.

Task 2:
Cut out the net.

Fold it up to make the box.

Check whether each of your answers is correct and mark each one with a √ or a X.

Stick the top half of the sheet, and the net, in your book.

• *Your teacher has the answers to these.*

A BIG EDD GUIDE   page 256   Nets, Cubes and Volumes

Star Challenge 5 5

Shifting perspective

36 faces correct = 3 stars
30-35 correct = 2 stars
25-29 correct = 1 star

Task 1: Draw this net onto card. Make the cube.

Task 2: The pictures below are all ways of looking at this cube.

Fill in the missing letters.

Make sure that the letters are the right way up.

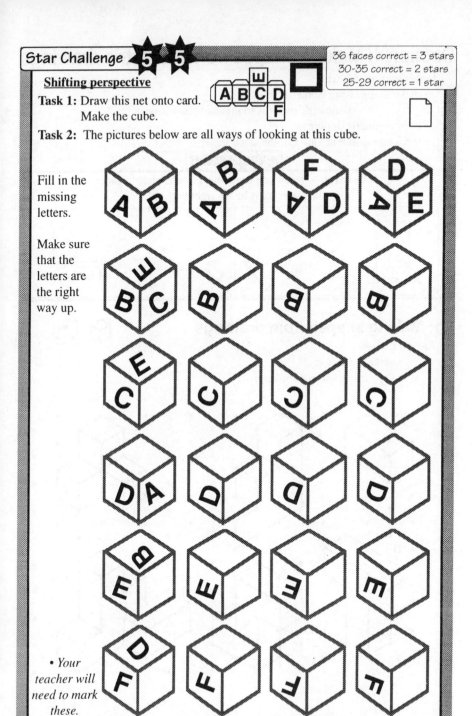

- *Your teacher will need to mark these.*

A BIG EDD GUIDE — *Nets, Cubes and Volumes*

Section 4: Making shapes from isometric drawings

In this section you will:
All individual work
- make shapes from isometric drawings
  (isometric paper is triangular spotty paper);
- copy isometric drawings;
- recognise different views of the same shapes.

DEVELOPMENT

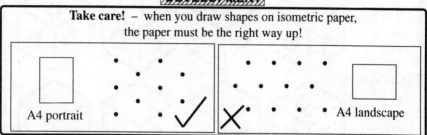

Take care! – when you draw shapes on isometric paper, the paper must be the right way up!

A4 portrait ✓   ✗ A4 landscape

D1: Making shapes from drawings

For each shape :
- *make the shape;*
- *copy the isometric drawing.*

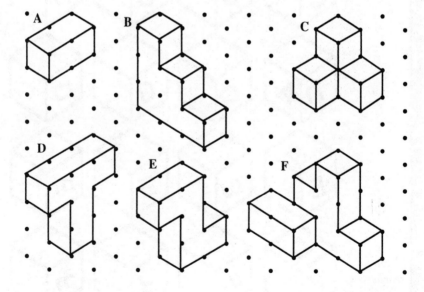

A BIG EDD GUIDE   page 258   Nets, Cubes and Volumes

P1: Different views

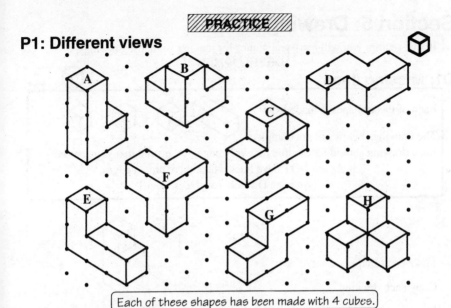

Each of these shapes has been made with 4 cubes.

Task 1: Guess which drawings are different views of the same shapes.

Task 2: Make each shape.
Use your shapes to check whether your answers were right.

Star Challenge 6

All correct = 1 star

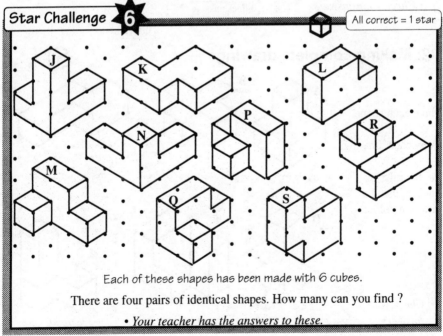

Each of these shapes has been made with 6 cubes.

There are four pairs of identical shapes. How many can you find?

• *Your teacher has the answers to these.*

A BIG EDD GUIDE   page 259   *Nets, Cubes and Volumes*

Section 5: Drawing shapes

In this section you will learn techniques for making isometric drawings.

DEVELOPMENT

D1: Missing lines

Each of these shapes is made from

The drawings below are not complete.
Each drawing should have a line for every edge of the solid that you can see.
It should NOT have lines where there are no edges.
[An edge is where two faces meet.]

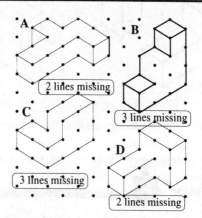

Make each shape.

Copy each drawing.

Put the missing lines in, using a different colour.

- *Check your answers.*

D2: Making complete drawings

Make each shape.

Copy each drawing.

Put the missing lines in, using a different colour.

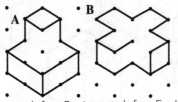

made from 5 cubes   made from 5 cubes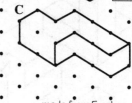

made from 5 cubes

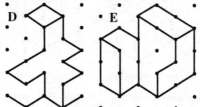

- *Check your answers.*

made from 6 cubes   made from 8 cubes   made from 6 cubes

A BIG EDD GUIDE   *Nets, Cubes and Volumes*

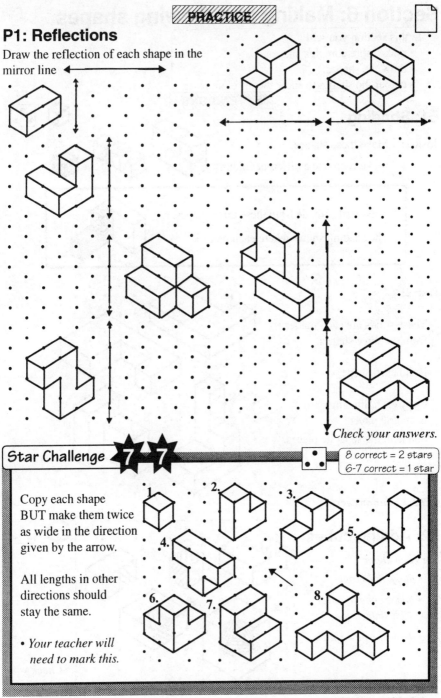

Section 6: Making and drawing shapes

In this section you will:
- make more complex shapes;
- draw the shapes;
- colour the shapes to show the different parts.

EXTENSIONS

E1: Shading

Task 1: Make these shapes.

Make each one a different colour.

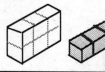

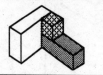

This solid is made from these three shapes.

The shading shows where each piece is.

Task 2:

These solids are each made from the three shapes.

Build each shape.

Copy each drawing onto isometric paper.
Shade in the separate pieces.

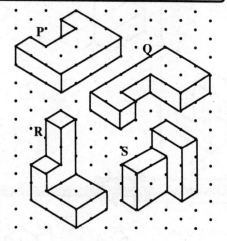

- *Check your answers.*

E2: Adding cubes

For each shape:
- *make the shape;*
- *add a cube to cover each shaded face;*
- *draw the new shape.*

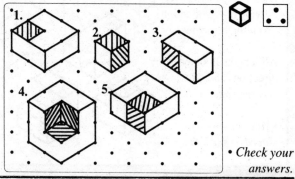

- *Check your answers.*

A BIG EDD GUIDE — Nets, Cubes and Volumes

Star Challenge 8

All correct = 1 star

Cube addition

For each shape:
- make the shape;
- add a cube to cover each shaded face;
- draw the new shape.

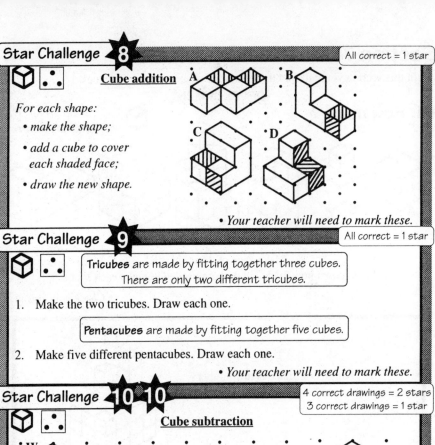

• *Your teacher will need to mark these.*

Star Challenge 9

All correct = 1 star

Tricubes are made by fitting together three cubes.
There are only two different tricubes.

1. Make the two tricubes. Draw each one.

   Pentacubes are made by fitting together five cubes.

2. Make five different pentacubes. Draw each one.

• *Your teacher will need to mark these.*

Star Challenge 10

4 correct drawings = 2 stars
3 correct drawings = 1 star

Cube subtraction

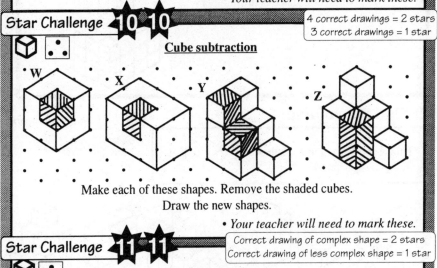

Make each of these shapes. Remove the shaded cubes.
Draw the new shapes.

• *Your teacher will need to mark these.*

Star Challenge 11

Correct drawing of complex shape = 2 stars
Correct drawing of less complex shape = 1 star

Creative shapes

Take 8 cubes. You must have at least three different colours.
Make a complicated shape. Draw it.
Shade it to show the colours you made it in.

• *Your teacher will need to mark this.*

A BIG EDD GUIDE — *Nets, Cubes and Volumes*

Section 7: Introducing volume

In this section you will find the volume of shapes made with cubes.

DEVELOPMENT

D1: How many ?

Small groups OR individual work

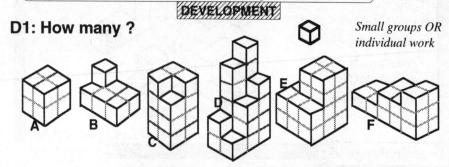

Make each of these shapes.
Write down how many cubes were needed to make each shape.

• *Check your answers.*

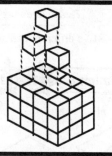

The **volume** of a shape is the number of cubes needed to make the shape.

D2: Find the volume

Individual work

This shape has volume 4 cubes.

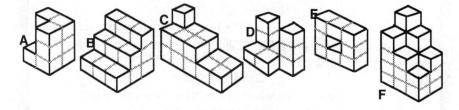

Find the volume of each of these shapes.

• *Check your answers.*

P1: Half cube problems

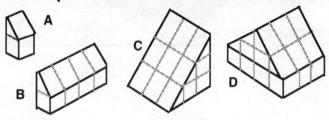

What is the volume of each of these shapes?

• *Check your answers.*

P2: Volumes of more complex shapes

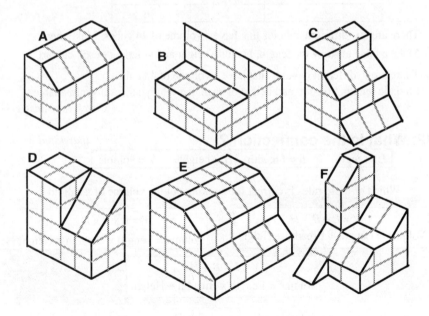

What is the volume of each of these shapes?

• *Check your answers.*

Section 8 : Volumes of cuboids

In this section you will investigate volumes of cuboids.

DEVELOPMENT

D1: Investigating cuboids

 Small groups OR individual work

A **cuboid** is a rectangular box.

Both these cuboids can be made from 12 cubes.

They each have a volume of 12 cubes.

1. There are four different cuboids that have a volume of 16 cubes. Make them.

2. This table contains the length, breadth and height of each cuboid.
   Copy and complete the table.

Length (L)	Breadth (B)	Height (H)	Volume (V)
16	1		16
8		1	16
	4	1	16
4	2		16

3. There are six different cuboids that have a volume of 24 cubes. Make them.

4. Make a table to show the length, breadth, height and volume of each cuboid.

5. There are 9 different cuboids that have a volume of 48 cubes.
   Find the length, breadth and height of each one. Put your results into a table.

   • *Check your answers.*

D2: What is the connection ?   *Individual work*

   L = length   B = breadth   H = height   V = volume

1. Which of these rules is correct for working out the volume of a cuboid ?

   | $V = L + B + H$ |
   | Volume = Length + Breadth + Height |

   | $V = L \times B \times H$ |
   | Volume = Length x Breadth x Height |

   | $V = L \times B + H$ |
   | Volume = Length x Breadth + Height |

2. Work out the volume of this cube: Length 5 Breadth 3 Height 2

   • *Check your answers.*

A BIG EDD GUIDE   Nets, Cubes and Volumes

D3: Finding volumes of cuboids

$$V = L \times B \times H$$
Volume = Length x Breadth x Height

Find the volume of each of these boxes in cubes:

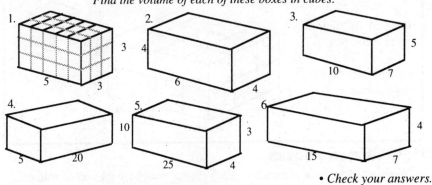

• *Check your answers.*

PRACTICE

P1: Too much information

Find the volume of each of these boxes.

Too much data has been given. Choose the data that you need.

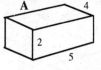 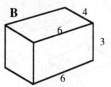 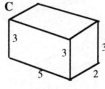

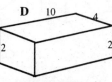 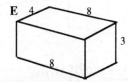 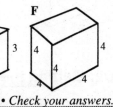

• *Check your answers.*

Star Challenge 12

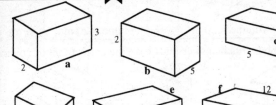

The volume of each of these cuboids is 60 cubes.

Find the value of each of the letters

• *Your teacher has the answers to these.*

A BIG EDD GUIDE   *Nets, Cubes and Volumes*

Section 9: Units of volume

In this section you will meet and use the common units of volume.

DEVELOPMENT

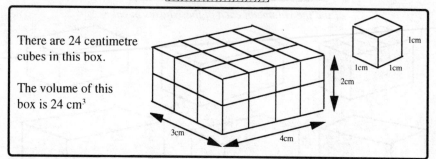

There are 24 centimetre cubes in this box.

The volume of this box is 24 cm³

D1: Centimetre boxes

Work out the volume of each box. Each answer must have the unit of volume.

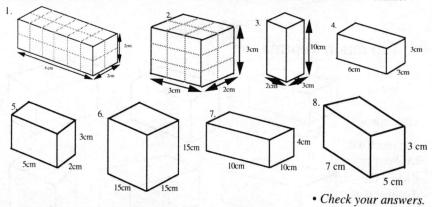

• *Check your answers.*

D2: Getting the right units

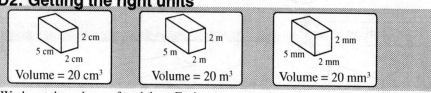

Work out the volume of each box. Each answer must have the correct unit of volume.

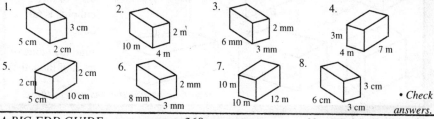

• *Check answers.*

A BIG EDD GUIDE — *Nets, Cubes and Volumes*

Section 10 : Cube challenges

In this section you will:
- try some very challenging cube problems;
- get very exasperated.

E1: The Soma cube

1. Make as many different shapes as possible using 3 cubes.
   Make each shape in just one colour.
   Make each shape in a different colour.

2. Make as many different shapes as possible using 4 cubes.
   Make each shape in just one colour.
   Make each shape in a different colour.
   [You should now have 10 shapes altogether.]

3. Take out the three cuboids (boxes). Put them on one side – they are not needed.
   Make sure that the seven pieces that you have made are *each* a different colour.

   > Get your teacher to check that your seven pieces are correct.
   > If they are not, you will never make the cube!

4. Make a cube from these seven pieces.
   This is the **SOMA CUBE**.

Big Edd

E2: The Diabolic cube

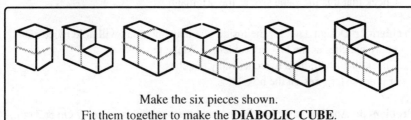

Make the six pieces shown.
Fit them together to make the **DIABOLIC CUBE**.

E3: The Steinhaus cube

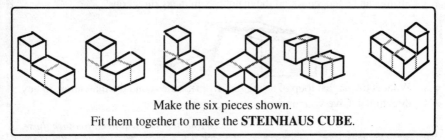

Make the six pieces shown.
Fit them together to make the **STEINHAUS CUBE**.

High Level Challenge Section
EXTENSIONS
YOUR TEACHER HAS THE ANSWERS TO THESE.

Ch 1: Nets for other solids `SECTION 2`   9-10 marks = 2 stars / 7-8 marks = 1 star

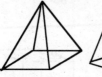
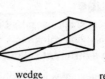

pyramid   prism   wedge   regular tetrahedron

1. Draw two different nets for the pyramid, the prism and the wedge. (6 marks)
2. A regular tetrahedron has four faces which are all equilateral triangles. Draw three different nets for it. (4 marks)

• *Your teacher will need to mark these.*

Ch 2: Matchbox problems `SECTION 2` 1 star for a correct answer to each problem : possible total 4 stars

Problem 1: Find a matchbox. Measure it.
Make two nets:
• one for the inside of the matchbox;
• one for the 'sleeve' of the matchbox.
Make a matchbox from your nets.
Check that it is the same size as the original box.

Problem 2: Design a net for the inside of a matchbox that will hold twice as many matches as the box in problem 1. Make the box.
Check that it will hold twice as many matches.
If it doesn't, re-design the box.

Problem 3: Another matchbox has outside measurements 12 cm, 7 cm & 3 cm. What is the total area of cardboard used in making the matchbox?

Problem 4: Here we are using the matchbox from problem 3.
String can be looped round the matchbox in many directions.

string

What is the largest loop of string that will fit once round the matchbox, in any direction? Give your answer to the nearest centimetre.

• *Your teacher will need to mark these.*

Ch 3: Colouring cubes

SECTION 3 — All correct = 1 star

How many different ways can you colour a cube so that it has ...
1. ... one red, one green and four blue faces.
2. ... one red, two green and four blue faces.
3. ... two red, two green and two blue faces.

Ch 4: Complimentary pieces

SECTION 4 — All correct = 1 star

Amongst these shapes are 3 pairs that fit together to make cubes.
Name the pairs.

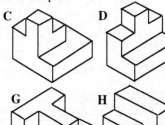
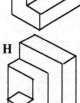

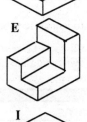
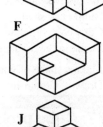

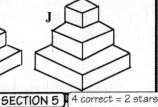

Ch 5: Outlines

SECTION 5 — 4 correct = 2 stars; 3 correct = 1 star

1. Make these two shapes. Make each a different colour.

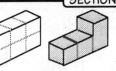

2. Each of these drawings is an outline of a solid made from the two shapes you have just made.

   Copy the outlines onto isometric paper.

   Draw in the missing lines and shade in the L-shaped piece.

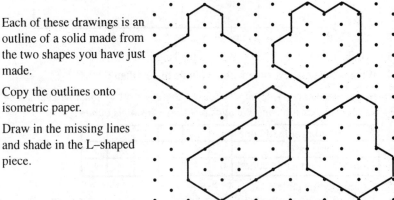

A BIG EDD GUIDE   page 271   *Nets, Cubes and Volumes*

Ch 6: Which is L and which is S ?

3 correct diagrams = 2 stars
2 correct diagrams = 1 star

SECTION 6

1. Make these two shapes.
   Make each a different colour.

This solid is made from these two shapes.
The shading shows where the S-shape is.

2. These solids are each made from
   the L-shape and the S-shape.
   Build each shape.
   Copy each drawing onto isometric paper.
   Shade in the S-shape.

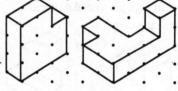

3. Make a shape of your own, using the L-shape and the S-shape.
   Draw it. Colour in the two pieces.

Ch 7: Cube problems

SECTION 8

6 correct = 2 stars
4-5 correct = 1 star

A **cube** is a box with square faces

1. Copy and complete this table:

Length (L)	Breadth (B)	Height (H)	Volume (V)
1	1	1	1
2			
3			
:			
:			
9			
10			

2. What is the volume of a cube of side 20 ?
3. A cube has volume 42875. What is the length of each side ?
4. What is the smallest cube with a volume bigger than 80 000 ?

When you make cubes from smaller cubes there are often some smaller cubes inside that you cannot see. We shall call these **'invisible cubes'**.

Number along side of cube	1	2	3	4	5	6
Volume of cube	1	8				
Number of 'invisible cubes'	0	0				

5. Complete this table.
6. Predict how many 'invisible cubes' there are in a cube of side 10.

Ch 8: Think carefully ...

SECTION 9 — 5 correct = 2 stars / 4 correct = 1 star

This box has been made from small cubes.

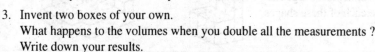

1. How many small cubes are there in the box?
2. An identical box is made from cubes whose edges are twice as long.
   How many of these cubes do you need to make the box?
3. Invent two boxes of your own.
   What happens to the volumes when you double all the measurements?
   Write down your results.
4. Investigate what happens to the volumes when you treble all the measurements. Write down your results and your conclusions.
5. If you multiply the length breadth and height of a cuboid by the same number, what happens to the volume?

Ch 9: Mixing units

SECTION 9 — 10-11 correct = 2 stars / 8-9 correct = 1 star

" The volume of this box is 6 cm^3."

" The volume of this box is 6000 mm^3."

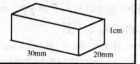

1. Both of these statements are correct. Explain how you get each answer.

Find the volume of each box. Make sure you put in the units of volume.

2. 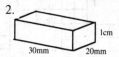 3.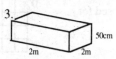

4. Cuboid with length 2 cm, breadth 5 mm, height 4 mm.
5. Cuboid with length 4m, breadth 2m, height 25 cm.
6. Cuboid with length 2 m, breadth 70cm, height 5mm.
7. The volume of a cuboid is 10 m^3. Its length is 5m. Its breadth is 4 m.
   What is its height?
8. The volume of a cuboid is 45 cm^3. Its length and height are both 15 cm.
   What is its breadth?
9. How many 1 mm^3 cubes are there in a 1 cm^3 cube?
10. How many 1 cm^3 cubes are there in a 1 m^3 cube?
11. How many 1 m^3 cubes are there in a 1 km^3 cube?

A BIG EDD GUIDE — *Nets, Cubes and Volumes*

Ch 10: Exploding Soma cubes

SECTION 10 — Clear diagram = 2 stars
SECTION 10

Draw a diagram to show how you made your Soma cube.

Ch 11: Making Soma shapes

SECTION 10 — 1 star for each shape

Fit the Soma pieces together to make each of these shapes.

Ch 12: Pentomino puzzles

Puzzle No. 1–5 = 1 star each
Puzzle No. 6 = 2 stars

Puzzle No. 1
Pentominoes are polyominoes made from five squares.
There are 12 different pentominoes.

Find them all. Draw them on 2 cm squared paper and use them to do the following puzzles. [Put your initials on the back and keep them in an envelope.]

Puzzle No. 2
These shapes have all been made by fitting together two identical pentominoes. Draw them.

Colour them to show which pentomino has been used for each shape.

Puzzle No. 3
Fit together …
   … three different pentominoes to make a 5 x 3 rectangle
   … four different pentominoes to make a 4 x 5 rectangle
   … six different pentominoes to make a 5 x 6 rectangle

Puzzle No. 4
Show me how you can fit these two pentominoes and three others into the 10 cm square

Puzzle No. 5
Show me how you can fit nine of the pentominoes into this cross. However – you cannot use the cross-shaped pentomino.

Puzzle No. 6
Show me how to fit all 12 pentominoes into a 12 x 20 rectangle.

A BIG EDD GUIDE page 274 *Nets, Cubes and Volumes*

Sum Number Fun Answers

Section 1 : Using a calculator   p5

D1: The calculator with the broken 3 key
For each Task :
- use a normal calculator to check that your method gives the correct answer
- check that your method doesn't use the 3 key

P1: Calculator crossnumber

P2: Solving problems
1. 453   2. £139   3. 305   4. 64   5. 43

Section 2 : Sum, difference, product   p8

D1: Arithmogons

1. 3, 2, 4
2. 5, 7, 1
3. 6, 2, 8
4. 8, 5, 9
5. 3, 7, 2
6. 4, 3, 9
7. 6, 4, 10
8. 15, 11, 20
9. 2, 3, 6
10. 3, 5, 11
11. 9, 4, 2
12. 12, 7, 8

Section 3 : Odd, even & consecutive numbers   p10

D1: Types of number
1. All of them   2. 49 57 17 4321   3. Odd numbers end in 1, 3, 5, 7 or 9
4. 18 54 2456732 3456 34   5. Even numbers end in 0, 2, 4, 6 or 8

Section 4 : Non-calculator techniques   p12

D1: Adding
1. 61   2. 399   3. 271   4. 511   5. 697   6. 815   7. 1002   8. 202
9. 49   10. 101   11. 67   12. 171   13. 312   14. 284   15. 236   16. 1065

D2: Multiplication using a table square
1. 21   2. 40   3. 63   4. 28   5. 56   6. 72   7. 42   8. 64
9. 35   10. 54

D3: Setting out multiplication sums
1. 45   2. 72   3. 94   4. 165   5. 384   6. 1064   7. 155   8. 441
9. 544   10. 1716   11. 3704   12. 924   13. 2350   14. 5432

D4: Setting out subtraction sums
1. 61   2. 39   3. 233   4. 18   5. 23   6. 18   7. 107   8. 194
9. 307   10. 133   11. 288   12. 348

A BIG EDD GUIDE   *Sum Number Fun*   ANSWERS

Section 5 : Techniques for division   p16

D1: Sharing with counters
1. 3   2. 2   3. 4   4. 2   5. 2   6. 3   7. 5   8. 3   9. 4
10. 2   11. 6   12. 4   13. 3   14. 7   15. 3   16. 5   17. 9   18. 7

D2: Division using the table square
1. 8   2. 3   3. 3   4. 3   5. 7   6. 8   7. 4   8. 6
9. 8   10. 8   11. 6   12. 5   13. 8   14. 9   15. 7

D3: Setting out division sums
1. 5   2. 6   3. 8   4. 4   5. 6   6. 9   7. 8   8. 8   9. 9   10. 4

Section 6 : Non-calculator techniques   p18

P1: Fill in the gaps

3	+	9	=	12		18	-	15	=	3		3	+	9	=	12		8	+	6	=	14		7	+	4	=	11		10	+	10	=	20
+		+		+		-		÷		x		x		x				-		x				-		+		+		x		or		+
12	+	1	=	13		3	÷	3	=	1		5	+	1	=	6		2	+	3	=	5		8	+	9	=	17		4	+	1	=	5
=		=		=		=		=		=		=		=		=		=		=		=		=		=		=		=		=		=		=
15	+	10	=	25		15	÷	5	=	3		15	-	9	=	6		16	+	3	=	19		15	+	13	=	28		40	+	10	=	4

P2: Little problems
1. 18   2. 8   3. 6   4. £20   5. 30

Section 7 : Some mental tricks   p26

D1: Finger counting
1. 21   2. 33   3. 52   4. 73   5. 41   6. 24   7. 44   8. 64
9. 131   10. 105   11. 73   12. 117   13. 84   14. 1323   15. 657

D2: Mental short cuts
1. 55   2. 96   3. 47   4. 33   5. 75   6. 77   7. 96   8. 73
9. 84   10. 92   11. 144   12. 136   13. 177
14. (a) + 100 then − 10   (b) + 500 then − 10
15. 147   16. 568   17. 1035   18. 45   19. 65   20. 126   21. 135   22. 66   23. 146

D3: Adding in pairs
A 20   B 30   C 30   D 22   E 25   F 31   G 60   H 80
I 65   J 82   K 67   L 91   M 340   N 430   P 395

Section 9 : Maths is more than just numbers   p28

D1: Getting the words right
1. 13   2. 10   3. less than 1000   4. your age + 2   5. 10   6. 10
7. 24   8. 15   9. 18   10. 40   11. 19   12. 433   13. 34   14. 72

D2: Getting some order
1. T   2. T   3. F   4. T   5. F
6. 2 < 3   7. 3 < 13   8. 34 > 27   9. 12 < 21
10. one hundred and one = 101   11. one thousand and one > 101

Introducing Area Answers

Section 1: Tiling and area   p 41

D1: Tiling

Tile	A	B	C	D	E	F	G
Number	6	4	12	9	16	4	6

D2: Tiling with 1cm squares
1. 4   2. 5   3. 5   4. 14   5. 11   6. 12

D3: Simple areas
1. 2   2. 4   3. 4   4. 5   5. 5   6. 6
7. $1\frac{1}{2}$ 8. 3   9. $2\frac{1}{2}$ 10. 2   11. $10\frac{1}{2}$

P1: Areas in cm²
1. 4 cm^2 2. 12 cm^2 3. 6 cm^2 4. 7 cm^2 5. 7 cm^2 6. $7\frac{1}{2} \text{ cm}^2$

Section 2 : Approximate areas   p45

D1: Squares and part squares
1. 10 cm^2 2. $2\frac{1}{2} \text{ cm}^2$ 3. 7 cm^2

D3: Awkward areas
P: will accept answers from 10 to 11 cm²
Q: answers from 8 to 9 cm²   R: answers from $4\frac{1}{2}$ to 5 cm²

Section 3 : Estimating areas   p46

D1: Estimating areas

Shape	A	B	C	D	E
Measured area	3	8	4	9	10

Section 4 : Areas of rectangles   p47

D1: Investigating rectangles

Task 4:

length	12	6	4	24	12	8	6
width	1	2	3	1	2	3	4

← Any 3 out of these 4

Task 5:   area of rectangle = length x width

D2: Areas by Rule

Area of A = 15 squares   Area of B = 32 squares   Area of C = 16 squares
Area of D = 20 squares   Area of E = 49 squares   Area of F = 40 squares
Area of G = 18 squares   Area of H = 50 squares   Area of I = 25 squares

D3: Measure and work out the area
1. Area = 8 cm^2 2. Area = 6 cm^2 3. Area = 12 cm^2 4. Area = 16cm^2
5. Area = 9 cm^2 6. Area = 21 cm^2 7. Area = 24 cm^2 8. Area = 30 cm^2

D4: Units of area
1. 15 cm^2 2. 24 cm^2 3. 150 cm^2 4. 12 mm^2 5. 30 mm^2 6. 20 m^2
7. 22 m^2 8. 24 km^2 9. 24 km^2

Section 5: Areas of compound shapes   p50
D1: Laying the foundations
1. Area 10 cm²   2. Area = 4 cm² ; Area = 4 cm²; Total area = 8 cm²

D2: Developing skills
1. 5 cm²   2. 14 cm²   3. 14 cm²

D3: Areas without measuring
1. 26 cm²   2. 32 cm²   3. 180cm²   4. 54 cm²

E1: Find the lengths
   a = 4, b = 4, c = 2, d = 5, e = 6, f = 14   Areas are 112cm², 99cm²,   38cm²

Section 6: Areas of right-angled triangles   p52
D1: Squares and half squares
1. ½ cm²   2.

| Area | 4 | 5 | 4½ | 3½ | 2 | 6 |

D2: Rectangles and half rectangles
   ΔF – D   ΔC – L   ΔE – G   ΔH – A   ΔI – B   ΔJ – K

D3: Areas of right-angled triangles
1. 6 cm²   2. 8 cm²   3. 8 cm²   4. 10 cm²   5. 5 cm²
6. 30 cm²   7. 18 cm²   8. 6 cm²

Section 7: Areas of parallelograms   p54
D1: Areas of parallelograms

1.
A	1	1	1
B	2	2	4
C	1	2	2
D	2	2	4
E	3	2	6
F	3	3	9
G	1	3	3

2.   Area = base x height

D2: Oops – wrong again !
   1. Dwork added the base and the height instead of multiplying them
   2. Mishrak measured the side – not the height

P1: Areas of parallelograms
   A 9 cm²   B 6 cm²   C 1 cm²   D 2 cm²
   E 6 cm²   F 12 cm²   G 3 cm²   H 6 cm²

Section 8: Areas of triangles   p56
D1: Parallelograms and half parallelograms
   ΔD – A   ΔB – F   ΔE – H   ΔG – C

D2: Rule for area of a triangle
1. 5 cm²   2. 12 cm²   3. 25 cm²   4. 9 cm²

P1: Areas of triangles

Triangle	A	B	C	D	E	F	G	H	I	J	K
Length	4	6	4	2	2	5	2	2	2	2	4
Height	2	2	2	2	3	2	2	3	1	1	2
Area	4	6	4	2	3	5	2	3	1	1	4

Task 2: 1. 6 cm^2 2. 9 mm^2 3. 10 m^2 4. $10\frac{1}{2} \text{ m}^2$

P2: No measurements given

	A	B	C	D	E	F	G	H	I	
base	3	3	7	4	6	4	3	5	7	all in cm
height	2	2	4	6	2	5	4	5	5	all in cm
area	3	3	14	12	6	10	6	$12\frac{1}{2}$	$17\frac{1}{2}$	all in cm^2

Section 9: Perimeters   p59

D1: Distance round the edge
1. 16 cm   2. 12 cm   3. 12 cm   4. 12 cm   5. 18 cm   6. 17 cm

D2: Finding perimeters
A 10 cm   B 12 cm   C 12 cm   D 14 cm
E 14 cm   F 12 cm   G 14 cm

P1: Different perimeters
Task 1: 4 units   **Task 2:** 6 units
Task 3: 2 shapes both with perimeter 8 units
Task 4: 4 different shapes – one with 8 units and three with 10 units
(2 different perimeters)

P2: Rectangle perimeters
1. 18 cm   2. 18 cm   3. 22 cm   4. 30 cm   5. 60 m   6. 40 mm

Journeys, Maps and Coordinates Answers

Section 1: Giving directions   p 76
D2: Youngsville, Tennessee
1. Grey's Avenue   2. St. Andrews Road   3. Dead End or Cul–de–sac

P1: Save Indiana Jones
2 TR 1   TL 2   TL 2   TR 2   TL 2   TL 3
TL 1   TR 2   TR 3   TR 6   TL 2

Section 3: Relative position   p 79
D2: North, South, East or West?
1. Cardiff   2. Glasgow   3. Brighton   4. Leeds   5. SW   6. W
7. SW   8. NW

P1: Around the counties
1. Flint   2. Derbyshire
3. Flint, Derbyshire, Shropshire, Staffordshire, Merseyside, Greater Manchester
4. N. Yorkshire   5. Tyne and Wear, Northumberland
6. Northumberland, N. Yorkshire, Cumbria, Tyne and Wear, Cleveland
7. Essex   8. Kent   9. Lincolnshire   10. Cheshire
11. Dorset   12. Greater Manchester   13. Wiltshire

D3: The Lake District
1. 10   2. 10   3. 40   4. 40   5. 40 km North
6. 40 km South   7. 5, 5   8. 5, 10, North   9. 15, West, 10, North
10. 10, East, 15, North   11. 20, East, 15 North   12. 10, West, $17^1/_2$, North
13. 20, East, 5, South   14. 15, West, 20, South   15. 15, West, 20, South
16. $7^1/_2$, West, $7^1/_2$, North   17. $7^1/_2$, East, $12^1/_2$, South

E1: Compass shapes
1. SE SE E N E W W SW

Section 4: Coordinates in the first quadrant   p 83
D1: Painting by numbers
1. 2   2. 6   3. G   4. V   5. J   6. (3,5)   7. (5,3)
8. (2,6) (1,2) (3,2) (3,6) | (7,4) (3,5) (2,3)
9. CHIRPY DOZEN   10. Instead of going across and then up, he went up and tried to go across – AND FELL

D2: Coordinates
1. (5,3)   2. (7,4)   3. N   4. E   5. PEAS   6. TUNA
7. STEAK   8. (7,7) (5,3) (2,7) (4,6) (7,4) (4,6) (2,1) (7,4) (7,4) (5,3) (0,2) (1,4) (1,4) (0,2) (2,1) (3,3)   9. (0, 0)

P1: Treasure Map
1. (8,5)   2. (4,4)   3. (2, $2^1/_2$)   4. Ailsa Craig   5. Pirates' Point
6. Longlass Lookout   7. ($1^1/_2$, 4)   8. Seething Swamp

A BIG EDD GUIDE

D3: Axes and coordinates

1. 2
2.

B	C	D	E
3	5	7	6
G	H	I	J
0	4	9	9

3. 3
4.

5. (0,6)
6.

L	M	N	P	Q
$(1\frac{1}{2}, 3)$	$(3\frac{1}{2}, 6)$	$(2\frac{1}{2}, 1)$	$(7\frac{1}{2}, 2\frac{1}{2})$	$(1\frac{1}{2}, 8\frac{1}{2})$

7. G or D 8. L or Q 9. K, M or D 10. A, E or H

Section 5: Plotting points   p 86

D1: Plotting pictures

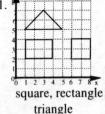

square, rectangle
triangle

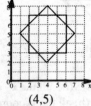

(4,5)
star *or* 2 overlapping squares

parallelogram, square
rhombus (*or* diamond)

P1: More pictures

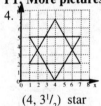

$(4, 3\frac{1}{2})$ star

bat *or* butterfly

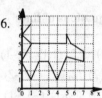

dog $(5\frac{1}{2}, 4\frac{1}{2})$

P2: Yet more pictures

7.   8. 9. 10. 11.

Section 6: Negative numbers and coordinates   p 89

D2: Extending the coordinate grid

A is (1,2)   B is (3,3)   C is (2,1)   D is (3,–2)   E is (1,–3)   F is (3,–4)
G is (–3,2)   H is (–1,3)   I is (–3,–2) J is (–2,–3)   K is –2,1)   L is (–1,–2)
M is (2,0)   N is (0,3)   P is (–1,0)   Q is (0,–4)

A BIG EDD GUIDE   page 281   *Journeys, Maps and Coordinates* ANSWERS

D3: Four quadrant picture sets

1.
2.
3.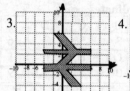
4.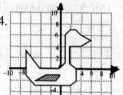

P1: Now you draw the grids

1.
2.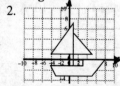

Section 7: Lines   p 92

D1: Related coordinates

1. (a) (2,6) (2,4) (2,3) (2,1) (2,–2) (b) all the x– coordinates are 2 (c) $x = 5$
2. (a) (1,1) (2,1) (4,1) (6,1)   (b) all the y–coordinates are 1
    (c) $y = 1$ (d) $y = 4$ (e) $y = -1$

D2: Equations of lines

1. $y = -2$

2. (1,4) (1,2) (1,1) (1,–1) (1, –3) $x = 1$

3. (3,–2) (2, –2) (–2,–2) (–3,–2) (–4,–2) $y = -2$

4. (–3,4) (–3,1) (–3, –1) (–3,–3) (–3, –4) $x = -3$

P1: Intersection of lines

1. (4, –2)   2. (–2,3)   3. (–2,–2)   4. (–4, 2)   5. (–6, 1)   6. (3,–4)
7. (7,–1)   8. (–2,–4)   9. and 10. lines do not cross because they are parallel

P2: Drawing lines

1.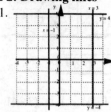
2.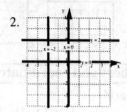

Shape Answers

Section 1: Triangles   p100

P1: Matchstick triangles

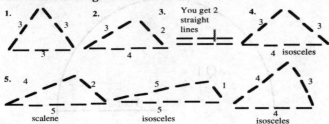

P2: Show me how

1. (square with one diagonal) or (square with other diagonal)
2. 2 lines
3. 4 lines
4. 8 lines

5.

No of Δs	2	4	8	16
No of lines	1	2	4	8

6. 32 lines

Section 2: Rectangles and squares   p103

D1: Truths, untruths and halftruths

A1: always true   A2: sometimes true
B1: always true   B2: sometimes true
C1: always true   C2: sometimes true
D1: always true   D2: always true
E1: always true   E2: sometimes true

D3: How many different rectangles can you find?

Task 1:

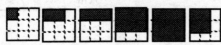

P1: Systematic counting

1.

1	4	9	16
0	1	4	9
0	0	1	4
0	0	0	1
1	5	14	30

Section 4: More polygons   p108

D1: Can you find ...... ?

1. E, J, H   2. A, G, M   3. B, F   4. I   5. K, L
6. F   7. A   8. J   9. C   10. K

D2: Make a regular hexagon

Section 5: Circles
D1: Introducing circles
These answers are drawn the exact size that yours should be.

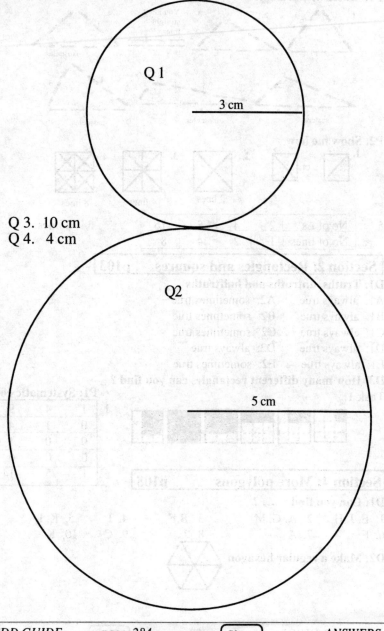

Q 1 — 3 cm

Q 3. 10 cm
Q 4. 4 cm

Q2 — 5 cm

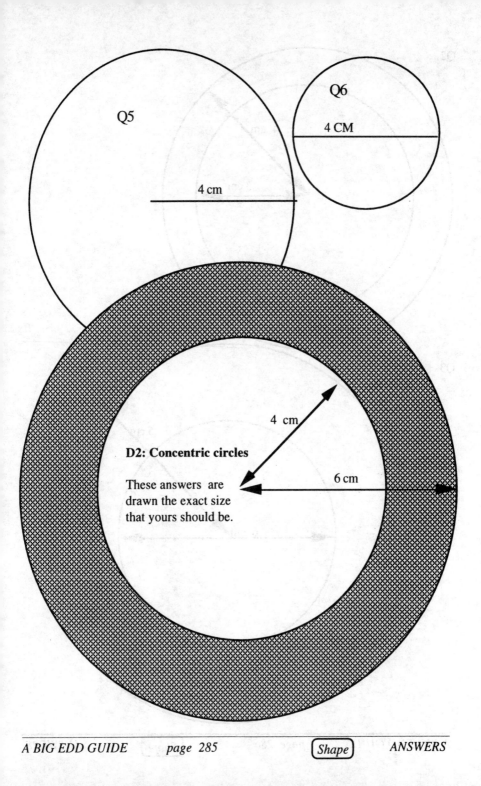

D2: Concentric circles

These answers are drawn the exact size that yours should be.

A BIG EDD GUIDE page 285 (Shape) ANSWERS

Q2.

Q3.

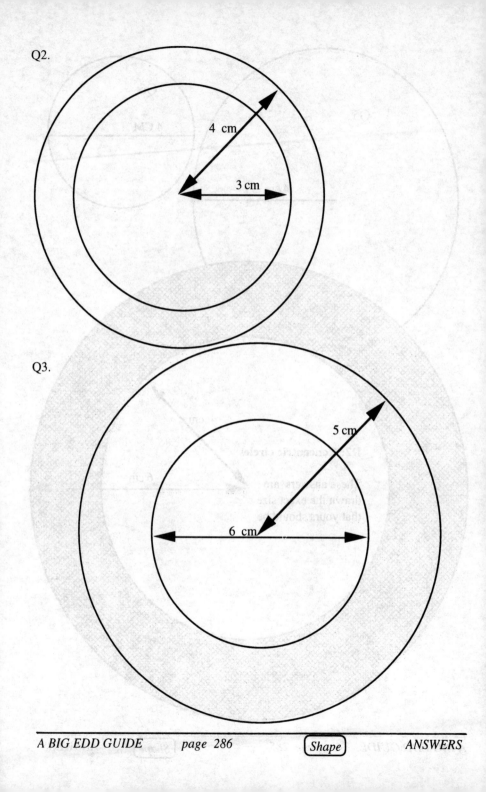

A BIG EDD GUIDE   page 286   Shape   ANSWERS

Fractions and Decimals Answers

Section 1 : Fractions of shapes p122

D1: Equal divisions
1. E   2. All of them   3. U: $\frac{1}{6}$ V: $\frac{2}{3}$ W: $\frac{3}{4}$ X: $\frac{5}{6}$ Y: $\frac{5}{12}$ Z: $\frac{3}{8}$
4. The ∆ has not been divided into 4 EQUAL parts

D3: How many squares do I shade ?
1. (b) $\frac{1}{4}$ 2. (a) 6 squares should have been shaded (b) $\frac{3}{4}$
3. (b) 3 squares   4. (b) 9 squares   5. (b) 6 squares
6. 6 squares shaded   7. 4 squares shaded   8. 5 squares shaded

D4: Shaded fractions

Shape	A	B	C	D	E	F	G	H	I	J	K	L
Sh. Fr	$\frac{1}{2}$	$\frac{1}{2}$ or $\frac{2}{4}$	$\frac{3}{4}$	$\frac{1}{3}$	$\frac{1}{2}$ or $\frac{3}{6}$	$\frac{7}{8}$	$\frac{7}{10}$	$\frac{2}{5}$	$\frac{2}{3}$	$\frac{1}{4}$	$\frac{3}{8}$	$\frac{1}{4}$

D5: Shaded and unshaded fractions

Shape	A	B	C	D	E	F	G
Shaded fraction	$\frac{1}{3}$	$\frac{1}{4}$	$\frac{3}{8}$	$\frac{1}{5}$	$\frac{5}{6}$	$\frac{2}{5}$	$\frac{4}{9}$
Unshaded fraction	$\frac{2}{3}$	$\frac{3}{4}$	$\frac{5}{8}$	$\frac{4}{5}$	$\frac{1}{6}$	$\frac{3}{5}$	$\frac{5}{9}$

P2 : Shady practice

A	B	C	D	E	F	G	H	I	J	K	L	M
$\frac{3}{5}$	$\frac{5}{12}$	$\frac{2}{5}$	$\frac{4}{8}$	$\frac{3}{5}$	$\frac{3}{5}$	$\frac{3}{4}$	$\frac{3}{5}$	$\frac{3}{5}$	$\frac{6}{9}$	$\frac{4}{6}$	$\frac{3}{6}$	$\frac{3}{6}$
$\frac{2}{5}$	$\frac{7}{12}$	$\frac{3}{5}$	$\frac{4}{8}$	$\frac{2}{5}$	$\frac{2}{5}$	$\frac{1}{4}$	$\frac{2}{5}$	$\frac{2}{5}$	$\frac{3}{9}$	$\frac{2}{6}$	$\frac{3}{6}$	$\frac{3}{6}$

N	O	P	Q	R	S	T	U	V	W	X	Y	Z
$\frac{4}{6}$	$\frac{2}{6}$	$\frac{4}{6}$	$\frac{3}{6}$	$\frac{2}{6}$	$\frac{6}{6}$	$\frac{5}{6}$	$\frac{4}{6}$	$\frac{4}{6}$	$\frac{4}{5}$	$\frac{3}{4}$	$\frac{2}{4}$	$\frac{3}{4}$
$\frac{2}{6}$	$\frac{4}{6}$	$\frac{2}{6}$	$\frac{3}{6}$	$\frac{4}{6}$	$\frac{0}{6}$	$\frac{1}{6}$	$\frac{2}{6}$	$\frac{2}{6}$	$\frac{1}{5}$	$\frac{1}{4}$	$\frac{2}{4}$	$\frac{1}{4}$

Section 2 : Equivalent fractions p 129

D1: Thinking in halves
1. $\frac{1}{2} = \frac{5}{10}$ 2. $\frac{1}{2} = \frac{4}{8}$ 3. $\frac{1}{2} = \frac{6}{12}$ 4. $\frac{1}{2} = \frac{8}{16}$

D2: Halves are very common fractions
1. T   2. T   3. F   4. T   5. T   6. F   7. T   8. F

9. $\boxed{\frac{25}{50}}$ $\frac{20}{\boxed{40}}$ $\boxed{\frac{11}{22}}$ $\frac{15}{\boxed{30}}$ $\boxed{\frac{9}{18}}$ $\frac{16}{\boxed{32}}$ $\boxed{\frac{7}{14}}$ $\frac{6}{\boxed{12}}$ $\boxed{\frac{50}{100}}$ $\frac{25}{\boxed{50}}$

P1: Equivalent Fraction Practice Exercises

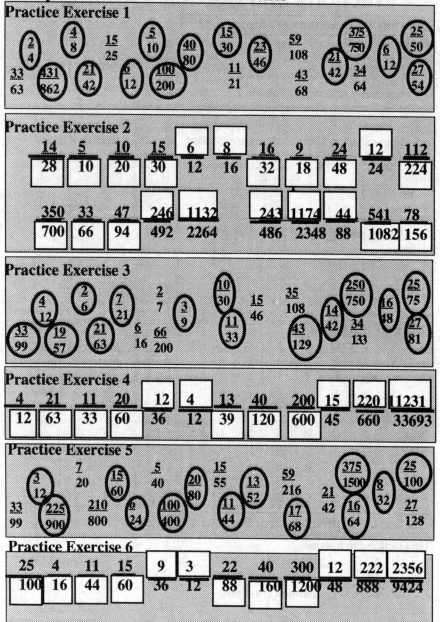

A BIG EDD GUIDE — Fractions and Decimals — ANSWERS

P2: Quarter-masters

$\frac{10}{40}$ $\frac{4}{16}$ $\frac{40}{160}$ $\frac{3}{12}$ $\frac{5}{20}$ $\frac{6}{24}$ $\frac{90}{360}$

Section 3 : Fractions of turns   p 132

E1: Fractions of turns
1. $\frac{1}{2}$ 2. 2   3. $\frac{1}{4}$ 4. 4   5. $\frac{1}{8}$ 6. $\frac{3}{8}$ 7. $\frac{5}{8}$ 8. $\frac{3}{4}$

E2: Equivalent fractions of turns
1. W   2. NE   3. $\frac{1}{4}$ 4. $\frac{1}{8}$
5. Directions: E   S   W   E   S   W   S
6. $\frac{2}{4}$ AND $\frac{4}{8}$ 7. $\frac{1}{4}$

Section 4 : Fractions of amounts   p 133

P1: Fraction practice

Batch A	Batch B	Batch C
1. 4	1. 5	1. 11
2. 3	2. 3	2. 2
3. 2	3. 3	3. 7
4. 6	4. 2	4. 5
5. 4	5. 5	5. 2
6. 5	6. 7	6. 2
7. 4	7. 3	7. 3
8. 10	8. 4	8. 1
9. 1	9. 1	9. 1

D1: Using a calculator …

Batch A	Batch B	Batch C
1. 40	1. 99	1. 118
2. 58	2. 79	2. 47
3. 32	3. 166	3. 19
4. 243	4. 219	4. 14
5. 68	5. 53	5. 25
6. 25	6. 73	6. 28
7. 28	7. 31	7. 19
8. 319	8. 41	8. 80
9. 39	9. 108	9. 143

D2: Fractions in action
1. 30 mins   2. 15 mins   3. 20 mins   4. 6 mins
5. 12 hours   6. 6 hours   7. 8 hours   8. 4 hours
9. 3 inches   10. 4 inches   11. 18 inches   12. 9 inches

D3: Using diagrams to find fractions
1. $\frac{1}{3}$ of 12 = 4   2. $\frac{2}{3}$ of 12 = 8   3. $\frac{1}{4}$ of 8 = 24. $\frac{3}{4}$ of 8 = 6
5. 3   6. 5   7. 10   8. 3   9. 9   10. 2   11. 4   12. 8
13. 2   14. 4   15. 10   16. 3   17. 6   18. 12   19. 6   20. 12

D4: More difficult fractions
1. 3   2. 9   3. 15   4. 21   5. 12   6. 8   7. 16   8. 6   9. 18   10. 20

P2: More difficult fraction practice

Batch A		Batch B		Batch C	
1. 2	6. 10	1. 2	6. 15	1. 5	6. 15
2. 4	7. 15	2. 10	7. 2	2. 15	7. £5
3. 10	8. 20	3. 5	8. 6	3. 25	8. £15
4. 30	9. £8	4. 10	9. 15	4. 35	9. 8 cm
5. 5	10. 12 cm	5. 5	10. 8	5. 3	10. £20

Section 5 : Common fractions and decimals   p 138
D1: Halves, quarters and three-quarters

1. $3.5 = 3\frac{1}{2}$ 2. $5.5 = 5\frac{1}{2}$ 3. $8.5 = 8\frac{1}{2}$ 4. $4.5 = 4\frac{1}{2}$
5. $9.5 = 9\frac{1}{2}$ 6. $10.5 = 10\frac{1}{2}$ 7. $6.5 = 6\frac{1}{2}$ 8. $15.5 = 15\frac{1}{2}$
9. $2.25 = 2\frac{1}{4}$ 10. $4.25 = 4\frac{1}{4}$ 11. $7.25 = 7\frac{1}{4}$ 12. $9.25 = 9\frac{1}{4}$
13. $1.25 = 1\frac{1}{4}$ 14. $6.25 = 6\frac{1}{4}$ 15. $8.25 = 8\frac{1}{4}$ 16. $14.25 = 14\frac{1}{4}$
17. $4.75 = 4\frac{3}{4}$ 18. $2.75 = 2\frac{3}{4}$ 19. $9.75 = 9\frac{3}{4}$ 20. $3.75 = 3\frac{3}{4}$
21. $6.75 = 6\frac{3}{4}$ 22. $5.75 = 5\frac{3}{4}$ 23. $7.75 = 7\frac{3}{4}$ 24. $10.75 = 10\frac{3}{4}$
25. $6.5 = 6\frac{1}{2}$ 26. $1.25 = 1\frac{1}{4}$ 27. $3.5 = 3\frac{1}{2}$ 28. $7.75 = 7\frac{3}{4}$
29. $6.25 = 6\frac{1}{4}$ 30. $2.5 = 2\frac{1}{2}$ 31. $2.75 = 2\frac{3}{4}$ 32. $25.5 = 25\frac{1}{2}$

P1: Mixed practice

Batch A:	1. 10.5	2. 7.25	3. 12.25	4. 13.75	5. 23.5
6. 17.75	7. 45.25	8. $9\frac{3}{4}$	9. $15\frac{1}{2}$	10. $16\frac{1}{4}$	11. $50\frac{1}{2}$
12. $21\frac{3}{4}$	13. $6\frac{1}{4}$	14. $13\frac{1}{2}$			

Batch B:	1. 14.25	2. 11.5	3. 17.75	4. 26.5	5. 12.25
6. 99.5	7. 22.75	8. $3\frac{1}{2}$	9. $14\frac{3}{4}$	10. $36\frac{1}{4}$	11. $21\frac{1}{4}$
12. $18\frac{3}{4}$	13. $4\frac{1}{2}$	14. $3\frac{3}{4}$			

Section 6 : Equivalent decimals and fractions   p 140
D1: Decimals and fractions

$0.3 = \frac{3}{10}$ $0.08 = \frac{8}{100}$ $0.005 = \frac{5}{1000}$ $2.6 = 2\frac{6}{10}$

$0.17 = \frac{17}{100}$ $0.04 = \frac{4}{100}$ $0.6 = \frac{6}{10}$ $0.003 = \frac{3}{1000}$

$0.67 = \frac{67}{100}$ $0.031 = \frac{31}{1000}$ $1.7 = 1\frac{7}{10}$ $2.11 = 2\frac{11}{100}$

$4.031 = 4\frac{31}{1000}$ $0.027 = \frac{27}{1000}$ $18.235 = 18\frac{235}{1000}$

Section 7 : Changing fractions into decimals   p 142
D1: Changing fractions into decimals

1. 0.2   2. 0.7   3. 0.4   4. 0.125   5. 0.15   6. 0.12   7. 0.625   8. 0.375

D2: Decimal tenths

1. 0.1   2. 0.3   3. 0.5   4. 0.9

5. $\frac{4}{10} = 0.4$ 6. $\frac{2}{10} = 0.2$ 7. $\frac{6}{10} = 0.6$ 8. $\frac{7}{10} = 0.7$

D3: Decimal hundredths

1. 0.01   2. 0.03   3. 0.05   4. 0.08

5. $\frac{7}{100} = 0.07$ 6. $\frac{6}{100} = 0.06$ 7. $\frac{2}{100} = 0.02$ 8. $\frac{9}{100} = 0.09$

Section 8: Decimal arithmetic p 144
P1: Decimal arithmogons

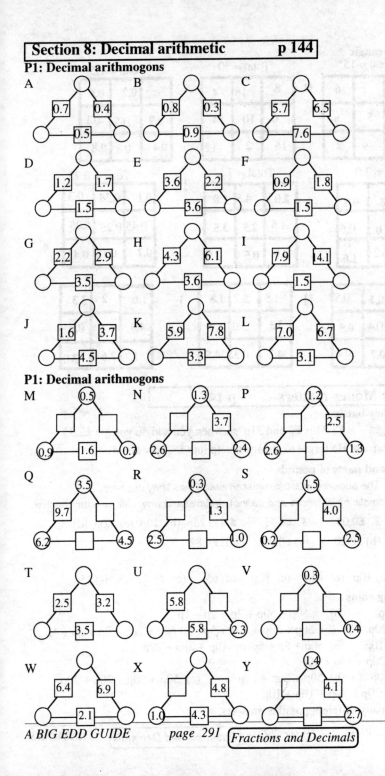

P2: Decimal magic

A — Total = 15

8	1	6
3	5	7
4	9	2

B — Total = 30

8	18	4
6	10	14
16	2	12

C — Total = 1.5

0.2	0.7	0.6
0.9	0.5	0.1
0.4	0.3	0.8

D — Total = 3.0

0.4	1.8	0.8
1.4	1.0	0.6
1.2	0.2	1.6

E — Total = 7.5

2.0	4.5	1.0
1.5	2.5	3.5
4.0	0.5	3.0

F — Total = 0.75

0.1	0.35	0.3
0.45	0.25	0.05
0.2	0.15	0.4

G

0.6	0.1	0.5
0.3	0.4	0.5
0.3	0.7	0.2

H

1.5	5.7	1.8
3.3	3.0	2.7
4.2	0.3	4.5

I

1.6	2	3.3
4.0		0.6
1.3	2.6	3.0

(centre of I: 2.3)

Section 9: Money matters   p 147

D1: The money battle
Sureshot is right   £2.31 is £2 and 31p so when you add 4p you get £2.35
Driller got it wrong. He forgot to change the 4p into £ (4p = £0.04)

D2: Pounds and parts of pounds
The answers must be written exactly as they are here.
If you have something different and cannot understand why, talk to your teacher.

1. £0.60   2. £0.08   3. £0.31   4. (a) 25p (b) 12p (c) 80p (d) 8p
5. (a) £0.75 (b) £0.20   (c) £0.09   (d) £0.82

D3: Change
1. 25p   2.(a) 10p (b) 45p (c) 80p (d) 65p (e) 4p   3. £0.25

E1: Changing coins
1. (a) £1 + 5p   (b)   50p + 50p + 2p + 2p + 1p
2. (a) 50p + 20p + 5p (b) 50p + 10p + 10p + 5p (c) 50p + 20p + 2p + 2p + 1p
3. (a) 50p + 10p   (b) 50p + 5p + 5p or 10p + 20p + 20p
   (c) 20p + 20p + 10p + 10p
4. (a) £1 + 10p   (b) 50p + 50p + 10p   (c) 50p + 20p + 20p + 20p
   (d) 50p + 20p + 20p + 10p + 10p
5. There are many different possible answers.

D4: Bill totals
Task 1: 1. £3.31   2. £9.90
Task 2: Second bill should be easier - because you could just put the figures onto a calculator

D5: Checking your bill
1. £4.65   2. £7.65   3. £5.17   4. £5.20

If you don't get these answers, ask your teacher to check your bills.

D6: Meet the @ symbol
1. 30p   2. £1   3. £1.20   4. £1.20   5. 48p   6. £12
7. £9.80   8. £47.809.   £3.90   10. £15.95
   £3.36   £10.48   £1.25   £13.77
   £5.30   £2.40   £0.48   £3.95
   £0.48   £4.00   £0.70   £1.57
   £18.94   £64.68   £0.25   £35.24
                          £6.58

Section 10: Related fractions   p 151
D1: Some common errors
1. Two halves make one whole. You can't split the kingdom into 3 halves.
2. If the cake is cut into halves, each half is the same size.

D2: Halves, quarters and eighths
The missing fractions are
1. $\frac{1}{4}$ 2. $\frac{3}{8}$ 3. $\frac{1}{2}$ 4. $\frac{3}{4}$ 5. $\frac{1}{4}$ 6. $\frac{1}{8}$ 7. $\frac{1}{8}$ 8. $\frac{3}{8}$ 9. $\frac{1}{2}$ 10. $\frac{3}{4}$

D3: Halves, thirds and sixths
The missing fractions are
1. $\frac{2}{3}$ 2. $\frac{5}{6}$ 3. $\frac{1}{3}$ 4. $\frac{2}{3}$ 5. $\frac{1}{6}$ 6. $\frac{1}{6}$ 7. $\frac{1}{6}$ 8. $\frac{1}{3}$ 9. $\frac{1}{3}$ or $\frac{2}{6}$
10. $\frac{1}{6}$ 11. $\frac{1}{2}$ 12. $\frac{1}{3}$

Handling Data Answers

Section 1 : Pictographs   p162
D1 : Traffic survey
1. 1 hour   2. 8 4 12 6 10 8   3. 48   4. 12

D2 : Teachers
1. 10 9 8 9 9   2. 9   3. 10
4. one subject has two teachers sharing the same class

D3 : Chips with everything
1. Friday 13th   2. 5 people
3. Number of meals 35 30 15 25 30 20   4. 155 meals

Section 2: Bar Charts   p164
P1: Lotta bottle
1. Monday   2. 6 pints   3. 9 pints   4. 14 9 12 13 6   5. £16.20
6. More on Monday to stock up for the week.
   Less on Friday as it would not keep over the weekend

P2: The return of the Pan–Galactic Explorers
1. 2034   2. 7   3. 5   4. 12
5.
8	7	5	2	6	8
4	5	13	16	7	3
12	12	18	18	13	11

6. 2037   7. Most crashes   8. 2035 (18 expeditions) or 2034

P3: Technology classes in Y9
1. 10 girls
2.
12	6	12	12	6
10	8	12	14	10
22	14	24	26	16

3. Food Tech.   4. 48   5. 54

Section 3: Information from tables   p166
P1: Sorting out the timetable
1. 7W   2. Mr. Bennett   3. Monday and Friday
4. Tuesday afternoon   5. 40   6. Form period & Library Skills
7. 5 periods   8. 6 periods   9. 3 periods
10. 12.00   11. 1h 15 min or 75 min   12. 8.55
13. 3.50   14. 6h 55 min or 415min   15. morning break

P2: May Days
1. Wed   2. 4   3. 21st May   4. Monday
5. 17 days   6. 3   7. 9th June   8. £200

P3: Luxury household goods
   1. 2   2. 3   3. Brown   4. 4   5. 4   6. 5   7. 9

A BIG EDD GUIDE   page 294

Section 4: Pie charts p169

D1: Reading simple pie charts
1. 20, 10, 10
2. 5, 5, 5
3. 6, 2, 2
4. 3, 6, 12
5. ½, 150, 50, 100
6. 45, 60, 75

D2: Recognising pie charts
1. B 2. C 3. A 4. E 5. D

D3: Working out simple angles
1. 120°, 120°, 120°
2. 90°, 90°, 90°, 90°
3. 90°, 90°, 180°
4. 45°, 45°, 90°, 180°
5. 90°, 90°, 180°
6. 90°, 90°, 90°, 90°

D4: Working out more difficult angles

1. 36
   360°÷36
   10°
   R: 200°
   B: 100°
   O: 60°

2. 18
   360°÷18
   20°
   P: 200°
   Y: 160°

3. 18
   360°÷18
   20°
   P: 300°
   G: 60°

4. 10
   360°÷10
   36°
   G: 108°
   R: 108°
   W: 144°

5. 6
   360°÷6
   60°
   O: 180°
   B: 120°
   Y: 60°

6. 24
   360°÷24
   15°
   B: 105°
   Pi: 75°
   G: 120°
   Pu: 60°

A BIG EDD GUIDE   *Handling Data*   ANSWERS

Angle Answers

Section 1: Turning p186

P1: Combining turns
1. 3/4 ↷
2. 3/4 ↷
3. 1/4 ↷
4. 3/4 ↷
5. 1/4 ↷
6. 1 ↷
7. 1/4 ↷
8. 1/2 ↷
9. 1/2 ↷
10. 3/4 ↷

D2: Recognising fractions of turns
1. 6/12 or 1/2
2. 3/12 or 1/4
3. 9/12 or 3/4
4. 9/12 or 3/4
5. 4/12 or 1/3
6. 8/12 or 2/3
7. 5/12
8. 11/12
9. 9/12 or 3/4
10. 12

P2: Following turning instructions   1. NE   2. N   3. E

Section 2: Describing angles p189

D1: Angles and how you describe them
Task 1: $1/4$ $1/2$ $3/4$ $1/4$ $1/8$ $3/8$
Task 2: 1   2   3   1 $1/2$ $1 1/2$
Task 3: 90°   180°   270°   90°   45°   135°

D2: Fractions of turns and degrees
1. 180°   2. 90°   3. 60°   4. 36°   5. 720°   6. 90°   7. 270°   8. 540°
9. 180°   10. 45°   11. 270°   12. 30°   13. 9°   14. 135°

D2: Tracing paper turn meter

Point	A	B	C	D	F	H
Fraction of turn clockwise	1/8	1/4	3/8	1/2	3/4	1
Degrees of turn clockwise	45°	90°	135°	180°	270°	360°

Point	G	F	D	B	E	C
Fraction of turn anti–clockwise	1/8	1/4	1/2	3/4	3/8	5/8
Degrees of turn anti–clockwise	45°	90°	180°	270°	135°	225°

P1: Clock angles
1. 90°   2. 30°   3. 180°   4. 90°   5. 30°   6. 60°
7. 30°   8. 120°   9. 120°   10. 240°   11. 270°   12. 300°
13. 330°   14. 150°   15. 150°   16. 330°

P2: Compass turns

Start	Finish	Direction	Angle turned through
E	S	c	90°
NE	E	c	45°
SW	W	c	45°
NW	NE	c	90°
NW	NE	a–c	270°
N	SE	c	135°
W	E	c	180°
W	SE	c	225°
E	SW	c	135°
NW	S	a–c	135°

Section 3: Comparing angles   p194

D1: Angle pairs

$\hat{Q} = \hat{H}$ $\hat{R} = \hat{A}$ $\hat{S} = \hat{B}$ $\hat{T} = \hat{D}$ $\hat{U} = \hat{G}$

$\hat{V} = \hat{I}$ $\hat{W} = \hat{E}$ $\hat{Z} = \hat{F}$ $\hat{X} = \hat{J}$ $\hat{Y} = \hat{C}$

D2: Ordering angles   P S U Q T R

Section 4: Measuring angles   p196

D2: Measuring work

1. 67° (will accept 65° – 69°)   3. 23° (will accept 21° – 25°)
2. 23° (will accept 21° – 25°)
4. 117° (will accept 115° – 120°) or 63° (will accept 60° – 65°)

D3: Measuring and labelling angles

Answers are acceptable that are within 3° above or below the given angle:

33° (accept 30° – 36°)   57° (accept 54° – 60°)   33° (accept 30° – 36°)

114° (accept 111° – 117°)   66° (accept 63° – 69°)

Section 5: Labelling lines and angles   p198

D1: Labelling

1. rectangle   2. HJK HIJ LMN XYZ   3. HIJ LMN   4. DEFG HIJK
5. EF   6. BC   7. YZ XZ   8. No   9. HIJK XYZ   10. LMN
11. Angle A   12. No   13. Yes   14. HJ   15. HJK HIJ   16. DF or EG

D2: Classifying angles

1. right   2. reflex   3. acute   4. obtuse   5. right
6. reflex   7. reflex   8. reflex   9. acute   10. obtuse

Section 6: The language of lines   p 200

D2: Parallel and perpendicular lines

1. T   2. F   3. F   4. T   5. T   6. T
7. F   8. F   9. parallel   10. perpendicular

Section 7: Angles on a line and at a point   p202
D1: Investigating angles on a straight line
1. You should have used 40° and 140°   2. You should have used 50°, 60°, 70°
3. You should have used 47°, 71°, 62°   4. Angles on a straight line add up to 180°
D2: Calculating angles on a straight line
    1. 60°   2. 100°   3. 140   4. 30   5. 110   6. 95   7. 45   8. 93
P1: Angles on a straight line practice
Batch A   1. $a = 30$ 2. $b = 40$ 3. $c = 150$ $d = 130$
4. $e = 120$ $f = 60$ $g = 120$ $h = 60$ 5. $i = 100$ 6. $j = 150$ $k = 90$
Batch B   1. $a = 50$ 2. $b = 100$ 3. $c = 40$ 4. $d = 90$ $e = 135$
5. $e = 120$ $f = 110$ 6. $g = 80$ $h = 140$ $i = 120$
D3: Investigating angles at a point 1. Should have used 160°, 110°, 90° 2. 360°
D4: Calculating angles at a point   1. 40   2. 110   3. 123 4. 95
P2: Angles at a point practice
1. $t = 90$ 2. $r = 110$ 3. $s = 160$ 4. $p = 140$ $q = 150$ 5. $u = 210$
6. $v = 20$ 7. $w = 30$ $x = 50$ 8. $y = 155$ $z = 30$

Section 8: Angles on crossed lines   p205
D1: Angles on crossed lines
1. $a = 40$ $b = 140$ $c = 140$ 2. $b = 80$ 3. $c = 130$ 4. $d = 165$ $e = 35$
5. $f = 120$ $g = 62$ 6. $h = 55$ $i = 60$ $j = 120$ 7. $k = 110$ 8. $l = 79$

Section 9 : Angles in triangles   p206
D2: Calculating angle in triangles
1. 80   2. 40   3. 55   4. 20   5. 35   6. 25   7. 99   8. 33   9. 21
P1: Angles in triangles practice
    1. A = 90   2. B = 50   3. C = 30   4. D = 114   5. E = 124
    6. F = 85   7. G = 130   8. H = 23   9. J = 35

Section 10: Special triangles   p208
D1: Special triangles
1. 60°   2.   3.   4.   5.
6. A&B   7. A & B   8. A&C   9. A&C
10. $a = 75$ $b = 30$ 11. $c = 30$ $d = 80$ 12. $f = 70$ $e = 40$ 13. $n = 30$ $m = 120$
D2: Working out the base angles (the equal angles)
    1. both 70°   2. both 40°   3. both 80°   4. both 50°
P1: A mixture of isosceles triangles
    1. $a = 30$ $b = 30$ 2. $c = 45$ $d = 45$ 3. $e = 55$ $f = 70$
    4. $g = 30$ $h = 30$ $i = 120$ 5. $j = 80$ $k = 50$ $m = 50$ 6. $n = p = q = r = 80$

Section 12 : Drawing angles   p211
D1: Constructing triangles
1. 3 cm & 3.3 cm   2. 51° & 4.1 cm   3. 57°   4. 5.2 cm

Number Patterns Answers

Section 1: Investigating square numbers   p226

D1: Investigating square numbers
5. 36, 49   6. 1, 4, 9, 16, 25, 36, 49, 64, 81, 100
7. (a) 36 (b) 100 (c) 121   (d) 400

D2: Squaring numbers

2	3	7	9	5	12	0	1	8	4	6	2	10	11
4	9	49	81	25	144	0	1	64	16	36	4	10	121

P1: Calculator squares search
    1. 4 x 4   2. 8 x 8   3. 12 x 12   4. 13 x 13   5. 15 x 15
    6. 22 x 22   7. 5   8. 29   9. 89

P2: Sum squares

$2 = 1 + 1$ $17 = 1 + 16$ $20 = 16 + 4$ $106 = 81 + 25$ $10 = 1 + 9$
$5 = 1 + 4$ $\lceil 50 = 25 + 25 \rceil\lceil 25 = 9 + 16 \rceil$ $145 = 64 + 81$ $104 = 100 + 4$
                $\ \ or\ 1 + 49\ $ $or\ 25 + 0$
$13 = 4 + 9$ $80 = 16 + 64$ $125 = 36 + 49$ $26 = 1 + 25$ $169 = 25 + 144$
                                  $or\ 121 + 4$
$18 = 9 + 9$ $65 = 64 + 1$ $85 = 81 + 4$ $52 = 16 + 36$ $313 = 169 + 144$
$8 = 4 + 4$ $74 = 25 + 49$ $61 = 36 + 25$ $202 = 81 + 121$

Section 2: Cubes and squares   p229

D1: Investigating cube numbers
    5. 1, 8, 27, 64, 125, 216, 343, 512, 729, 1000

D2: Cubing numbers

2	1	5	6	9	10	12	15	20
8	1	125	216	729	1000	1728	3375	8000

P1: Calculator cube search
    1. 2 x 2 x 2   2. 3 x 3 x 3   3. 10 x 10 x 10   4. 11 x 11 x 11
    5. 14 x 14 x 14   6. 30 x 30 x 30   7. 25 x 25 x 25

Section 3: Powers   p231

D1: Powers
1. 4 to the power of 5
2. 7 squared (7 to the power of 2 will do but 7 squared is better)
3. 6 to the power of 4
4. 5 cubed (5 to the power of 3 will do but 5 cubed is better)
5. 9 to the power of 7   6. 3 to the power of 8
7. 11 squared   8. 10 to the power of 6
9. 9^6 10. 14^5 11. 6^4 12. 2^3 13. 15^2 14. 27^4

D2: Calculating powers of numbers
1. 9
2. 25
3. 100
4. 196
5. 676
6. 8
7. 343
8. 1000
9. 125
10. 3375
11. 1296
12. 32
13. 3125
14. 2401
15. 512
16. 4096
17. 256
18. 64

P1: Finding the powers
1. $25 = 5^2$
2. $27 = 3^3$
3. $8 = 2^3$
4. $1000 = 10^3$
5. $32 = 2^5$
6. $64 = 2^6$
7. $64 = 4^3$
8. $125 = 5^3$
9. $36 = 6^2$
10. $216 = 6^3$
11. $243 = 3^5$
12. $625 = 5^4$
13. $16807 = 7^5$
14. $14641 = 11^4$
15. $279841 = 23^4$
16. $24137569 = 17^6$

P2: Sums of powers
1. $2^2 + 3^2 = 4 + 9 = 13$
2. $4^2 + 6^2 = 16 + 36 = 52$
3. $5^2 + 12^2 = 25 + 144 = 169$
4. $8^2 + 11^2 = 64 + 121 = 185$
5. $3^2 + 2^3 = 9 + 8 = 17$
6. $4^3 + 15^2 = 64 + 225 = 289$

Section 4: Triangle numbers   p233

D1: Investigating triangle numbers
2. 1, 3, 6, 10, 15, 21
3. $T_1 = 1$
   $T_2 = 3$
   $T_3 = 6$
   $T_4 = 10$
   $T_5 = 15$
   $T_6 = 21$
4. 4
5. 5
6. $T_2 + 3 = T_3$
   $T_3 + 4 = T_4$
   $T_4 + 5 = T_5$
   $T_5 + 6 = T_6$
   $T_6 + 7 = T_7$
7. 5
8. 6
9. 7
10. 28

E1: Connecting squares and triangle numbers
2. (a) $\Delta 1$ & $\Delta 2$ (b) [diagram]   (c) $T_1 + T_2 = \Delta$

Section 5: Divisibility   p235

D1: Divisibility
A: Yes B: No C: Yes D: No E: No F: No G: Yes H: Yes I: No J: Yes

D2: What does 'divisible by' mean ?
1. No 2. Yes 3. No 4. No 5. Yes 6. Yes 7. Yes 8. No
9. Yes 10. No 11. No 12. Yes
13. 35 63 49 56 21 84
14. 40 16 24 92 12 108 52
15. 39 26 65 117 195 351 299

D3: Numbers that are divisible by 2, 5 or 10
1. 60 30 70 100 40 300 240 450   2. A number that is divisible by 10 ends in 0
3. 55 70 80 20 85 900 225 15   4. A number that is divisible by 5 ends in 0 or 5
5. 16 24 28 40 68 120 678 2472
6. A number that is divisible by 2 ends in 0,2,4,6 or 8

D4: Using divisibility rules
Task 1: 70 170 290 3390
Task 2: 85 70 95 215 4545 170 290 205 275 570 3390
Task 3: 24 70 38 22 452 666 8432 252 170 290 746 570 3390 542

Section 6: Multiples   p238
D1: "Divisible by" and "multiples of"
1. 20, 30, 40, 50   2. 12, 15, 18   3. 20, 25, 30, 35, 40, 45, 50, 55
4. 21, 28   5. 45 30 75 60

D2: Multiples of 3 and 9
1. Yes   2. Yes   3. No   4. Yes   5. Yes   6. No   7. No   8. Yes
9. Yes   10. Yes 11. Yes 12. No 13. Yes 14. Yes 15. Yes

Section 7: Factors   p240
D1: Guzzintas and factors
1. Numbers in boxes are 1, 2, 4, 8 : The factors of 8 are 1, 2, 4, 8
2. Numbers in boxes are 1, 2, 3, 4, 6, 12 : The factors of 12 are 1, 2, 3, 4, 6, 12
3. True   4. True   5. 1, 2, 3, 6   6. 1, 3, 5, 15   7. 1, 5, 25
8. Numbers in boxes are 1, 2, 4, 5, 10, 20 : The factors of 20 are 1, 2, 4, 5, 10, 20
9. Numbers in boxes are 1, 2, 3, 4, 6, 8, 12, 24 :
   The factors of 24 are 1, 2, 3, 4, 6, 8, 12, 24

D2: Factor pairs
1. $6 \div 2 = 3$ 6 is divisible by 2   2 is a factor of 6
   $6 \div 3 = 2$ 6 is divisible by 3   3 is a factor of 6
2. $6 \div 1 = 6$ 6 is divisible by 6   1 is a factor of 6
   $6 \div 6 = 1$ 6 is divisible by 6   6 is a factor of 6
3. 1 & 10   2 & 5   4. 1 & 18   2 & 9   3 & 6   5. 1 & 20   2 & 10   4 & 5

D3: A systematic way of getting all the factors of a number
1. 1, 15, 3, 5   2. 1, 24, 2, 12, 3, 8, 4, 6   3. 1, 30, 2, 15, 3, 10, 5, 6
4. 1 25, 5   5. 1, 36, 2, 18, 3, 12, 4, 9, 6   6. 1, 40, 2, 20, 4, 10, 5, 8
7. 1, 49, 7   8. 1, 48, 2, 24, 3, 16, 4, 12, 6, 8

Section 8: Prime numbers   p243
D1: The factor table

1.

Number	Factors	Number of factors	Number	Factors	Number of factors
5	1, 5	2	14	1, 2, 7, 14	4
6	1, 2, 3, 6	4	15	1, 3, 5, 15	4
7	1, 7	2	16	1, 2, 4, 8, 16	5
8	1, 2, 4, 8	4	17	1, 17	2
9	1, 3, 9	3	18	1, 2, 3, 6, 9, 18	6
10	1, 2, 5, 10	4	19	1, 19	2
11	1, 11	2	20	1, 2, 4, 5, 10, 20	6
12	1, 2, 3, 4, 6, 12	6			
13	1, 13	2			

2. 2, 3, 5, 7, 11, 13, 17, 19

Nets, Cubes and Volumes Answers

Section 1: Cubes and nets of cubes p250
D1: Examining cubes
1. 6 2. square 3. 3 4. 12 5. Yes
6. 9 7. 8 8. 3 9. 3 10. 6

D2A: From hexominoes to nets
The 11 possible different nets of a cube are given in 2B

D2B: A systematic investigation to find *all* the nets of a cube

1. 2. 4. 6. 7. 8. Not possible (as in Q 4)

Section 2: Nets of many shapes p253
D1: Examining cuboids
1. 6 2. No 3. Some rectangles, some squares
4. 12 5. No 6. 8 7. 3 8. 3

D2: Nets of cuboids
A and B are nets

P1: Making boxes

Section 4: Making shapes from isometric drawings p258
P1: Different views
A&E, B,F&H, D&G

Section 5: Drawing shapes   p260

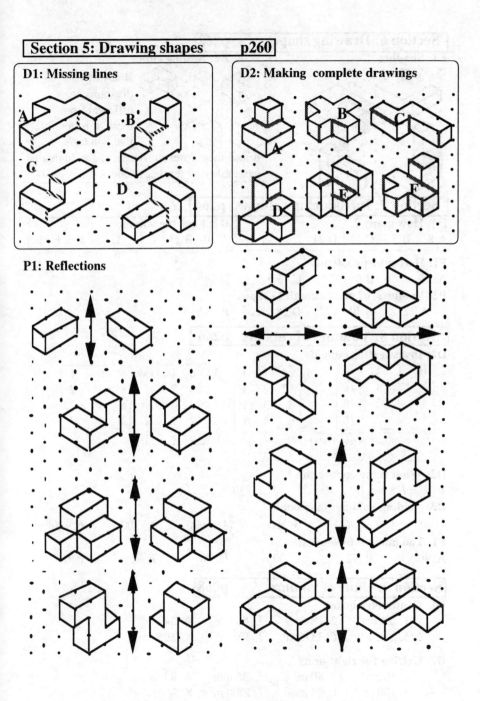

Section 6: Drawing shapes p262

E1: Shading

E2: Adding cubes

If any of your diagrams are different from these, it is possible that you have drawn them from a different angle. In this case, ask your teacher to check them.

Section 7: Introducing volumes p264

D1: How many ?
A 8   B 7   C 15   D 21   E 26   F 18

D2: Find the volume
A 10   B 18   C 17   D 9   E 8   F 21

P1: Half cube problems
A 1.5   B 6   C 13.5   D 24

P2: Volumes of more complex shapes
A 22   B 40   C 21   D 28   E 65   F 23.5

Section 8: Volumes of cuboids p266

D1: Investigating cuboids

2.
16	1	1	16
8	2	1	16
4	4	1	16
4	2	2	16

The numbers in each row can be in any order.

4.
24	1	1
12	2	1
8	3	1
6	4	1
6	2	2
4	3	2

5.
48	1	1	&	8	6	1
24	2	1		8	3	2
12	4	1		6	4	2
12	2	2		4	4	3
16	3	1				

D2: What is the connection ?
1. $V = L \times B \times H$ 2. 30

D3: Finding volumes of cuboids
1. 45   2. 96   3. 350   4. 1000   5. 300   6. 420

P1: Too much information
A 40   B 72   C 30   D 80   E 96   F 64

Section 9: Units of volume p268

D1: Centimetre boxes
1. 24 cm³   2. 18 cm³   3. 60 cm³   4. 54 cm³
5. 30 cm³   6. 3375 cm³   7. 400 cm³   8. 105 cm³

D2: Getting the right units
1. 30 cm³   2. 80 m³   3. 36 mm³   4. 84 m³
5. 100 cm³   6. 48 mm³   7. 1200 m³   8. 54 cm³